The Nonprofit Challenge

The Nonprofit Challenge

Integrating Ethics into the Purpose and Promise of Our Nation's Charities

Doug White

palgrave
macmillan

THE NONPROFIT CHALLENGE
Copyright © Doug White, 2010.

First published in 2010 by
PALGRAVE MACMILLAN®
in the United States—a division of St. Martin's Press LLC,
175 Fifth Avenue, New York, NY 10010.

Where this book is distributed in the UK, Europe and the rest of the world,
this is by Palgrave Macmillan, a division of Macmillan Publishers Limited,
registered in England, company number 785998, of Houndmills,
Basingstoke, Hampshire RG21 6XS.

Palgrave Macmillan is the global academic imprint of the above companies
and has companies and representatives throughout the world.

Palgrave® and Macmillan® are registered trademarks in the United States,
the United Kingdom, Europe and other countries.

ISBN: 978–0–230–62392–7

Library of Congress Cataloging-in-Publication Data

White, Douglas E., 1952–
    The Nonprofit Challenge : integrating ethics into the purpose and promise
of our nation's charities / by Doug White.
        p. cm.
    ISBN 978–0–230–62392–7
    1. Nonprofit organizations. 2. Nonprofit organizations—Finance.
3. Nonprofit organizations—Moral and ethical aspects. I. Title. II. Title:
Nonprofit challenge.

HD62.6.W495 2010
338.7′4—dc22   2010013320

A catalogue record of the book is available from the British Library.

Design by Newgen Imaging Systems (P) Ltd., Chennai, India.

First edition: October 2010

10 9 8 7 6 5 4 3 2 1

Printed in the United States of America.

With Gratitude

*Even though we are alone to put thoughts
on paper, no author writes without
invaluable assistance:*

*Alice Baker
Roberta d'Eustachio
Laurie Harting
Bill Josephson
Naomi Levine
Marianne Pisarri
Eric Swerdlin
Dale Willman
John Yodsnukis*

*Thank you.
You know why.*

Though goodness without knowledge is weak and feeble, yet knowledge without goodness is dangerous, and that both united form the noblest character.

John and Elizabeth Phillips
From the Original Deed of Gift to
Phillips Exeter Academy
May 17, 1781

Contents

Introduction

The world of nonprofits is larger and more varied than you might think. Public charities and foundations total well more than one million organizations, by far the largest category among the many within the larger nonprofit world, which consists of almost 2 million organizations.[1] Most people use the words "nonprofit" and "charity" interchangeably.

Each charity has its own charter and goals. Offering up one characteristic or another—or even a set of characteristics—and declaring it to capture the essence of that world would be futile, misleading, and a disservice to the unique and wonderful work performed by the nation's charities.

The gamut is both wide and deep: Governance, fundraising, and internal management take up a lot of time at charities, but the public is aware of charities primarily through their services and programs, how they serve society. The number of ways they help people is pretty staggering. Types of organizations include the arts, education, the environment, animal protection, health care, medical research and disease prevention, legal services, international affairs, religion—and more. There are so many, in fact, that when the IRS determines whether charities should be granted tax-exempt status, it refers to a database that has many types and subtypes of categories—a taxonomy—within the nonprofit world.[2]

Many people think of charities as groups that help the poor. Yet the taxonomy includes types of organizations that often have, or seem to have, little to do with the poor. When we think of schools, colleges, and universities, we don't usually think of charity because costs are so high. The same is true of hospitals. For many people, the idea of "charity" is at odds with the high costs associated with hospitals. Especially these days; in fact, for several years now, Congress has been debating whether some hospitals should continue to receive the tax benefits that charities and their donors receive because so many are thought to be so wanting in the amount of care they provide to the poor. It's the same with museums. No one goes into the Metropolitan Museum of Art in New York City or the Getty

Museum in Los Angeles and confuses it with an organization whose primary purpose is to help the poor.

These types of organizations, and many more, are often so wealthy, with operating budgets in the millions and endowments in the billions, that they seem like anything but charities. But they are. That's in addition to those we more naturally think of as providing charitable assistance for the poor: religious organizations, social services agencies, and shelters for the homeless.

Nonprofits are large and small, some with vast amounts of money at their disposal and others that don't know how the light bill will be paid next month, and many make a profit—but they all share the same space in our society. What makes them part of the nonprofit sector is that they serve society in ways that neither government nor private enterprise can.

"Serving society" is a broad identity, however, so to truly understand why so many seemingly disparate organizations can fall under one umbrella, it is important to realize that the umbrella was built by Congress. Practically any activity that anyone can think of that does not fall under the category of government or business—anything that might be construed as charitable—can be found in the category of nonprofits.

The goal of this book is to explore the differentness of the charitable world and to determine if there is a unique ethos that applies—or ought to apply—to the way charities work. Perhaps there is something within the perplexing labyrinth of purpose that we can identify, something that informs how society is served in an unpolitical and unbusinesslike way, a way of looking at the world unique to charities that I'd like to call the "nonprofit ethos." If it is true that the motives that drive at least some people are not financial or political, and while it is also true that executives who lead charities are not paid as well as their for-profit counterparts and cannot exercise political influence, then it follows that the roots of leadership and citizenship within the nonprofit environment must be found within another ethos. To find that ethos, it is necessary to look at the broad issues confronting the nonprofit world. That look will reveal some practical issues—tax complexities and fundraising challenges, for example—but they are just supporting players in the real drama of getting inside the hearts of charities. After all, they uniquely serve society with love. Philanthropy, the margin that marks the difference between financial health and financial ruin at almost every charity in the country, means "love of humanity." It is the mind-bendingly complex human dimension, therefore, that ought to interest those who care about the nation's nonprofits.

Nonprofits and For-Profits

The term "nonprofit" is misleading. Nonprofits are permitted to make a profit. That's not their purpose, but they are allowed to make money. A surprisingly large number of charities have more revenues than costs, often receiving more money in fees, gifts, and investment revenue than they spend to operate their programs, pay salaries, and maintain their buildings. Some nonprofits earn enormous profits. The ones you are most familiar with, the largest nonprofits, are the organizations that tend to make the most money.

For its fiscal year of 2008, Harvard University—the President and Fellows of Harvard College, as it is formally known—generated revenues of more than $6.7 billion and expenses of less than $3.5 billion. A $3.2 billion profit in one year isn't bad for a nonprofit organization. Part of the reason for the profit that year was that Harvard's investment portfolio, of which the lion's share is the endowment, generated investment income of a little more than $4.2 billion. In the same year, the J. Paul Getty Trust, the private foundation that runs the Getty Museum, generated revenues of $444 million, most of that from its investments, and had expenses of $368 million. That was a profit of almost $76 million. Again, endowment income helped make the difference. The Getty earned about $440 million from its investments.[3]

It's not only the big, well-known charities that make a profit. By basically aiming a dart at a list of charities—that is, by choosing some names randomly—I found the Global Business Coalition on HIV/AIDS, Tuberculosis, and Malaria in New York City, which had a profit in 2007 of a little more than $126,000. Another, the Gift of Life Bone Marrow Foundation in Boca Raton, Florida, reported revenues of slightly more than $6.5 million in 2007 and expenses of $5.65 million, a profit of $850,000.

These two charities don't have the kind of endowment that Harvard and the Getty have and so it's not always the income from a large endowment that helps balance the books. Nevertheless, the revenue generated from endowments can be a large reason why charities can get by without charging as much for providing services as it costs them. Generally, the spread is larger for the wealthier

charities; that is, the bigger a charity, the more likely its endowment will provide a significant amount to offset its expenses.[4]

So if nonprofits are actually profitable much of the time, what
distinguishes them from profit-making enterprises? If there is one
characteristic that applies to all nonprofits, it's that none of them
has any shareholders. In the philanthropic world, fundraisers like
to say that, because there are no real investors, donors are the
"investors" in charities and that the "profit" is in the good charities do with their donated dollars.

But, while the definition and characteristics of a nonprofit are
useful to know from a legal perspective, they don't tell us anything about what most people care about: What the charity does
to serve society.

Key to understanding the nonprofit environment is understanding that nonprofits provide a broad range of services and programs
so broad that almost everyone in America is or at one time was
touched by the nonprofit world in one way or another. In fact, it
would have to be a very isolated individual in American society
to claim that he or she has never been affected by a charity. If
you've ever been to a religious service, or if you attended a college, or have visited an art museum, or been in the hospital, you've
bumped into a charity—and if your heart has ever been moved by
its work, you've been affected.

Ethics Starts Here

Just as in business and government, there are scandals in the world
of charities. William Aramony, United Way's former overpaid
chief executive officer—the man whose fraud and deceit were so
egregious, at least as measured by the standards of the nonprofit
world, that he singularly introduced the modern era of public
charity scrutiny—was convicted of 25 counts of illegal conduct
in 1992. Most of the convictions related to the interstate trans-
portation of fraudulently obtained money; the most serious was
that Aramony used United Way money for personal benefit.[5] Peter
Diamandopoulos, the former president of Adelphi University, was
fired in 1997, just after the New York State Board of Regents fired
the entire board of directors, for his lavish spending and salary, to
say nothing of how he demoralized the entire campus. Not many
liked the idea that he was being paid more than the president of
Harvard—he was the second highest paid university president in

the country at the time—and they liked even less that one trustee defended Diamandopoulos's pay by saying that it didn't take as much effort to run Harvard as it did to run Adelphi. He also punished at whim those who disagreed with him. The morale got so bad that a group of faculty, alumni, and others formed "The Committee to Save Adelphi," whose singular goal was to rid the university of its president.[6]

Bad as all that is—and there are many more examples—either one of these characters would have a hard time achieving the same level of notoriety as some rotten apples in the business world. Consider, for example, the late Ken Lay, the former head of Enron, the poster child for corporate wickedness. Lay's legacy makes any nonprofit leader's—indeed, any other business tycoon's—look like that of a Boy Scout in comparison. And no nonprofit head, no matter how corrupt, has destroyed (and it is hard to imagine that it would be possible) the lives of so many thousands of investors—and of those who depended on them financially—by vaporizing more than $20 billion, the result of the continuous four-decade journey of deceit, exposed in December 2008, by Bernard Madoff.[7]

If the business world has its rotten apples, government can claim just as much, or more, notoriety. Power, more than money, is the engine of sin in Washington and the state capitols, although money usually plays an accompanying, as well as motivating, role. In fact, scandal is a prominent American tradition among publicly elected officials. Disgraced politicians have been with us at least since the early 1800s, and chances are that someone holding a sliver or more of the public trust has recently been shown to be less than straight—or worse—with the public. An alarming number of well-known and otherwise highly regarded politicians, beginning with Thomas Jefferson, reaching through to some of those in office today, have been associated with breathtaking scandal.

Comparatively speaking, one might suppose, nonprofits aren't all that bad. But when things go wrong at a charity, it's different, not because of the public trust—public trust permeates every organization in one way or another—but because we have a sense that charities should be above that nonsense. They're too good, too innocent. But there it is.

*   *   *

In the midst of so much that grates on decency, however, the Wall Street or Washington, D.C., standard is a wanting measure to use for the nation's charities, whose sole purpose in this world is to *be* good and to *spread* that good.

To be sure, most people who work at charities do a pretty good job. At any individual charity it is likely that the staff works hard, and the trustees, or board of directors, use their volunteer time to provide enough oversight that the charity doesn't lose its tax exemption and to ensure that it stays on course in working toward its mission. For the most part, charities serve their communities well. This could be said of all organizations and their workers, of course, but it is true that the people who work at charities generally have a different internal purpose inspiring their work. They tend not to think as much about what they earn as their counterparts in business do, and, as they are generally prohibited from endorsing candidates or from taking positions on legislation, they tend to feel freer of the politics of serving society than those in government service. It's a different ethos.

But over the years, for a variety of reasons addressed in this book, more and more charities are losing their way. The news stories of fraud and deceit are growing, both in number and seriousness. Part of it is that the media are more sophisticated and attuned to what is going on in the nonprofit world—the news about charities is not as boutique as it was for so long, and certainly it is often found elsewhere than in the society pages—but financial pressures have worked to make the world of charities a different place from what it was until the 1980s. And so we learn, almost every day, of a new scandal: the charity that plays fast and loose with the tax laws, the charity that takes another to court in a power grab for part of a dead man's estate, the donor who claims a charity did not honor his mother's wishes, and others.

Part of human nature is the desire for power, influence, and financial reward, and charities, as they have grown in stature and size, are today almost as likely to be a magnet for people who want to fulfill those desires as anyplace else. What started out in this country as a loosely formed group of organizations that paid no one's salary—the Frenchman Alexis de Tocqueville called them *associations* when writing up his report after his nine-month tour around the United States in the early nineteenth century—turned into something far less loose and far more corporate by the twenty-first century. The nonprofit sector is responsible for 10 to 12 percent of our Gross Domestic Product (although no one really knows, so imprecise are the data). Large charitable gifts are in the news almost every day. Annual charitable contributions in the

United States exceed $300 billion. Within a $15 trillion national Gross Domestic Product, that may not seem like much, but it is, and the numbers are growing every year. With giving reaching new heights and many individual gifts getting larger and larger every year—to say nothing of the amount of money generated for the economy by nonprofits—it is no wonder that the nonprofit sector looks a lot like big business.

We've got three philosophically distinct sectors in society—government, business, and nonprofits—and, although too many people who work in and otherwise serve charities don't seem to realize it, the nonprofit world is as important as the other two. It's not a look-alike to the business sector. It never will be, and it's got to stop trying.

The Ethical Sector

The central thesis of this book is that charities occupy the ethical sector in our society. Yet, based on recent formal surveys as well as informal cocktail party banter, you'd be hard pressed to find the words "ethics" and "charities" used in the same sentence. That has to change. People need to start thinking of charities in the context of the tangible good they do for society and less about the amount they spend on fundraising costs and other overhead. The nonprofit world needs to be seen as the *ethical leader* of society, and that won't happen without a lot of hard work on the part of each individual organization, as well as of the groups that are comprised of those organizations. Charities that don't do the right thing aren't always acting *un*ethically, but, if there's a neutral zone, charities don't belong there. As participants in the most humanity-based sector of society, charities must erase that gap by holding themselves to a higher standard than they do now. Even though—perhaps because—charities are as susceptible to malfeasance as any other type of organization, they must constantly ask themselves what steps they can take to make things better.

*   *   *

How can charities take the lead? Why *must* charities take the lead?

There's no choice. Not really. Not with the growing drumbeat of bad news. Charities are accumulating more and more money, and questions about where that money goes are increasing. Why, for example, does so much of it stay in the charities' investment accounts, their endowments? What is the measurable or qualitative impact that charities have on their communities?

The public is more demanding than ever before. The economic crisis that began in the late 2000s has only sharpened people's skepticism. "Transparency," "accountability," and "conflict-of-interest" are today's buzzwords at meetings of the executives who work in the nonprofit world, but for so many charities they remain only buzzwords and not real action items that result in an ability to make hard decisions in the right way. And the reason for that is the absence of a nonprofit ethos.

The nonprofit ethos is certainly not social marketing, a benign-sounding but somewhat misleading term that's far more about marketing than it is about the social good. Born in the 1970s and often associated with selling ideas as opposed to products, social marketing is supposed to be more about the audience being marketing to than the organization that's doing the marketing. It's meant to connote a good for society, which perhaps is supposed to take the edge off the raw idea of greedy, capitalistic selling. Selling and capitalism, of course, are hardly dirty words—a great deal of the world's success depends on them—but when the public mood moves away from companies who make too much profit or who make it for too few at the expense of too many, those companies often try to find refuge in the veneer of goodness in charities.

Corporations want to partner with charities. So do politicians. Often enough, the political donation that comes from a questionable source is given to charity; money going to charity seems to have been "cleansed." But how can charities maintain that clean image if they see those same characteristics—materialism and fraud—when they look in the mirror? To be the go-to for good, you have to be good. You have to live up to the image and the expectation.

People in business primarily try to make money for their firms. People in government make laws (Congress) and interpret them (the courts) and ensure they are executed (the regulators) so that society can function. Charities...well, they're here to make society better in ways that neither government nor business can. Can you imagine government trying to take care of all the social needs of the nation's citizens? That's been the plan in Europe for centuries, but many Europeans are finding that even the highest acceptable tax rates (and in some European countries, that's pretty high) can't do the job. That's why some of them are right now scrambling to figure out how to insta-grow a charitable ethos. European charities, such as England's Oxford University, traditionally never raised funds, but do today because government money is no longer enough.

Or can you imagine businesses doing the work of charities? We call them *nonprofits* for a reason.

Charities have to stop thinking in terms of profits and growth. They have to stop paying exorbitant salaries to their top executives for fear that someone—somebody who might not be all that good anyway—might leave. They have to stop thinking about next quarter's profits at the expense of what it needs to accomplish next year, or 5—or 25—years from now. They have to understand that their mission—their purpose on this earth, to say nothing about why they get such great tax breaks—is something more than a marketing strategy or a public-relations gimmick. The goals and mission of most charities are long term. Quarterly financial results are not the best indicators of whether a program is doing well. And charities, even those that expect or hope to be around for a relatively short period of time (by a short period of time, I mean charities that hope to accomplish their mission within the next several generations or so) don't find much guidance in metrics that measure results in mere months or even a few years.

A Compact with the Public

Does anything capture the essence of charities? For me—as I take into account how many charities there are and the number of people who support them, as well as the hundreds of billions of dollars that they receive in donations and the enormous social purpose they serve—the most important issue at charities is how they broker their deal with the public. That is, my base line of thinking about the nonprofit sector isn't about the money or the type of mission, but about the promise. We give these unique organizations our hearts and our pocketbooks, and the government legislates in their favor. In return, what do we get? Do we get honesty, responsibility, respect, fairness, and compassion? Do we get those characteristics that, relieved of making profits for shareholders, staff and directors should keep in mind—qualities that Americans hold in the highest esteem[8]—as they run their organizations?

For the most part, yes. To be fair and honest—two qualities of the ethical mindset—of the charities that ask for your money, only a few run into trouble. A few more might be on that list if anyone was caught or anyone cared about the problems that might exist, but the vast majority is doing a good enough job. That is, they're not running off with your money and spending it foolishly. It doesn't necessarily mean they pass the test of meeting all the qualities charities should—which is what this book really addresses.

But is it good enough that the "vast majority"—for example, 99 percent—of charities are doing a good job? Of the almost two million tax-exempt organizations and other entities in America, about 1.1 million fall into the IRS's 501(c) (3) category.[9]

Ninety-nine percent of one million is a little over 990,000; that leaves 1.1 percent, if the assumption is in the ballpark or about 10,000 charities that aren't doing a great a job. In fact, no one knows exactly the number of badly run charities, but because of the special compact charities have with the public—they exist to do good—one badly run charity, one case of fraud, or one case of embezzlement is one too many and ought to grab the attention of the attorney general of the state where the charity is located, the IRS, Congress, and the public.

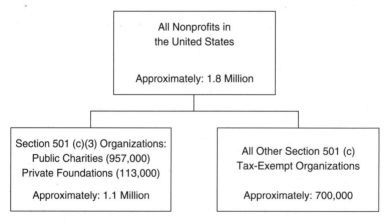

Figure I.1   Tax-Exempt Organizations.[10]

It is rare for an organization to lose its charitable status. The IRS just doesn't have the staff to audit very many charities.[11] One person in authority at the Charities Bureau, the office in charge of charity oversight at the New York State Attorney General's office, has said that she often learns of a charity's problems—a board member ran off with all the money, or the charity spent lavishly on activities unrelated to the charity's mission—by reading the newspaper. As that office is understaffed, so is the IRS office in charge of charities.

No matter the number, charities today are facing more problems than ever before. What we have is an important sector of our society—judged either by the heart or the wallet—that no one can precisely define or whose effectiveness can be accurately measured, and yet it is a sector about which many people have growing concerns. The challenge is to understand the promise of the nonprofit world as it affects everyone, while at the same time appreciate the good of charity through each of our personal perspectives.

* * *

This book's focus is on charities, the organizations you're most familiar with, the places you donate to: colleges and universities, museums, hospitals (most of them), homeless shelters (for people and animals), the environmental groups, social service organizations, the groups that oppose abortion—as well as those who support a woman's right to choose—and churches, synagogues and mosques. It's about those kinds of places; the kind that ask people for money to advance their mission.

One more thing: include in the category of charities, as I've just described them, those organizations that everybody knows as *foundations*. Technically, they're charities too but for the most part foundations don't raise money. They give money away because they have a lot, usually because one person provided most of it; think of names like Rockefeller, Ford, Mott, and Gates. The rules governing how they operate are a little different from those governing public charities, the groups that raise money from the public, but foundations are charitable organizations; they fall under the IRS Code—familiar to almost everyone who works with charities—*501(c)(3)*.

* * *

This book is about the special place charities occupy in society, how they need to be true to that place and their struggles to that end, and how, by being true, they can help the rest of society. It's about harnessing an ethical imperative that is unique to charities to find humanity in society.

So often people excuse their bad behavior by saying it was legal: "I broke no law" is so common a refrain that you know it can't mean much. Unless you're pathologically cynical, you feel a loss every time you hear the phrase and rue the emptiness of its hypocrisy. The matter is certainly obfuscated when what's legal is equated with what's right. For that matter, the person making the claim is often wrong—some would use the word "lying"—about the legality of his or her actions as well; no more than the first automated step in the way some people are taught to react to the light exposing their bad behavior. Lying is the opposite of telling the truth, and telling the truth is one of the most revered values people want to see in other people. As elusive as that quality may seem in the government and business sectors, although even there it doesn't have to be, it is also elusive in the nonprofit sector.

But since it's the best we have, the nonprofit world is examined here through the prism of ethics. As Rushworth Kidder, the president and founder of the Institute for Global Ethics, has said repeatedly, at bottom everything is about ethics. It's also true that ethics permeates everything, that ethical decisions drive everything else,[12] and that everything is connected to everything else.

Right now, unfortunately, not many people at charities see it that way. Too many think that finance, fundraising, board governance, programs, and the other areas of pursuit at a charity are wholly discrete activities. Fix one thing, and go on to the next. But, despite how an organization chart makes it seem like an organization is filled with discrete boxes, it's really not. Whether charity leaders want to admit it or not, each activity is connected by a system of values that permeates the mechanical aspects of all other activity at a charity.

Many professions have codes of ethics. Associations of charities, as well as many individual charities, also have behavioral codes, but as with so many voluntary rules, they are often ineffective or, even, intentionally ignored. Given charities' place in society—they exist primarily to promote humanity—this is striking, but codes are only as good as the people who wrote them, who promise to abide by them, and who have anything to say when the code is violated. That's why we are, or should be, upset when we read of egregious lapses anywhere, but most particularly at charities. To read of those lapses means at least that someone has identified them and tried to do something about them, but many more go unaddressed. Board members and key staff are too often unable or unwilling to confront difficult issues. We must come to understand that *every* decision of consequence to others is a function of an intention—good or bad. We have to be asking ourselves: What is at the root of that intention? How do we make that root a positive beginning of the decision-making process?

*   *   *

This book offers a framework for discussing ethical behavior and I'd argue that of the three sectors of society, the nonprofit world has the strongest claim to thinking about ethics most clearly and most effectively. After all, while both government and commerce do wonderful things for society and for individuals, their founding purpose is not, as it is for nonprofits, explicitly to call upon the love of humankind as the underpinning for whatever they do.

In fact, mere kindness is inadequate in government and business. The knowledge that humans are not all that inherently good has forced the formation, as a system of checks and balances, of the laws within whose guidance many individual actions are directed or prohibited. The legal system—you can't kill, you can't steal—serves to keep people nonviolent, and perhaps even, depending on how you define it, civilized: You don't have to depend merely on another person's kindness to understand that he won't shoot you on a busy street. However imperfect they often are, laws help a lot.

Even so, society doesn't run particularly well right now, and it's not entirely because the laws aren't strict enough or because people aren't making enough money. It's because we lack a common ethos—a way to think and feel, where the resulting decision, come what may, can be respected by everyone.

Such an ethos doesn't exist right now, even though the issue is as simple and old and common—and compelling—as the quest for understanding the difference between right and wrong. "The Nonprofit Challenge" describes a way for those employed at a charity, who serve on a board, who volunteer at a charity, or anyone else who cares about charities to address problems and disagreements—even the most severe and dividing—with intelligence, compassion and dignity, as well as with authority.

Certainly, as you must already know at some level of your consciousness, a strong, aggressive move toward ethical behavior won't be found in the whorls of business or the pettiness of government.

Where, then, if not at charities?

Section I

The Shifting Perceptions of Allies and Regulators

Chapter One

The Public's View

Describing the suffering among England's inhabitants in 1852, thus acknowledging that things weren't what they should be for such a wealthy country as England, the *London Times*, in a story headlined "Destitution in London," wondered why "one person out of twenty of the inhabitants of this luxurious metropolis is every day destitute of food and employment, and every night without a place for shelter or repose." Still, following the criticism—of the government, of society in general?—the article decreed, rather protectively, "Let us not be interpreted as casting a slur upon English charity—its schools, its hospitals, its benevolent institutions..." for, in fact, "there is no charity like English charity—there is no country in the world where such strenuous efforts have been made to relieve the destitution and minister to the wants of the suffering classes."[1]

Tell that to Alexis de Tocqueville who, after his extensive tour, concluded that the United States—not England or anywhere else in Europe—had the lead on effective charitable organizations based on the work they did and how they were organized.[2] There may have been no charity like English charity for the *London Times*, but the poor, according to Tocqueville, were better off here. No doubt we had our destitute souls roaming the streets too, but there were fewer of them, either because they received better services in America or perhaps as a result of our unique get-it-done culture. Or maybe it was just the perspective of one man, who had his own views about the way government ran things in imperial Europe, likening what he saw here, including our nonprofit associations, to a breath of fresh democratic air.

Some decades later, in 1896, the Englishman Hillaire Belloc, upon completing his own visit to the United States, said, "the most conspicuous feature which foreigners observed in America's public affairs was generosity: I suppose that the total sum of public benefactions from rich men in Philadelphia during the last century amounts to something like ten times the public benefactions from rich men in any city of similar size in Europe."[3]

So, according to two men who had given the matter some thought, not only were American charities doing a better job than those in Europe, donors in the United States were more generous. Since then, charities in America have lived the public relations dream, and the pedestal upon which they have been perched has grown mightily.

But that is changing.

A Little History

Charitable giving on a national scale was first reported in an annual compendium of a variety of topics called *Appleton's Annual Cyclopedia*, a publication that began its life during the Civil War. It began tracking charitable gifts and bequests in 1893. In that year, donors across the country were recorded as having made charitable gifts totaling $20 million. The names and amounts listed in those years tell instructive stories. In the 1896 edition, for example, readers learned that the estate of Leland Stanford—the railroad tycoon, leader of the Republican Party, governor of California, and United States senator—had been settled, allowing his $2.5 million bequest to seed what would become Stanford University.

Five years later, after his wife Jane died, the 1901 edition of the cyclopedia listed her gift to the university of $18 million, much of that no doubt the unspent remainder of her husband's bequest to her. Their generosity, according to the *New York Times*, made Stanford—its full and proper name is Stanford University Board of Trustees of the Leland Stanford Junior University—"the wealthiest educational institution the world has ever known." Mrs. Stanford also left to charity, according to the cyclopedia, one million acres of real estate worth $12 million. Her San Francisco home, worth $400,000 was converted into a museum.

The Stanford gift was a big reason that charitable gifts in the United States for the first time exceeded $100 million dollars in 1901, but that year's edition of the cyclopedia lists many other names, and each of them provides the seeds for some remarkable stories. Along with the record-breaking amount, the enduring names of philanthropic giants made 1901 a remarkable year in the nonprofit world.[4]

That year the public learned that

- George Sheldon, along with his siblings, gave money for a library building at St. Paul's School in Concord, New Hampshire.

- Edward Tuck supplemented his $350,000 gift a year earlier to Dartmouth College with an additional $100,000 to build what became the Tuck School of Business, ranked by the *Wall Street Journal* in 2007 as the top business school in the United States.
- John Rockefeller gave several gifts, mainly to educational organizations, including $300,000 "for the foundation in New York City of the Rockefeller Institute for Medical Research."
- Andrew Carnegie made numerous gifts to several organizations, including "for a technical school at Pittsburg, Penn., $2,000,000 with a promised endowment of at least $25,000,000."
- And from Josephine Sophie Newcomb, a New York resident at her death, a "bequest to Tulane University, the residue of her estate, estimated at $1,500,000. She had previously given the university about $1,000,000." (In chapter 6, we will take a look at an important development in this gift more than a century after it was made.)

There were anonymous gifts, too. Among the dozens mentioned in the cyclopedia is one for Harvard University, a "gift from a friend for a new building, $100,000," and for Northwestern University, a "friend" gave $15,000.

Not everyone was as convinced that such gifts were a sign of Americans' inherent generosity, however. Amid the newspaper stories about what all that generosity meant, there were rumblings of what it might not have meant. Chauncey Depew, a New York businessman and politician, questioned the assumed altruism of the wealthy donors. "The large public gifts made in this country by the rich constitute for them and our institutions a valuable kind of insurance." The editors of the *New York Times* were certain he meant those words pragmatically, as, for example, "insurance against injury to property rights through attacks from anarchists."[5] This was the era of the Robber Barons, after all, and the wealthy had reason to worry.

Although anarchists didn't get the barons, the government would soon reign in their ability to create monopolies. Despite the rugged individuality that characterizes the American spirit, government concern about the distribution of wealth is as old as wealth itself in this country. At the turn of the twentieth century, individual affluence was taking on new dimensions. That affluence and those dimensions are central players in the development of American philanthropy.

Perhaps as part of a first-strike strategy in an effort to divert the public's and the government's attention, charities became important outlets for the wealthy in the late 1800s. Looking at the prominent industry names of the day—Astor, Carnegie, Fisk, Frick, Rockefeller, and Vanderbilt, as well as Stanford and others—in an era that was practically defined by the pursuit of unrestricted wealth, with no regulations and no taxes, even the casual observer will see their prominent and public connection to the great foundations that were established then, names we recognize today principally for their connection to philanthropy.

By the humanitarian and equal-opportunity standards that have developed in the United States over the past century, the ruthlessness that otherwise characterized many of those men's lives would have ruined their reputations. But, without ever being paid a dime for the sycophancy, newspapers at the time performed the kind of attention-diverting work that paying clients of a public relations firm could only dream of. And why not? Society itself was the beneficiary. As a result, the original John Rockefeller is today far better known for his charitable endowments than for his brutal, inhumane tactics to quash legitimate competition to Standard Oil, tactics that were so brazen that in 1890 Congress passed antitrust legislation that today is still a clarion call for curbing such behavior.[6] Charity was and, as we will now see, continues to be the convenient laundering agent used to cleanse and enhance reputations.

Taking Advantage of the Positive Perceptions of Charity

It seems that whenever the world learns that someone in public life has received ill-gotten money, once the game is up and there's no other way out, he or she proclaims that the money will be donated to charity. This is often done with a sanctimonious undercurrent, as if diverting the money to charity breaks the tie between the money's tainted origins and the recipient's implied corruption. Charity is the refuge to wash away implications of dirty yesterdays.

In 2009, while the world was still reeling from the severe economic downturn that began in late 2007, the investment house Goldman Sachs announced that it would pay its executives billions of dollars in bonuses. It wasn't the smartest of public relations moves: Many experts felt Goldman itself was partly responsible for causing the collapse, and it had dubious financial underpinnings as well. So, when the firm belatedly got wind of how the move would play in the papers, Goldman tried to influence public perception by announcing that it would also donate up to a billion dollars to charity.[7]

* * *

One of the more dispiriting moments I've had as an advisor to charities was when I was asked in 2006 to review a list of contributors to determine which ones would be good candidates for estate commitments. That is, who among regular donors might be the best prospects to make a large gift when they died? I was looking for donors with the potential for gifts in the million-dollar-and-up range. This type of review is common as charities often solicit their most loyal annual supporters, even those whose previous gifts are, relatively speaking, small—even those who have made gifts of less than $10,000—for eventual multi-million dollar commitments.

Because these lists tend to be alphabetical and updated less frequently than they should be, the name of the first prospect I saw was that of Jack Abramoff. Abramoff, a former Washington lobbyist who became notorious in the mid-2000s for his complex snake-oil escapades—such as defrauding American Indian tribes of tens of millions of dollars and attempting to corrupt public officials—was sentenced to serve time in prison after pleading guilty to fraud, conspiracy, and tax evasion. Part of his public image was his alleged charitable work. It appears that he used the nonprofit world not to benefit society, but himself. Two charities were prominent in that façade: Eshkol Academy and the Capital Athletic Foundation, neither of which is still in existence.

* * *

Abramoff established Eshkol Academy in 2002 as an all-boys Orthodox Jewish day school in Columbia, Maryland. But it was really never a school—Abramoff used it only as a convenience, as seen in his own words in an email to a colleague in 2003: "Please make sure the next $1M[illion] from Coushatta for me goes to Eshkol Academy directly. Please tell them that we are 'using the school as our conduit for some of activities.' "[8] In 2004 it closed before it could get going; it never had enough money. Many of the teachers filed a lawsuit after the school shut down, just a month before graduation toward the end of its second year, because they weren't paid for several months. Right after the school opened in the fall of 2002, the first principal quit without an explanation.

"The school was totally unable to function as an educational institution," according to Samuel Whitehill, a former teacher. "It was like a Greek tragedy."[9] As a charitable endeavor—which is what Eshkol was established to be—the school failed miserably.

Eshkol's principal source of income was the Capital Athletic Foundation, an organization set up by Abramoff for youths who wanted to pursue athletics, but which seemed to be used primarily as a pass-through for his own illegal activities. Because of Abramoff's notoriety, the Center for Responsive Philanthropy, a foundation watchdog in Washington, D.C., conducted its own investigation of Abramoff's activities and in 2005 the group offered some salient observations:

> Given what is known about Abramoff's philanthropic work, it all reads like a satire from *The Onion* [the satirical newspaper], but it's true. The Capital Athletic Foundation's [tax] filings are a gold mine of dubious money laundering hiding behind the mask of a charitable foundation. Where was the Internal Revenue Service? Where was the self-regulatory fervor of the nation's foundation trade associations? Maybe the foundation sector leaders missed the Capital Athletic Foundation because Jack Abramoff failed to join their organizations and sign their statements of ethical standards. Someone should have caught, called out, and convicted Jack Abramoff for his misuse and abuse of philanthropy.[10]

*   *   *

Then there were Tareq and Michaele Salahi, the couple who, despite not being among those on the guest list, showed up at President Obama's first state dinner in November 2009. Regardless of whether they were actually gate-crashers, these people used charity to enhance their own reputations—reputations that had been built not on hard work and good deeds, but mainly on trying to glide through society's more elite circles. Not that anyone who was legitimately in those circles seemed to know much about them.

In 2006, they established an organization called The Journey for the Cure Foundation. Its website went blank the day after the *Washington Post* ran a detailed article explaining that the charity was illegitimate. Purportedly, it was all about raising money from the public so that it could distribute gifts to organizations like the Washington, D.C., area offices of the National Multiple Sclerosis

(MS) Society and the Leukemia & Lymphoma Society. The foundation had given $5,000 to the National MS Society in 2007, but its 2008 profit-and-loss statement showed that it gave nothing to the National MS Society in that year, and only gave $680 to the Leukemia & Lymphoma Society; $20 was donated to the United States Navy Memorial Fund. In fact, the foundation's expenses were over $22,000 that year and its revenues were only $19,000.

While a total of about $700 went to charities, a third, $7,200, was spent on "professional fees," which probably means that the Salahis paid themselves this amount. Approximately one quarter of the budget, or $5,400, was spent on "travel," and a similar amount, almost $6,000, went to "fundraising and meals."

How much of its budget did the foundation spend on its charitable mission that year? Three percent.[11]

The foundation had not registered with the state of Virginia, and the state warned the public that contributions "to such an organization could be used for noncharitable purposes." According to the *Post* article, only a few days before the White House state dinner—three years after it was required to—the foundation finally registered with Virginia authorities.

Presumably, those revenues that were supposedly going to charity came from the Salahis' big event: the Land Rover America's Polo Cup, whose website said that it is "being patroned by every President of the United States," even though the *Post* found "no record of any president attending any of the polo cups." As well, there were many allegations of shoddy business dealings and tastelessness. "The portrait of the couple's twin entities," one of which was a charity, "is marked by financial disarray, potentially false or misleading claims, broken friendships and bitter court filings."[12]

Jack Abramoff and the Salahis aren't the only ones who have used the good name of charity for their own nefarious ends. Many people use their association with charity as a way to garner legitimacy.

*   *   *

With this as backdrop—its reputation so clean that the unscrupulous will go to great lengths to use charity to hide their bad deeds or to establish or enhance their credibility—the question arises as to what people really think of charity. In the glare of increasing public scrutiny, should charities be worried about their reputations? We have a better handle on that today than ever before because media accounts have become both more numerous and more critical.

Media Perceptions of Charities

When you compare the story about the Stanford gift in the 1890s and the ones reporting on the mega-gifts of the early twenty-first century—such as Dorothy and Donald Stabler's $334 million bequest to Lehigh University, and Helen Kimmel's $156 million gift to New York University's Medical Center[13]—it may seem that not much has changed in the way the public hears news of philanthropy. But, in fact, much is different. Even though when it comes to donor-centric stories, reporters are still essentially reverential, coverage that is more critical of charities has begun to emerge.

Prior to the late 1980s there certainly had been information aplenty about the more technical aspects of philanthropy, mainly through tax newsletters—publications written by attorneys and accountants who specialize in the technicalities of charitable giving—but nothing was available that put all topics relating to philanthropy and charitable organizations under one roof, a place where those employed or volunteers at nonprofits could go for comprehensive information about their world.

Although the nuances of complex gifts remain the subject of the specialty newsletters, journalism-based outlets began to emerge in the late 1980s. The growth of interest of all things philanthropic inspired the creation in 1988 of the *Chronicle of Philanthropy*, which would become the first principal outlet of comprehensive reporting on the important nonprofit issues of the day. With the tag line, "connecting the nonprofit world with news, jobs and ideas," the *Chronicle of Philanthropy* quickly filled a void by addressing a growing appetite for a publication devoted solely to issues of the philanthropic world.

Since then, several other publications also have begun to regularly report on the world of philanthropy. The *Nonprofit Times* and the *Philanthropy Journal* are such outlets. Created by veteran journalist Todd Cohen, the online publication *Philanthropy Journal* is a product of the A. J. Fletcher Foundation in Raleigh, North Carolina. Well-done, comprehensive, and highly intelligent, the site is another in a line of examples of the growth and sophistication in philanthropy and nonprofit journalism. The *Philanthropy Journal* describes its vision as helping "people understand, support and work in the nonprofit and philanthropic world, and help them recognize and solve social problems."[14] The *Nonprofit Times* is still mostly a paper product and competes with the *Chronicle of Philanthropy*. In addition, there are several other sites and many blogs that analyze and gossip about many other aspects of the world of nonprofits and their supporters.

The country's larger newspapers also keep an eye on the general-interest philanthropy stories. A few of those include the fight over the estate of Brooke Astor, the New York City socialite and philanthropist who died in 2007 at the age of 105; the controversy involving the will of Leona Helmsley, the flamboyant hotelier (she provided mightily for her dog); and the legal dispute between Princeton University and the son of one of its largest benefactors over the matter of how the gift income was being used. These stories, and others that also find space in the major publications, usually have in common a lot of money and not a little drama.

*   *   *

On a single day—I happened to see the following on August 31, 2009—in addition to its story about a $20 million pledge for the University of Miami Medical Institute, the *Chronicle of Philanthropy* reported that the residents of Auburn, California, were upset to learn that the town had agreed to name its park after William Shockley, winner of the 1910 Nobel Prize in Physics, whose views on race and intelligence were controversial, but who, in his will, had donated the 28 acres of land that the town had turned into the park. There were also interviews with Bill Gates and his father, as well as with the California philanthropist Eli Broad, about their views of philanthropy. In the same issue, readers could also learn that that the long-running PBS show *Reading Rainbow* was being canceled because of a shortage of money and donors, and that, even though the stock market and the economy were doing poorly worldwide, charity fundraisers in Europe were more optimistic than their American counterparts.[15]

That the amount of news relating to nonprofits and philanthropy has been growing, and that journalism is growing up, are good developments. An example of a critical story about philanthropy was when the *Los Angeles Times* researched the endowment portfolio at the Bill and Melinda Gates Foundation and discovered many investments in companies that contradicted the

purposes of the foundation.[16] That is not to say that the foundation's investment managers were doing anything wrong, but it has
been a steady development over the years that newspapers and
broadcasting outlets have begun to look at a gift or a charitable
entity more critically than ever before. John D. Rockefeller would
have a tough time these days keeping his image clean.

The bell curve of journalistic examination has moved away
from pure adoration or regurgitating a press release. A gift of
some millions of dollars to a charity will always catch the awed
eye of any journalist, but, while donors are lauded for their good
deeds, either their ideals or the real purpose of the gift is more
likely to be critically examined than ever before. That goes for
charities too.

By the end of 2009, the *Boston Herald* was skeptical enough
about high salaries at nonprofits that it wrote a story with the
headline, "Charity Heads Home." It began with this: "As the
worst recession in decades stripped thousands of Bay State workers of their jobs, a small group of people saw greenbacks continue
to fatten their paychecks."

An accompanying article described the perks at charities. That
story started this way: "A *Herald* review of scores of Boston-area
nonprofits has found a small number that don't hesitate to gener-
ously lend a hand...to their own leaders, that is."[17]

The paper's research revealed that a number of social service
agencies—which are not the most financially secure segment of
charities in the land; compared to many universities, museums
and hospitals, they run on shoestrings in the land—paid their
executive directors in excess of $400,000. The article named the
Massachusetts Housing Investment Corporation (MHIC), which
helps finance affordable housing projects; Vinfen, a mental-illness
service provider; Oxfam, the international relief organization; and
the May Institute, a service provider for those with autism. One
organization, The Education Resources Institute, a student-loan
information provider and lender, paid its head $600,000 a year.

The *Herald* also discovered that some organizations in Boston
with comparable operating budgets paid salaries to their executive
directors that were not comparable. Action for Boston Community
Development (ABCD) and the Boston Foundation both have operating budgets of about $130 million, but ABCD's president was
paid less than half of the head of the Boston Foundation. Another
example was the Pine Street Inn, a homeless shelter, which paid
its executive director half of what MHIC paid its director, even

though the Pine Street Inn's $32 million annual budget is nearly five times that of MHIC.

"You have to pay for talent," is the refrain heard often in connection with the criticism of high executive pay at charities. Indeed. Oxfam America said it would have "a greater impact if we pay salaries that attract and retain the leaders with the right set of skills and experience."[18] Yet the large and growing number of media stories that are critical of charities often originate in the discovery of how much a charity's leader is paid and people intuitively sensing that it's too much.

The editors at that celebration of capitalism, *Forbes Magazine*, intuitively think there's a problem. They discovered that a lot of talent at the larger charities—that is, the elite universities, hospitals, and museums—is getting paid handsomely. Responding to the 2009 nationwide nonprofit salary survey conducted by the *Chronicle of Philanthropy* and after listing the top salaries, Forbes said there were critics, among whom the magazine surely counted itself, who are, "Shocked and appalled at these exorbitant executive salaries," that those critics believed that "the IRS should put a cap on the salary a nonprofit CEO can earn."[19]

*   *   *

Increased public skepticism about the behavior of charitable organizations based on media stories such as those mentioned above has become real enough that Marion Fremont-Smith, an attorney and a senior research fellow at Harvard's Kennedy School of Government, and her colleague Andras Kosaras searched through press reports between 1995 and 2002 to prepare a report on nonprofit fraud. The search produced 104 reports of newsworthy criminal activity during that time. Fifty-four of those involved breaches of fiduciary duty.[20] Fiduciaries at a charity are its directors, trustees, and corporate officers; in other words, the people who are in charge.

Another survey, of news reports published in 2003, examined the wrongdoing of charity employees other than fiduciaries, from bookkeepers to executive directors, and it showed that there were 32 newspaper reports of criminal incidents at charities.[21]

Is this a high rate of crime? Perhaps not, when you consider the total number of charities in the United States. But Fremont-Smith thinks her survey results of wrongdoing "indicate a persistent degree of criminal activity."[22] Regardless of whether these reports show a lot of or "just" a little wrongdoing in the nonprofit sector, it is no wonder that people today trust charities less today than they did in the past.

The charitable pedestal is wobbling.

*   *   *

Sometimes donors are actually criticized for making a gift. In August 2009 the financier and philanthropist George Soros, through his foundation, the Open Society Institute, announced that he would donate $35 million to the state of New York to permit approximately 850,000 low-income school children to benefit from a four-to-one matching program that the federal government had established as part of its economic stimulus program. The prevailing reaction was this: What a great day for the state's poor students, who could use the money—$200 per child—to pay for school supplies. New York's governor David Paterson said the money was a "critical boost for families preparing for school in September."

A few days later, however, the state's senate Republican leader, Dean Skelos, criticized the gift, saying that it was a bad idea because it didn't restrict the spending to back-to-school shopping. "It's a plan that's ripe for fraud and abuse," he claimed. Whether there would be abuse or, if, as another critic said, "It exemplifies the federal stimulus approach at its worst," that reaction is the kind of thing that has been happening to philanthropy over the years: Such donations are no longer seen as acts of altruism.[23] Today, they are far more often seen as financial transactions edged with a purpose.

*   *   *

The idea of asking people for money to support a charitable cause is rather profound, filled with depth and purpose, but when producers in the entertainment industry get involved, it can seem almost silly. When NBC aired *The Philanthropist* in the summer of 2009, the world saw how far the television industry has to go before any meaningful representation of the world of philanthropy is ready for prime time. If shows like the popular and respectable *Law and Order* dramatize the otherwise dull proceedings of courtroom battles,[24] they at least are true to their subject. The *Philanthropist* wasn't. It was sappy and had nothing to do with the way people are motivated to give either their time or their money. It was much more about the lead character loving himself and not loving humanity. Bad acting and a bad script didn't help either. One blogger called it the "television program philanthropy loves to hate." For good reason, wrote William Schambra, the director of the Bradley Center at the Hudson Institute in Washington, D.C. Why? "Because the program challenges the central premise of American philanthropy: that it is—and should be—turning into a profession."[25] All and all, this was a genteel criticism of a crass portrayal.

The superficiality of the *Philanthropist* was out of whack with the depth and seriousness of what philanthropy actually offers. While newspapers have come a long way, entertainment producers either cannot grasp the importance and real impact of the nonprofit world or they don't think their audience can. Intelligent dramatic discourse examining the seeds of altruism does not yet exist.

Yet despite these signals of a general distrust and misperception about the work charitable organizations do, the public is coming to understand that the nation's charities are an essential ingredient in today's society. Donors are making larger gifts that have more impact than ever before, and organizations are operating on larger and larger budgets. Professionals, many of them credentialed or degreed for the purpose, are hired to raise money.

And all of that is good. Even though that has the effect of dulling the shine, its compact with the public means charity should be held to a far higher standard than it has been in the past. Even though some media outlets are less observant and critical than others, their collective impact has been that people are more aware of the issues facing charities, and whether an organization is functioning poorly. Everyone wants media coverage, but it is axiomatic that when things are publicly shown to have gone wrong, the people involved blame the media. It's possible that problems exposed at a charity are the result of a novice journalist unfairly attempting to create a reputation on the back of the sector least expected to do wrong. But that's not usually the case, and charities cannot and should not try to escape what is true and well known: an independent lens—not only because of its independence but because it can be intelligently critical—is healthy for society.

Public Opinion Polls

A National Nonprofits Ethics Survey conducted in 2007 found good news and bad news regarding the way people feel about charities. The good news was that the public thinks charities on the whole behave more ethically than for-profit organizations or government. "Nonprofits have the strongest ethics standing over any other sector," according to the survey. The most telling of the bad news was that "integrity in the nonprofit sector is eroding" and that "misconduct is on the rise—especially financial fraud."[26] In fact, people said they think that financial fraud at charities is actually higher at nonprofits than at for profits or in government. That may seem inconsistent with the notion that charities have a strong ethical standing, but that happens in surveys when an issue is approached in different ways. It may be that people want to think good things about charity, but that they are also concerned.

Boards receive a good deal of the blame for all this. "Boards, while very important in shaping the perceptions of employees with regard to ethics," the report said, "are not taking advantage of their influence to set clear ethics standards for their nonprofit organizations. Where boards have heavy influence, we also see high levels of misconduct."[27]

So, while the ethical climate at charities was healthy in 2007, according to the Ethics Resource Center, it was deteriorating.

Similarly, a 2008 survey conducted by the Wagner Graduate School of Public Service at New York University concluded that, "charitable confidence has not risen significantly since it hit bottom in 2003, Americans remain skeptical of charitable performance, the considerable drop in the ratings of helping people poses a serious challenge to the sector's distinctiveness as a destination for giving and volunteering, and estimates of charitable waste remain disturbingly high."[28] Confidence in charities dropped dramatically after 9/11, when the public learned that the Red Cross had been siphoning gifts intended for the victims to other purposes.

A Harris Interactive poll conducted in 2006 found that "one-third of adults have less than positive feelings toward America's charitable organizations." About the same number thinks "the nonprofit sector in America has pretty seriously gotten off in the wrong direction."

But here's the really damaging kicker: While a majority of adults have "positive feelings toward nonprofits" and the vast majority—92 percent—of households contribute to charity, only one in ten "strongly agrees that charitable organizations are honest and ethical in their use of donated funds."[29]

Then there's the issue of cost. Fraud at charities is a costly business. A study conducted in 2008 indicates that approximately $40 billion is stolen from charities every year by their employees. The data came from the Association of Certified Fraud Examiners, which found that "all organizations," including nonprofits, "lose on average six percent of their revenue to fraud every year." The underlying assumption is that charities are no different from for-profit businesses when it comes to stealing. Even though it may be surmised, as it was, that since all groups were lumped together, the number might be lower for charities and *higher* for businesses. Unfortunately, there is no is no way to know—and, right now, no reason to think charity employees are more honest than those anywhere else. It may well be that charities actually experience a higher rate of theft because the financial controls at the average charity may not be as sophisticated as those at a business. For nonprofits, with total revenues of approximately $65 billion, that means $4 billion. "It's a surprisingly large number," said Paul Light, a professor of public service at New York University who does surveys of public confidence in charities. "We really need to take a good hard look at what's going on in these organizations."[30]

But the situation is not entirely dire: An organization called Indiana Nonprofits, a joint project of the Center on Philanthropy at Indiana University and Indiana University's School of Public and Environmental Affairs, issued a report in February 2009 entitled "Are Nonprofits Trustworthy?" It found that "three-fourths of the respondents said they trusted nonprofits or charities...to do what is right most or just about all the time, compared to only about one-fifth who felt that way about the federal government."

That, of course, isn't exactly the highest bar by which to measure success, but, overall, nonprofits came in first in the trustworthiness category among a group that also included business, local government, and state government. The report said that those who trusted nonprofits least included respondents "over the age of 65, separated or living with someone, African-American or minority status, retired, have no more than a High School degree, live in households with no more than $35,000 in income, rent their home, live in a rural community, and are undecided about their choice for President." That left the affluent white people—who constituted about 85 percent of the Indiana respondents, a little over half of whom had a college degree—as having the most trust in nonprofits.[31]

In 2008, the Charity Commission in England conducted a study on public trust and confidence in charities. The study found that, as in the United States, Brits have a relatively high level of confidence in their charities, and many of them—85 percent— also give to charity. Also, as with the Indiana study, perceptions of charities vary among people in different ages, socioeconomic categories, and ethnicity.

Most important, though, were what was identified as key drivers of the public trust. The most important positive driver is the "belief that charities spend their money wisely and effectively." The next two were "the belief that charities ensure that a reasonable proportion of donations make it to the end cause" and "that fundraisers are ethical and honest." Other positive drivers include the belief that charities are regulated and controlled to ensure that they work for the public benefit, having personally experienced what a particular charity does, and a belief in the charity's cause. Interestingly, the belief that charities make a positive difference to the cause they work for "actually has a much lower impact on people's overall trust" than the other drivers.

The study showed that the vast majority of the public thinks that charities play an "essential" or "very important" role in society; also, that most people—83 percent—acknowledge that they have benefited from a charity in some way; however, "almost three in five people—59 percent—admit to knowing very little about how charities are run and managed."[32]

Foundations—an important source of revenue for public charities—are beginning to weigh in on the issue of trust too. Melissa Berman, the president and chief executive officer of Rockefeller Philanthropic Advisors, a group whose mission is to help potential donors to make worthwhile philanthropic choices, addressed trust in the organization's 2008 annual report. After noting that trust in both government and financial institutions has deteriorated, she wrote, "This trust deficit is also crippling for the philanthropic and charitable sector. Nonprofits now have far more cause to worry that a donor's pledge has little or no meaning. Donors have to worry that nonprofits have not invested their money with proper safeguards, or that they are not financially sound enough to sustain their mission."[33]

What to make of all these attitudes and perceptions? Since nonprofits exist solely to do good deeds and don't profit or govern, you might wonder why as much as 25 percent of those surveyed, as seen in the Indiana study, think nonprofits are trustworthy either only some of the time or almost never. That the public perception of charities is that they are no worse than government or business should provide no solace as to how we think charities are operating. That particular bar is too low to be meaningful. If the other two sectors can better the nonprofit sector at what should be one of its greatest strengths—trustworthiness—then what's the point of even having a nonprofit sector? We may as well give it up and watch from the sidelines as the crucial needs of society, unaddressed by those other two sectors, inexorably become fully neglected altogether.

What *Is* Charity?

Clearly, there's the growing question in the public's mind about whether charity is a force for good. The concern is burdened by something quite fundamental: Marion Fremont-Smith, in addition to chronicling fraud at charities, acknowledges that no one has really nailed down what the word *charity* means. This is one of the few instances where the difference between the words *charity* and *nonprofit* is important: nonprofit has a clear legal definition, while for most people charity is a concept of the heart.

A charity in many people's minds is an organization that serves the poor and is poor itself. But that's not the type of place where most charitable donations end up. Robert Reich, the secretary of labor under President Clinton, notes that many philanthropic gifts go "to culture palaces: to the operas, art museums, symphonies and theaters where the wealthy spend much of their leisure time. Donors] also give money to the universities they attended and expect their children to attend, perhaps with the added inducement of knowing that these schools often practice a kind of affirmative action for 'legacies.'" To Reich, it is appropriate that a contribution to "the Salvation Army is eligible for a charitable deduction. It helps the poor. But," he asks, "why, exactly, should a contribution to the already extraordinarily wealthy Guggenheim Museum or to Harvard University?"[34] The public perception of such a simple issue as what constitutes a charity, in the sense of an organization that deserves help from the public because it helps the poor, is up in the air. Even someone so steeped in philanthropy and finance as Robert Reich is can't put his finger on it.

In fact, to many people, a place like Harvard is no charity. Any organization with such a large financial cushion—Harvard's endowment was valued at $38 billion before the severe market decline beginning in the fall of 2008 diminished it by approximately 30 percent—has to fight hard to convince people that it is the kind of organization that, from a public policy perspective, should be in the same category as homeless shelters, which have no endowment at all and struggle just to keep the lights on.

From the perspective of the money management skills required to run most charities, it is excusable if some people think that running Harvard is very much like running a Fortune 500 *for-profit* business. Some charities—large universities, such as Tulane and Stanford; museums, such as the Museum of Modern Art and the Getty Museum; and hospitals, such as the Mayo Clinic and Massachusetts General Hospital—feel more like corporate entities than nonprofits, and they have attracted people with the same ethos as business managers have, where the bottom line is the most important value. It is no wonder that the media include not only fawning narratives about donors but critical stories that focus on the problems charities not only face but incur. And they do much to bring their problems to themselves.

The growing criticism isn't only about how "bad" charities are getting. It's also about our expectations and the image charities have in our hearts, an image we almost certainly will never let go of. For it is against this standard of purity—not of government or commerce—that we measure our hopes and dreams for this one segment of our lives that we refuse to think of as anything but innocent. While the day-to-day of the nonprofit world isn't entirely innocent—even though we expect a charitable ethos from those who work at charities, they still must deal humanly with problems—for all but the most cynical charity is still that good thing in society that generates unadulterated hope. Although that hope is often mirrored in the public accountings of charities, those accountings also expose cracks in the mirror.

Charities today must deal with a more complex world than they used to. In addition to highlighting the good deeds they do, charities must do far more than they have been doing to combat poor perceptions. They must not only avoid fraud and other scandals, they must act out the honor they claim by aggressively, preemptively fighting fraud. If the label "charity" is to mean anything, the mandate must be to act ethically.

The sooner charities do that—the sooner they raise the bar on themselves—the better, because there are those who are convinced that charities can't do it by themselves. As we have seen, the nonprofit world is filled with a growing tension. That tension, brought about by perceptions that call into question purpose and law at charities, has made its way to the corridors of regulatory power. It may seem discordant that in a quest for the ethical sector to improve, some would feel that it will require the efforts of lawmakers and regulators, but that's what we have. In addition to the public and the media, the nonprofit world has looking over its shoulder—and sometimes right in its face—the courts, Congress, the IRS, and the legislature and the attorney general in every state.

As they fight increased regulation, charities would be wise to keep in mind that laws have their ethical underpinnings. Violations of generally accepted ethical norms are often best corrected, at least by those for whom answers are to be found in such places, with laws and regulations.

Chapter Two

Regulating and Scrutinizing Charities

Charities that don't want more regulation may think they don't have much to worry about. In a world of decreasing state and federal budgets, and in a sector that generates little in taxes[1] and with so many other regulatory priorities—it may seem that no one in the corridors of power has much appetite for serious regulatory oversight or, certainly, for imposing reform.

But that would be a mistake. Regulators may be struggling financially, but they will rise to the occasion—even if only sporadically—if they think it commands the public's best interests. Are there some regulators who are politically sensitive and use a less-than-pure compass to decide what groups to chase down? Sure. But don't mistake that for the absence of a sense of responsibility—which, feeble as it may sound, often finds its resolve in the cries coming from the media. Public perception of charities—as measured by increased, intense media scrutiny and polls indicating the public's lack of trust—has shifted. So, too, has the perception of the regulators.

Because of limited staff and other priorities, regulators are often not able to unearth what goes wrong at charities as often or as easily as news reporters can. The media, in effect, act as an arm of the regulator. Enough stories of wrongdoing sniffed out by a reporter hot on the trail of a few leads pointing to fraud, and regulators are sure to pay attention.

* * *

There were periods in the first decade of this century when the charitable climate was not good: In late 2001, the Red Cross came under fire for mishandling donations meant to help 9/11 victims; in 2003, the *Washington Post* in a series of articles accused the Nature Conservancy of making insider deals with its major donors that took advantage of the tax laws by offering to sell pristine land only to insiders close to the charity; that same year, a Supreme

Court case highlighted how much money many charities spend on telemarketing services, amounts that *weren't* being used for the charity's mission; and, in 2007, the head of Smithsonian Institution was in the midst of explaining to the public, and to Congress, why he made so much money and spent so much more money on matters unrelated to the organization's mission.[2] Throughout the decade, less publicized but still troublesome transgressions involving scam artists, dubious car-donation schemes, and imprecise gift-valuation practices seemed rampant.

For the regulators, these problems seemed to highlight the extent to which the laws as well as the practices of the nonprofit sector were out of synch with its public purposes. Even before some these issues came to light, Senator Charles Grassley, who at the time was the chairman of the Senate Finance Committee, recognized a need for change. In 2004, he said he was going to propose legislation based on the "various charitable abuses" his staff had been investigating.[3]

Whether regulators don't have the time or staff they need to do a thorough job or charity officials and fundraisers simply want them to stay away doesn't make much difference. As for the assumption that charities are the "good guys," regulators have begun sending the message that enough has come to light to suggest otherwise. Charities need to wake up to this new reality. The days of hiding under the radar are over.

*   *   *

Yet if we were to take a poll, we would almost certainly discover that the nonprofit sector overwhelmingly opposes any further regulation. The consensus would be that, between the federal government—the Congress and the IRS requiring that charities complete a complex form explaining their finances and meddling with the valuation of gifts—and the state governments—the attorney general who pays attention to the operations of charities—there are enough laws on the books regulating the way charities operate. The protests go like this: "Leave us alone. There's no need for any more paperwork." "What right do government agencies have to intrude? We're the good guys." And the resistance is aimed not only at government efforts; even those from within the industry—*voluntary* efforts—are suspect.

In 2005 the Johns Hopkins Center for Civil Society Studies reported that "more than 95 percent of nonprofit groups had undergone an independent financial audit within the past two years and have established internal procedures to ensure their financial accounting is solid." This led Lester Salamon, the center's director, to dismiss the critics' claims, saying that the problems are "not anywhere near as heinous as the anecdotes in the newspapers seem to imply."[4]

In response to Congress's growing interest in regulation, Independent Sector, a group that represents several hundred charities, issued a report in March 2007 that recommended several steps charities could take to better govern themselves.[5] But Adam Meyerson, the president of the Philanthropy Roundtable, an association of donors, corporate giving officers, and foundation trustees and staff responded to those recommendations with skepticism:

> First, we have concerns about specific proposals. In particular, we fear that some of the draft principles take a "one-size-fits-all" approach to setting rules for a very diverse sector, are an invitation to arbitrary enforcement, or would require private organizations to reveal publicly their internal decision-making processes.
>
> Second, we are concerned about how the proposed principles would be administered and enforced. Independent Sector doesn't explain what it means by "self-regulation." And there are some forms of self-regulation that would be seriously harmful to the foundation world and to charitable giving.[6]

There is no acknowledgement in Meyerson's entire 2,000-word response to Independent Sector's report of any wrongdoing on the part of charities. The above quotation is not taken out of context; it reflects the essence of the message. It's true that in his opening paragraph, Meyerson expresses gratitude for Independent Sector's attention to the issue, but it is very pro forma, so much so that one has to question its sincerity—especially because he otherwise does not admit that anything is wrong.

That attitude concerns regulators, as it should. A sector that touts itself as representing the best of society ought to be more receptive to suggestions to correct problems that are as clear as day to anyone who pays attention.

One commentator, however, felt the report didn't go far enough. Pablo Eisenberg, a fellow at Georgetown University, said of the Independent Sector report, "Nonprofit leaders have produced a timid, uninspired report, long on mild, safe suggestions," and accused Independent Sector of bowing "to pressure from nonprofit groups that do not want to be overly burdened by regulations." He asserted that "it should be possible" for Independent Sector "to produce more than a mouse of a report."[7]

Michael Peregrine, an attorney at the law firm of McDermott Will & Emery, laid out his version of the issue in a speech at the 2009 meeting of the National Association of Attorneys General and the National Association of State Charity Officials in Dallas, Texas. He placed the ongoing controversies concerning the governance and business practices of the high-profile nonprofit organizations on " 'front burner' legal feasibility issues" that are occurring "at an extraordinary pace." He also underscored the growing sense that "existing statutes and regulations may be insufficient to provide effective oversight of nonprofit organizations, particularly those that are structurally and/or financially sophisticated." The message was clear: Charity oversight needs to be stepped up.

Peregrine also cited as a driving force in the need for change the public's loss of confidence in the integrity of charitable organizations. "More than ever before, nonprofit governance is operating within an environment of skepticism, in which the bona fide charitable nature of organizational activities will not serve as a shield for non-compliant activity. Furthermore, governance must be prepared to respond to an emerging, broader climate of corporate accountability that may sharpen finger-pointing at the board."[8]

Combine that with newspaper accounts and a shifting, more demanding attitude in Congress, at the IRS, and among state attorneys general than ever before about how charities behave and their role in society, and you have an unprecedented level of official skepticism in what for so long has been a benignly neglected world.

Taking Issue with The IRS

The tax laws that affect charities are passed by Congress. They are enforced and, where necessary, interpreted by the IRS. Notable among these laws are those related to charities' tax-exempt status. Tax-exempt status means that a charity can make investments without paying tax on the gain and that donations made to a charity are tax deductible for donors. There are many laws that govern the ways nonprofits and charitable giving work, and, as in many ways taxes affect the rest of society, they can be complex. In fact, the complexity of the tax code for tax-exempt organizations means that the IRS—an organization whose sole purpose is to collect taxes, an irony when you think how much time they spend on nonprofits—must carefully monitor all transactions designed to reduce or eliminate taxes.

The basic idea is that, when the government tries to balance its need to collect taxes with what is lost in the charitable sphere—taxes on income and realized investment gains, as well as deductions for gifts—it wants to be sure that the monies diverted from the public account benefit society by at least that same amount. In other words, charities' tax-exempt status and donors' deductions mean lost government revenue, and Congress wants to make sure that when the treasury foregoes that money, it goes to a cause that Congress has approved.

The IRS plays the role of a police officer to enforce the laws, except, unlike the police, it has considerable interpretive and decision-making power where the law is not clear. Usually, when the IRS denies a charitable income tax deduction, it is because of something straightforward: The donor did not make the gift before December 31 but took the deduction anyway. Or the donor overvalued a gift; many gifts are not straightforward, and complex calculations are needed to ascertain their value.

One area of vagueness has been in the valuation of noncash gifts. Publicly traded stocks are no problem because their value comes across the stock exchanges every day, but other assets, such as land, for example, are more difficult to value. Although it has a meaning in the IRS Regulations—the price that would be agreed on between a willing buyer and a willing seller, with neither being required to act, and both having reasonable knowledge of the relevant facts—value is hard to pin down. Until the mid-1980s, which is when a valuation process was established, there wasn't much the IRS could do, other than through the audit process, about overstated valuations of gifts. The value of artwork, for example, was notoriously overstated until the mid-1980s; the IRS's art panel estimates that back then the average overvaluation of donated art was almost 1,000 percent. That is, a $100,000 deduction for a gift of art to a museum would likely be reduced upon audit to a value of only $10,000.

In response, the IRS established the qualified appraisal methodology, a way for all noncash gifts—not just artwork—to be valued and reported. The methodology isn't an exact science, but the rules do require that a professional and disinterested appraiser value the asset, and then sign his or her name on a form that the donors sends to the IRS. The amount can be compared to the deduction the donor claims. The IRS doesn't audit everyone, of course, but now it has a much better idea of the actual value of the assets donors are deducting. As part of the process, the IRS also requires charities to report sales of donated assets that are made within three years after the gift was received, the theory being that the IRS can compare the gift's claimed value as a donation to its actual market value. Large differences, which for some reason tend to show that the donated value was much higher than the amount it sold for, and not the other way around, raise a red flag. The qualified appraisal rules haven't done away with the need for audits, but, far more than in what is now the distant past, the IRS is likely to notice when a charity sells a donated parcel of property for less than what the donor deducted.

*   *   *

The U.S. Tax Court adjudicates disputes involving charitable deduction claims.

Much of the time, when they are notified by the IRS of why a deduction has been denied, donors see the error of their ways and pay the lost tax and, usually, a penalty. But that's not the way all donors react. Some argue with the IRS and take their case to court—and so, when there's a dispute over taxes, and there are many, they are resolved in tax court, which is a federal court.

While it may seem that the IRS is omnipotent, it loses a lot more cases than you might think when it's up against taxpayers. Like the Supreme Court, the United States Federal Tax Court has issued landmark decisions that have defined the rules within which donors and charities operate. How to apply those rules in specific situations often remains unclear, however.

Easements, for example, are important sources of charitable deductions. An easement permits another person or company to use property for a specific purpose, such as when a public utility is permitted to run its telephone lines on private property. A conservation easement, the type we're talking about in the world of charitable deductions, is a special restriction on property that prevents it from being used for commercial purposes. A perpetual easement means that the property can never be developed. In 2002, Kiva Dunes, a development company in Alabama, placed a perpetual conservation easement on a golf course it owned and then donated the easement to the North American Land Trust. Kiva Dunes claimed a charitable income tax deduction of a little more than $30.5 million. The IRS denied the deduction altogether and also imposed penalties because it felt the transaction was incorrectly valued.

The owner of Kiva Dunes said he would see the IRS in court.

While an easement is a good thing for people who want to enjoy the natural beauty of a property, it also has the effect of reducing its value; that is, the value that otherwise would be realized from its "highest and best use," a real estate phrase that captures the idea of the potential for property to provide the seller with the maximum profit. Both the IRS and Kiva Dunes offered up experts who appraised the easement property given that condition. Both appraisers used the same methodology but based their calculations on different economic assumptions.

After a lengthy and meticulous mathematical comparison of all the economic and financial factors and confirming all the numbers, the judge bought the argument of the company's appraiser—not the IRS's.

Court documents provide a clue as to why. The court noted that the IRS's appraiser,

> Philip Paulk is a Member of the Appraisal Institute. He has spent a substantial portion of his appraisal career in Atlanta, Georgia. Mr. Paulk recently moved to, and has offices in, Birmingham, Alabama, 250 miles from Kiva Dunes Golf Course. Mr. Paulk has no particular expertise in Baldwin County, and he has been to the Baldwin County, Alabama, area only twice in connection with his appraisal of the easement.

Compare that to its assessment of the appraiser for Kiva Dunes:

> Mr. Clark is a professional real estate appraiser and has decades of experience in Baldwin County. He has lived and worked in the immediate vicinity of the subject property for 22 years and owns and has owned property on the Fort Morgan Peninsula. Mr. Clark performs more appraisal work in Baldwin County than any other appraiser, and he has a great depth of knowledge of the comparable properties used in valuing the easement and of the surrounding local real estate market.[9]

For an appraiser, experience and familiarity with the area where the property is located are essential. After a few adjustments imposed by the court, Kiva Dunes was able to claim a deduction of a little more than $28.6 million. The IRS lost that one.

It's important to realize that the IRS doesn't necessarily have the last word, and donors armed with what they think are legitimate arguments will often feel emboldened to take on the IRS in court.

Applying for Nonprofit Status

Most charities today are organized as corporations, and states approve and regulate corporations. Each state sets the rules that guide the language for the nonprofit's by-laws, establishes a minimum number of people to serve on its board, and dictates other administrative matters affecting the organizational components of the nonprofit. Thus, the first stop for an organization on the way to becoming a nonprofit is at the office of the secretary of state.

After a charity is approved at the state level, it then must apply to the federal government—to the IRS—for its tax-exempt status. The approval process is slightly arduous; the application is a little more lengthy and complicated than a personal tax return. Usually a charity waits several months before receiving its tax-exemption letter.

The wait will almost always be worth it, however. The IRS has the easiest grading system in the universe. All the IRS looks for, in reality, in addition to the proper corporate structure, is that the organization is doing something approved as a charitable activity. Almost every application for tax-exempt status—about 98 or 99 percent—is approved. "Obtaining recognition by the IRS as a public charity is an embarrassingly easy thing to do," says a report written by Stanford students in October 2009. "It is hardly an exaggeration to say that when it comes to oversight of the application process to become a public charity, nearly anything goes." Rob Reich, the Stanford professor who oversaw the study, said, "It seems utterly implausible that anyone can be doing due diligence in any way that constitutes a serious review of the applicant, let alone keep an eye on them after they are approved."[10]

And except for the applicants, the high rate of approval doesn't play as good news. "Especially during these tough economic times, it's troubling to hear we are increasing the number of these organization at such a rapid pace," said Representative Xavier Becerra, a California Democrat who pays attention to nonprofit issues.[11]

The IRS, as you might imagine, takes a different view. Lois Lerner, the director of exempt organizations at the IRS, says that the process has been improved since she got to the agency in 2001. These days, different applications for different types of charities are looked at differently: "We don't need to take the same kind of look at a large hospital and at a local soccer group." As for the scrutiny of applicants, she says, "We're asking them questions and looking at things like whether they seem to be able to go forward" and "educating them so they know what responsibilities they have if they're approved."[12] She has a point. In 2001, the rejection rate was 1 percent; in 2008 it was 2 percent—a 50 percent increase in being declined. But still, getting tax-exempt status is very easy.

The Stanford study used the numbers to essentially mock the types of charities that are approved. It named sixty organizations approved in 2008 whose missions might seem to the public bizarre or not best addressed in the guise of charity. Monticello Graduation Party, organized to "provide a chemical free graduation party for the graduating seniors of Monticello High School on their graduation night," is one example; Planet Jelly Donut—whose website says it "spreads the common belief that the core essence of the human spirit is goodness"—is another; and yet another is The Grand Canyon Sisters of Perpetual Indulgence, a "Missionary Order of an International Order of Sisterhoods of the 21st Century Drag Nuns" that has assumed "a role for the Gay, Lesbian, Bi-sexual, Transgender and Gay Friendly Individuals within our community."[13] To quell any doubt about how accepting these nuns are, the group says that they "do not discriminate...due to sexual orientation, fetishes, marital status, national origin, race, physical imitations, or religious beliefs."[14] Of the 50,000 or 60,000 nonprofit applications accepted by the IRS each year—the number peaked at almost 70,000 in 2007—thousands are for activities most people have never heard of.

To try to find a connection between the number of acceptances and the type of charity that gets accepted, however, might be folly. One of the key justifications for establishing a charity in the United States is that there are so many endeavors that are useful to society that neither government nor the for-profit world can address.

The 990

Every year, charities have to file a financial report with the IRS. It's the 990, a form that many people outside of the nonprofit sector have become much more aware of in the past years. Essentially, charities must report their financial activities on the 990. Not only is the 990 complicated and—many people who work at charities feel—intrusive, the information contained in it is available to the public.[15] The public's right to the information is absolute, as is the charity's obligation to provide it. On the top right-hand corner of the first page of the form, are printed the words: "Open to Public Inspection." They appear in white lettering against a blocked black background, for emphasis.

The 990, which was revised for the first time ever in 2008, asks for what the IRS thinks is essential information about the charity's financial condition. It is also an attempt to determine that the charity is working within the guidelines of its tax-exempt mission. By reading the form, the public can learn about the charity's total budget, including the amount of money that it spent on overhead and fundraising. Over the past several years, people have been interested in calculating the percentage of fundraising costs as they relate to the overall budget and the amount that was raised. The general perception is that the lower the fundraising costs and overhead, and the more money to programs, the better.

A charitable organization's investments show up on the 990 as well. In addition to the annual operational budget, asset data are listed so that people can see just how financially healthy a charity is. A charity may have made a profit or experienced a loss during the fiscal year, and so it is important to also see a summary of all its assets. The 990 reports liquid investments, such as stocks, bonds, and cash; illiquid investments, such as land and buildings; and other assets and obligations that affect the charity's bottom line.

The 990 also shows how much the organization's key staff earn. As noted in chapter one, the pay package of the heads of some charities has become the subject of many of the critical stories in the media recently. The *Chronicle of Philanthropy*, as well as a few other newspapers and magazines, now annually reports on the highest paid people at a charity. Some presidents at large universities earn more than a million dollars a year. The heads at some of the larger hospitals earn even more than the highest paid university presidents. Interestingly, though, the head isn't always the highest paid person at a charity. Sometimes, one of the elite professors at a university makes more than the president; at universities with well-known athletic programs, the football or basketball coach might make more—much more—than anyone else. All of this is reported on the 990.

The form also asks for the names of the trustees and key employees and their salaries. In 2008, supplemental schedules were added to the form—37 in all—some of which an organization must be prepared to submit. For example, one section relates to political campaign activities; another, to whether the organization had any overseas staff.

The 990 also shows whether anyone at the charity loaned money to any of its staff or board members, or if anyone might have a conflict of interest. This is to alert the IRS to the possibility that someone may be benefiting unfairly—and illegally—from the charity. The term is for this *private inurement,* and the idea is that because a charity, as it is "owned" by the public, cannot be a vehicle for unseemly gain on the part of any one individual that is associated with it. As the IRS puts it, "No part of the net earnings of a section 501(c)(3) organization may inure to the benefit of any private shareholder or individual. A private shareholder or individual is a person having a personal and private interest in the activities of the organization."[16] Charities, of course, do not have shareholders, but the provision extends to members of the board of directors, the executive director, or other key employees.

The IRS also asks questions about governance: whether the charity has conflict-of-interest policies, for example, and how the chief executive's compensation was established. These questions can lead to problems, as each—and there are others—calls for an interpretation that is often far too subjective, and the truth of the answer requires far more narration than the 990 allows for.

This makes many wonder what the true purpose of the 990 is. Is it simply a financial accounting to ensure that money is being spent well? Or, because financial decisions are, at root, values and ethics decisions, is it an attempt to get inside the way charities work? That is, in addition to providing basic financial disclosure, does the IRS want to use the 990 to learn if a charity offers meaningful programs and practices good governance so that it serves society as a servant in the voluntary sector?

There's something else, actually: Anyone looking for a charity's soul, anyone who wants to truly evaluate a charity, must look elsewhere. Charities are unique organizations that way—they have a soul, or they should, in a way that for-profit entities cannot and never will. This intangible but real fact poses a problem for regulators. They may have much legitimate work to do, but their work will never connect mere legal behavior with the activities charities undertake to tug at anyone's heartstrings—which is why people have such love affairs with charities.

Rating Charities

Nonprofit organizations don't have the equivalent of a Securities and Exchange Commission to look over their shoulder. There's no Dow Jones or other market index, which measures the value of individual publicly held companies, for charities. There's no Morningstar, which measures the value of mutual funds, for charities. Furthermore, the oversight roles of the states' attorneys generals and the IRS actually do not include helping the public see the differences among charities.

Therefore, another type of overseer has emerged: the ratings agencies. Think of them as unofficial regulatory stepchildren. The ratings agencies analyze the information in a 990—some of it anyway—to calculate the value of a charity. One agency, the Better Business Bureau Wise Giving Alliance, asks for additional information directly from the charity.

The center of attention is on the ratio of total budget to program expenses, as well as on the relationship between a charity's budget and its fundraising costs. But looking at those ratios isn't the best way to evaluate a charity. On the one hand, it helps to know if a charity is in the red and has been for the past decade. It also helps to know how much it costs the organization to raise money, what its executive director is being paid, and other financial components of a charity's operations. But even after its massive update in 2008, which was designed to elicit more information than before then, the 990 still doesn't provide the kind of information that provides comprehensive understanding of a charity's work. Besides, some charities don't tell the truth on the 990. And the information on it is dated; because of the time lag and the filing extensions, which charities take full advantage of, the typical 990 that the public sees is at least one year old and often it is two years old. Using a rating organization to determine the value of a charity is akin to deciding who you want to marry based solely on an analysis of the contents of your prospective mate's 1040, ignoring the potential cultural affinity and intellectual companionship as well as the chemistry that make for a strong relationship. The emotional attachment people feel to charitable causes is not beside the point in an evaluation of a charity. Indeed, it is often *the* point.

In a better world, intelligent, caring, and informed individual donors would take on the role of assessing charities for themselves. Comparing a university to a soup kitchen on a similar scale or set of criteria, as the ratings agencies do, does not make sense—the missions, constituencies, financial operations, and impact on the community, however community is defined for each type of group, are so vastly different. Deciding which one to donate to based on fundraising ratios completely misses the point, which is to find a charity worthy of your support. The analysis takes into account the first layer of considerations by showing tangible financial indicators of health. The second layer is based on impact, and it's this that is so far so unquantifiable. Even if we could quantitatively measure an outcome—a person's satisfaction after being fed a good evening meal, a direct correlation between a particular university's college degree and success in life—there are many ways to interpret those outcomes, and the process is itself subjective and personal. The financial indicators aren't all that quantitative either: that a soup kitchen has no endowment, for example, is not necessarily a sign of financial failure, although a university, to be financially viable these days, needs a strong endowment.

Donors should look to their hearts first to determine the kind of causes they wish to support. The choice of charity begins with that. Then they should become familiar with its work—by talking to the people who work and volunteer at the charity, including members of the board, and getting an understanding of all the ways the charity helps its community. Potential donors should ascertain for themselves the extent of the charity's commitment to its community and how it actually gets help—in the form of food or classroom experience, or whatever the charity does—to those it serves. Ratings don't do a very good job of that. We would do ourselves a favor, despite our love for lists and rankings, by understanding that charities are not like stock quotes, football scores, political elections, or anything else whose results can be calculated pretty much by punching numbers into an adding machine.

How we can gain an understanding of charities is a problem that is all the more acute for those who don't have time for or are not making a big enough gift to warrant an in-depth exploration of the charity's inner workings.

One of the ratings organizations, Charity Navigator, which calls itself "the nation's largest and most-utilized evaluator of charities,"[17] does discuss the limits on evaluations. "We do not recommend using our ratings," its website says, "as the only factor in deciding whether to support a particular organization."[18] It even approaches the issue of not addressing program effectiveness: "We hope over time to expand the information we provide donors, and that includes developing a methodology for measuring an organization's output. For now we're still seeking a methodology that would allow us to apply a uniform standard to all charities...."[19]

But until someone figures out how to impose a uniform standard on the heart, the ratings system as we know it is probably here to stay, and the value of charities are held hostage primarily to a derivative of the financial information found on the 990.

And the nonprofit world has one more overseer.

The IRS and Governance

Over the past several years, the IRS has come to see its role as larger than merely collecting 990s and, except for the occasional audit, filing them away. Its vision is not about only fighting bloated deductions, either. The IRS sees itself more and more as another pair of eyes on governance issues.

Governance is, of course, the provenance of the board of directors and, to put it mildly, charities are enduring a governance crisis. In 2005 The Urban Institute, a nonpartisan research organization in Washington, D.C., conducted what it said was a "first-ever national representative survey of over 5,100 nonprofits" and found that 70 percent of them found it difficult to recruit board members.[20] As governance can be generally defined as the exercise of authority and control at an organization, it has important implications to how well an organization is run, which in turn affects the ability of a charity both to comply with IRS regulations and to accomplish its aspirational goals or transform itself into a true leader in the community.

By the way, addressing what has become an acute issue, the report stated:

> that among those nonprofits that say they did not engage in transactions with board members or affiliated companies, fully 75 percent also say they do not require board members to disclose their financial interests in entities doing business with the organization, and thus, respondents may have been unaware of transactions that do exist.[21]

Sarah Ingram, the commissioner of tax-exempt and government entities at the IRS, explained as much in a 2009 speech at the Georgetown University Law School. Building on the Service's initiative toward more and better oversight, she acknowledged that the connection between governance and tax compliance at a nonprofit organization is not altogether clear, and that there are many who don't feel the agency should attempt to involve itself in governance issues.

> These critics often note that effective governance arises from intangibles—the dedication and diligence of responsible officers and board members—rather than from the adoption of numerous rules and procedures. These, in their view, can pile up on top of each other to such an extent that they prevent good governance rather than promote it. Knowing who is right in this discussion is not easy.[22]

No, it isn't. But if people in the nonprofit world ultimately accept the validity of the IRS's effort to help them on the road to better governance, the question will become how valid the information is by which the IRS makes decisions. Even in her hopeful state, where she imagined a better partnership with the nonprofit sector, Ingram implied that anything substantive would not be coming soon. "We are going to start asking agents, at the end of each examination [of a charity]," she said, "to fill out a check sheet about certain of the examined organization's governance practices and internal controls. The check sheet is intended to...gather information about whether the organization had, and used, any internal controls." That sounds undefined—and, as it comes from the mouth of the person in charge of charities at the IRS, a little scary—but she insisted that the effort would be useful.

"Let me be clear—we will be gathering objective data, not subjective views," she said. "And we will do this over time. As we collect enough information to be interesting, we'll share it with the community, and everyone can have a go at it. I appreciate that this is not a statistically valid way of proving anything about good governance. With unlimited resources we would undertake a study that would meet that standard. But this tally by our agents will tell us something, and we will read the results in conjunction with the studies that various members and observers of the tax-exempt sector have undertaken."

To the concern that the IRS might use this information to begin involving itself in the actual management of a charity or to enact a micro-oversight process that an employee or a board member at a charity might reasonably infer from her comments, Ingram said she thinks that oversight will be limited. The IRS is not likely to be interested in deciding which restaurants the board might dine at or which copiers to buy.

> I'm not interested in trying to usurp the business judgment of an organization's officers or board of directors or trustees. Nor am I a micro-economist concerned with whether an organization is maximally efficient in the way it provides its charitable services to the public. I do think, however, that a tax-exempt charity should actually provide charity; it should provide some meaningful and measurable benefit or service to the public.[23]

This is key. What has begun to erode over the years is the public's sense that charities are primarily about serving the public. With all the stories we've heard about rogue leaders, combined with ratings services deciding just how efficient charities are and ought to be, regardless of whether the information generated by those services actually hits the mark, questions relating to good governance and mission do arise. The IRS sees itself in a key position to address those concerns.

But it's a road to be traveled carefully.

"Governance…is not mathematics," said Ingram, perhaps already aware of the concerns not only of critics of the IRS but of people who try to run their charities well.

"There is not only one right answer or way of doing things. In my view, one of the great strengths of the nonprofit sector is that it is a great engine of experimentation and new ideas. There can be, and should be, many varieties of good governance, many right answers." Ingram didn't provide any examples of what she meant by "good governance" or "right answers," presumably because she realizes that they cannot be condensed to a simple list and that charities have to figure those things out by themselves.

Nor, she said, should the IRS "intrude on areas under the jurisdiction and supervision of the attorneys general or charity officials of the states."[24]

*   *   *

Just what is *good governance*, then? This has been debated by many people, including those at BoardSource, a nonprofit in Washington, D.C., that helps charities around the world figure this out. One of the key components, which is also hard to define, is leadership. It's not just about managing the budget and financial picture and hiring the right executive director; it's about looking to the future and…leading.

Ingram described the concept. "What do I understand that term to mean from a federal tax perspective? I am speaking of a number of key organizational and operating principles that the IRS has already articulated, and that find their origin in the Internal Revenue Code. They are not expressly laid out in the Code, nor do they need to be, but the principles of governance that are of concern to the IRS should derive from the requirements for tax exemption."

The principles are as follows:

- The organization should clearly understand and publicly express its mission. This helps assure that the organization provides a public benefit and does not drift away from a charitable purpose. It helps an organization avoid practices that are inconsistent with tax-exempt status.
- The organization's board should be engaged, informed, and independent, and have real responsibility and authority. It must, for example, be able to implement, within the organization, the rules against inurement and self-dealing.
- The organization should operate with complete transparency. Board decisions should be reflected in minutes; records of the information that supported decisions should be retained for reasonable periods; whistleblowers should be protected; and each year's Form 990 should be complete, accurate, and prepared in good faith.

Another set of key good governance principles are those relating to the proper use and safeguarding of assets. These principles are supported by policies and practices that address executive compensation, that protect against conflict of interests, and that support independent financial reviews.

Ingram's IRS thesis is not about a complex set of rules, but about "guiding principles." "Not a battleship bristling with guns, but a sturdy lighthouse with a bright and steady beam."[25]

Even though nothing specific has been proposed, the IRS has officially announced its intentions to be in the game, broadening its idea of oversight to uncharted territory—not only a place it has never before gone, or claimed the right to go, but where careful and thoughtful minds, undistracted by a need for tax-code compliance, have themselves yet to settle and civilize in a way within which all charities can comfortably and industriously operate.

As new as Ingram's sentiments may seem, there is some history. In a 2009 memo to its employees the IRS listed regulations, citations and court cases that have in the past spoken to governance issues, citing the following court cases:

- The Levy Family Tribe Foundation: In 1978 "the Tax Court found that all of the directors and officers of an organization were related and it could not find the 'necessary delineation' between the organization and these persons acting in their personal and private capacity."
- Merle E. Parker, the Foundation for Divine Meditation: In 1966, the 8th Circuit Court of Appeals "concluded that one individual who had 'complete and unfettered control' over an organization had a special burden to explain certain withdrawals from the organization's bank account."
- United Libertarian Fellowship: In 1993, "the U.S. Tax Court stated that 'where the creators control the affairs of the organization, there is an obvious opportunity for abuse, which necessitates an open and candid disclosure of all facts bearing upon the organization, operation, and finances so that the Court can be assured that by granting the claimed exemption it is not sanctioning an abuse of the revenue laws.' "
- Wendy L. Parker Rehabilitation Foundation: In 1986 "the organization was found not to meet the requirements of section 501(c)(3) of the Code. The foundation was formed by the Parker family and benefits inured to Wendy Parker (who was related to all directors). While the family's control over the organization did not in itself preclude exemption, it highlighted the inurement of earnings to the Parker family."
- Western Catholic Church: In 1979 "the court considered an organization with three directors (the founder, his wife, and their daughter) among a membership base of five. The small size of the organization was held to be 'relevant,' with the court finding private inurement and private benefit because of the 'amount of control' the founder exercised over the organization's operations and the 'blurring of the lines of demarcation between the activities and interests' of the organization. The court observed that 'this is not to say that an organization of such small dimensions cannot qualify for tax-exempt status.' "[26]

In theory, the line between good governance and tax compliance will be clear and objective. If this will be so, it will be the first time ever that some level of standardization relating to the concept of "good governance" from an entity with authority will materialize. As Ingram said, there are many critics of the idea, but as things now stand—no one with credibility denies this—governance at charities is not at an optimum place. Chapter 7 examines some of the issues facing boards of directors; for now, it is sufficient to take note that the IRS, in addition to performing its traditional role of ruling on direct tax-related questions—which is to say, most often, questions relating to a donor's tax-*deductions* and a charity's tax-*exemption* status—it will look to enhance tax compliance by evaluating fundamental, albeit the far more difficult to define, components of governance.

Regulators Are on the Case

In 1969 Congress passed its most sweeping reforms of nonprofit laws—before or since. The Tax Reform Act of 1969 established private foundation rules, including a minimum charitable payout requirement of five percent, and a four percent excise tax on net investment income. Congress also raised the deduction limitations for donations to operating private foundations and public charities from 30 percent of adjusted gross income, where it had been set five years earlier, to 50 percent of adjusted gross income. These were matters of a technical nature, however, and none of those changes deterred Congress from its strong support of the charitable world. In 1995, Congress held hearings that resulted in new laws exempting charities from investing and antitrust restrictions that affect the business world.[27]

Today, however, that support might not be as forthcoming. Those laws were passed before the growing onslaught of media stories focusing on misconduct, when charities had more strength and the perception was more positive.

Recently Congress has been growing more doubtful about the purity of charities.

In 2004 the Senate Finance Committee asked its staff to prepare a report on the ways charities might be reformed. Among its considerations were requiring charities to undergo a review every five years to renew its charitable status. Right now, charities have that status forever, unless the IRS revokes it. For that to happen, though, the charity has to engage in egregious misconduct. The report also said that charities that accommodate tax shelters would lose their tax exemption, and that any benefit a charity received from such a transaction would be taxed at a rate of 100 percent.

The report also called for stricter penalties for self-dealing, a process by which the leaders of a charity use the charity for their own personal interests. There also would have been a limit to the amount private foundations can pay their trustees and a limit on amounts paid for travel, meals, and accommodations. Most charities don't pay their trustees anything—when they do, it's usually just to cover travel expenses to the meetings—but over the years, many private foundations, especially the small family foundations, have begun paying their board members a salary. Congress got concerned when it realized that most board members are related family members, and salaries could go through the roof for the few hours they spent three to four times a year deciding how much they should give to their private schools and colleges. Never mind that the usual scenario was that the board decided upon the same charities every time they met and often did no due diligence on them. Often, it was feared, most of the board time was spent socializing.

The report also wanted to incentivize private foundations to give more money away.[28]

The following month, after hearings on the issues raised by Finance Committee staff members, the Finance Committee began to consider charity performance, board governance, nonprofit spending, sweetheart deals, and enforcement.[29]

The Pension Protection Act, passed in 2006, tightened up appraisal requirements and provided more comprehensive guidelines on how donor-advised funds should operate. It also addressed some specific issues; for example, it prohibited tax deductions for "charitable contributions of taxidermy property (a work of art which is the reproduction or preservation of a dead animal)."

That taxidermy item may seem strange. Charles Grassley brought up the stuffed animal issue in his opening remarks at an April 2005 Senate Finance Committee meeting on reforming nonprofits and charitable giving. Addressing the tax gap—the amount of taxes that are owed but not collected, an amount estimated to be approximately $300 billion each year—Grassley homed in on the abuse of the charitable deduction. He said:

> We've become familiar with the problem of individuals taking big tax deductions based on estimates—often pie-in-the-sky estimates—for gifts of closely held stock, in addition to real and tangible property that is given to charity. What we see too often is the charity receiving a very small amount of support, at best, from

this kind of gift, at the same time the taxpayer gets a tremendous benefit from the tax deduction.

I have here a Spring Bok from South Africa. Unfortunately, some people think its name is "Free Buck." The Spring Bok is known for its ability to leap when startled. Boy, were we startled when we learned of this new tax scam. The story in this morning's *Washington Post* makes me think that many people think the "tax" in taxidermy is meant to allow them to write off safaris to Africa as tax deductions if they give away a stuffed animal. This type of scam gives new meaning to the term tax "game."

I expect the Internal Revenue Service to be very active in big-game hunting when it comes to this particular tax shelter. Mr. Commissioner, I would suggest the next head that needs to be mounted—figuratively, of course—is the appraisers who've been promoting this scam. This taxidermy problem is just one example of what we're seeing too often when it comes to certain tax deductions for gifts to charity. Similar problems with valuation exist throughout the tax code. Finding solutions is part of slicing away at the tax gap.[30]

At the same meeting, Senator Max Baucus, the ranking Democrat on the Finance Committee, said, "This proliferation of sloppy, unethical, and criminal behavior is unacceptable." "It has led to a crisis in confidence. It has hurt fund raising by legitimate charities. And it overshadows the good work done by the majority of civic-minded groups."[31]

The tax deductions for gifts to charitable organizations add up to a sizable amount. As mentioned earlier, the IRS estimates that the tax gap every year, the amount of tax revenue that is lost to taxpayer noncompliance, is about $300 billion.[32] About $15 billion of that can be accounted for by abuse by charities and donors each year.[33] It's not surprising that this amount figures prominently when Congress discusses charitable reform. Although $15 billion is only 5 percent of the nation's total tax gap, it is approximately 25 percent of $60 billion, the total approximate amount deducted for charitable giving.[34] Spending a billion or so more at the IRS than is done now on tracking down charity abusers would make economic sense.[35] The effort would also be consistent with the desire on the part of many charities to encourage donors to properly account for and value their gifts.[36]

*   *   *

These are fighting words. Congress and attorneys general may sometimes seem to be asleep when it comes to addressing wrongdoing at charities, but they are ready to be nudged into action when they feel the need. The rhetoric over the past several years from regulators should be seen as a precursor to a larger battle, one that won't be won by charities if they continue to deny their responsibilities as public institutions that are responsible and answerable to the public.

Although the fervor ebbs and flows, if charities don't do more to regulate themselves—to act ethically in the absence of specific and restricting laws—Congress will revisit the issue of imposing specific and restricting laws, undoubtedly with more vigor and determination than before.

Section II

How the Quest for Money Affects Nonprofits

Ch 3:

Very difficult to quantify impact of giving - industry-wide,
  and vs. other possible futures for the money.
People like to give, it makes them happy, its emotional. They give
  because they are asked. Most gifts are small. Larger, super gifts
via foundations on indiv. giving.
  Lots of statistics on who gives to what and how much.

Chapter Three

Philanthropy is Big—But Does It Have a Purpose?

Fantastic wealth and philanthropy should go hand in hand: The names Andrew Carnegie, John Rockefeller, and Edward Harkness come quickly to mind; they were fantastically wealthy men who devoted a great deal of time to the "work" of philanthropy during their lifetimes. Bill Gates established the William H. Gates Foundation (now the Bill and Melinda Gates Foundation) in 1994 with $94 million, and over the next decade, thanks to market growth and additional gifts, it became world's largest philanthropic foundation,[1] with assets of $30 billion. In 2006, Warren Buffett made it even bigger. He made the commitment of a lifetime, also making his philanthropic mark while he is still breathing, when he pledged $31 billion more to be added over several years to the Gates Foundation.[2] Gates's and Buffett's intention was that the money would be used to finance health and education initiatives among the world's most disadvantaged peoples.

It wasn't just the money that made Buffett's historic addition important. His gesture was a merger of philosophies as much as it was one of assets. That two of the richest men in the country pool their significant resources for the common good sends a signal: The relationship between the two became a unique partnership, and ego took a back seat. Gates and Buffett demonstrated that they share a common charitable ethos. Buffett, who has said that the "market system has not worked in terms of poor people,"[3] worries about whole swaths of humanity; his beliefs and ideals, perhaps propelled by that concern, guide him to help humanity through his philanthropy. That's not typical of the way lots of businesspeople think, but it is how philanthropists think.

Because there are only two first and second richest people in the country, everyone else has to make his or her philanthropic mark less dramatically than Gates and Buffett. Still, that leaves a lot of room for fanfare—where lesser amounts of money still make waves—and the amount of giving to American charitable organizations indicates that Buffett and Gates are not alone in their philosophy. Philanthropy commands a lot of money, and it plays a major role in the financial success of charities.

Donating Today: The Big Picture

In the United States, charitable contributions total more than 1.5 percent of the GDP; this is twice the percentage of GDP in Britain, and ten times what the French give. Although charitable giving dropped a little during the recession that began in late 2007, Americans remain the most generous people on the globe when it comes to charity.[4]

In 2008 Leona Helmsley, the head of the Helmsley Hotel Chain in New York, topped the list with her bequest of $5.2 billion. Her entire gift went to the Leona M. and Harry B. Helmsley Charitable Trust, to support the care and welfare of dogs. James LeVoy Sorenson, an inventor of medical devices, came in second with his bequest of $4.5 billion to the Sorenson Legacy Foundation, which funds a variety of charitable causes, including the arts and education. The highest-ranking living donors in 2008 were Peter Peterson and Joan Ganz Cooney. Peterson co-founded the Blackstone Group, a financial firm in New York, and Cooney, Peterson's wife, co-founded the Children's Television Workshop (now the Sesame Workshop). Most of the money went to the Peter Peterson Foundation, which, as its website says, is "dedicated to doing our best to promote responsibility and accountability." The sixth largest gift, $300 million from David and Suzanne Booth, went to a public charity as opposed to a foundation—the business school at the University of Chicago.[5]

These gifts are compiled on a list of the top 50 charitable donations in 2008. The gift ranked 50th was $30.5 million, donated by David F. Bolger to The Valley Hospital in Ridgeway, NJ.[6] Of course, there is no list of the smallest gifts to charity. If there were, it would be a long and important list. For while it is true that most gifts are not in the million-dollar-plus category, most charities are quite happy to accept gifts of $100 and less. Even though the 20/80 rule applies to charitable donations—20 percent of the donors give 80 percent of the money—the other 80 percent, in addition to being responsible for a solid chunk of giving, includes many loyal donors, some of whom will one day be large donors.

Most people who invest in for-profit companies do so passively through their retirement programs or through mutual funds, and they are usually happy with only an increase in asset value or a steady investment income. They don't really care if the companies they are invested in do much besides make money. Observers of the big picture will argue that successful for-profit businesses do their part to make the world a better place, but for the investors, it's really all about personal gain.

People who support charity, on the other hand, are usually engaged in one or more levels of the organization's work—as donors, board members, or volunteers (although serving as a board member is a volunteer activity at almost all charities in the United States). According to Independent Sector almost nine of ten American households make charitable donations and over 25 percent of adults volunteer their time to charitable organizations.[7] The individual return for them is a sense of satisfaction that is not monetarily based. Appeals like "Please give this child a better future" or "Save the whales" are what most people respond to when deciding to give money to a charitable cause. Their decisions are typically not based on a thorough understanding of all the work a charity does. Larger donors usually want more information, and they will make the effort to get some of it. Still, other than in fundraising appeals, the maze of information about charities—the programs they run and their effectiveness, as well as the way they operate and are governed—is complex, and it often doesn't get through or register to most people. It's enough that they believe that the work done by the charitable organizations matters.

* * *

We've come a long way since 1893, when *Appleton's Cyclopedia* began recording charitable gifts. The estimated total of all charitable donations in the United States back then was $20 million. In 2008, it was more than $306 billion. According to *Giving USA*, a publication that tracks donation data and trends, the annual average growth of charitable giving since 1967 has been approximately 7.3 percent. Compared with the average annual inflation rate of 4.6 percent during that same time, charitable giving has positively galloped along.[8]

But despite this American largesse, in 2006 the IRS reported that only about 14 percent of nonprofit revenue consisted of philanthropic support.[9] The lion's share of the rest came from what is categorized as "Program Service Revenue," which means tuition, bills, admissions charges, subscriptions and other fees that people pay for services at a charity. As a percent of revenue, the larger charities rely less on donations than smaller ones. For charities with $50 million or more in assets, nongovernment charitable contributions accounted for 10 percent of all revenue; for charities with less than $100,000 in assets, the number was 49 percent.[10] Although the dollars have certainly changed since 2006, the ratios almost certainly have not changed much. And remember that these statistics are based on *reported* donations. The Senate Finance Committee estimates that only a quarter of all taxpayers itemize on their income tax returns. That means millions of people donate to charity each year without the reward of a tax deduction.

It is worth remembering that giving totals are estimates; they are useful, but they are not exact. According to the IRS, in 2006, before the Buffett gift to the Gates Foundation, the 240,000 charities that filed a 990 reported about $200 billion in private donations.[11] *Giving USA*, however, reported that Americans donated $295 billion that year. The difference in these two figures can be accounted for, in part, by the many small and religious-based organizations that raise money but are not required to file a 990. Also, while the IRS numbers are based on the amounts reported on individual tax returns, *Giving USA* makes an estimate each year using its own methodology, with conclusions drawn from "econometric studies using tax data, government estimates for economic indicators, and information from other research institutions."[12] The IRS's numbers are exact but incomplete; *Giving USA* is more comprehensive but less exact.

Of the more than $300 billion donated to charity every year, about 75 percent of that comes from individual donors during their lifetimes, five percent from bequests, and the rest from foundations and corporations.

The organizations that receive the most money receive a lot of money. In an annual survey called "The Philanthropy 400," the *Chronicle of Philanthropy* provides statistics by ranking the charities that received the most money during the year from donors. The first and second charities on the 2009 list (which reported the rankings for 2008) were the United Way Worldwide, which received over $4.2 billion, and the Salvation Army, which received almost $1.9 billion. The charity ranked last in the survey, International Medical Corps, received approximately $47.5 million.[13]

According to the Center on Philanthropy at Indiana University, 70 percent of all households in America make at least one charitable gift each year, and the average donation per household is a little over $2,000. Taking into account all households that donate, each supports an average of 2.7 charities and donates 2.6 percent of its income cumulatively to those charities. Interestingly, households with higher incomes give less: Those with more than $100,000 give an average of 2.2 percent of their income while those with less than $50,000 give an average of 4.2 percent—almost double.[14]

The Big Donors

Megagifts come from megadonors, and charities tend to spend their time cultivating them. From that perspective there is good news: there are a lot of rich people in the United States. In what it calls its "World Wealth Report," Merrill Lynch and the Capgemini Group found that in 2009 the number of people in the United States with at least one million dollars of investable assets—High Net Worth Individuals (HNWI)—was approximately 2.86 million.[15] Since much of their money is invested in the stock market, fortunes rise and fall: from 2007 to 2008, the number of HNWI fell dramatically—18.5 percent—[16]and then rose the following year by 16.5 percent. There is no dearth of capable prospects for charities.

That does not mean that all wealthy donors are increasing their giving. A key finding in a study conducted before the recession by the Center on Philanthropy at Indiana University and Bank of America found that giving among the ultra-wealthy—those with more than $5 million of disposable assets—dropped almost 10 percent between 2005 and 2007, from an average of almost $89,000 to a little over $80,000. Hit the hardest were arts organizations, with a drop among the ultra-wealthy from 13 percent of their giving to 4 percent.[17] The top reason put forth in the report for the drop in giving was that these very wealthy donors no longer felt connected to an organization.

Another concern was that they were deciding to support other causes, something that seems to be supported by the Council for Aid to Education, an organization that tracks gifts to educational organizations. CEA reported that in 2007 gifts to universities from people who did not attend those schools have increased dramatically. While alumni still donate more to their alma maters than non-alumni—$8.4 billion and 5.7 billion that year, respectively—there was a 14 percent increase in non-alumni giving over the prior year. The general theme of an online forum that met to discuss the trend was that many donors are eschewing their wealthy alma maters, often those with endowments of over $1 billion, to make gifts to universities and other organizations that are far less wealthy and just as deserving. Those donors often feel that their gifts will accomplish more at those organizations.[18]

Other organizations provide some drill-down on the numbers. For example, the Institute for Jewish and Community Research (IJCR) in San Francisco analyzed over 8,000 gifts of $1 million or more made to 4,000 organizations between 2001 and 2003. According to the study, which was published in 2007, "higher education, health, and cultural arts organizations receive the lion's share of the largest gifts." The study found that higher education received 37 percent of the gifts and 44 percent of the dollars from gifts of $1 million or more. When the gifts were $10 million or more, higher education received "an even bigger share with 46% of gifts and 47% of dollars."[19] This puts some flesh on the *Giving USA* report showing that 14 percent of all charitable giving goes to education. *Giving USA* does not distinguish between "education" and "higher education," and it does not distinguish among different gift sizes and their destinations.

We also learn from IJCR that health and medical causes received 14 percent of the gifts and 19 percent of the dollars from donors of more than $10 million or more, an increase over the totals the group compiled between 1995 and 2000.

But then there's this: *Giving USA* shows religion, with 34 percent of all gift dollars, to be the second highest recipient after education, while IJCR reports that religious causes received only three percent of the large gifts and that none of the 110 largest gifts were destined for religion. The differences were not due to the different time periods covered in each survey, but the different sets of data that were applied. Religion gets more small donations than most other sectors of the charitable world, but they add up to a lot. Another interesting and parallel tidbit from the IJCR study is that approximately 55 percent of megagift dollars came from private foundations, and only 28 percent came from individuals.[20] *Giving USA* shows that individuals account for 80 percent, and foundations for 13 percent of all donated dollars.

Tomorrow's Donations: The Transfer of Wealth

The thesis in a study published in 1999 by The Center on Wealth and Philanthropy at Boston College was that between 1998 and 2052, the people in the current and coming generation are expected to create estates of somewhere between $41 trillion and $136 trillion by the time they die. These estimates are accounted for in different models of economic growth: the lower number assumes a 2 percent economic growth rate, the higher number assumes a 4 percent growth rate. Subtracting legal fees and estate taxes, the range of money to be left behind is between $31 trillion and $90 trillion. Of that, the report estimates, between $6 trillion and $25 trillion will be earmarked for charity. After 20 years, by 2017, the wealth transfer is estimated to generate somewhere between $1.7 trillion and $2.7 trillion for charity.[21] (In 2003, in the midst of an economic downturn that began in 2001, the authors of the report, Paul Schervish and John Havens, wrote an article defending their original numbers and explaining why the forecast was still valid.)[22]

The first thing to note, in addition to the mind-numbing totals, is that the study's standard deviation—essentially, the plus-or-minus error rate—is startlingly high.[23] Yet nonprofit fundraisers, not many of them as accomplished in research or statistical evaluation as Schervish and Havens, often talk about the coming windfall without focusing on the fact that if the range is between 6 and 25, the higher number is higher by a not insignificant 300 percent. It would be a little like asking your employer what your salary will be next year and being told, surely unsatisfyingly, that it will be somewhere between $100,000 and $400,000.

The report's conclusions, having endured the scrutiny of newspaper accounts and the authors' peers for over a decade—from the report's publication, in 1999, through 2010—seem sound enough. But mathematical accuracy or a competency in statistical and predictive analysis doesn't ensure relevance. The numbers may be generally accurate, assuming sound research, but it's hard to get a handle on what they mean.

To connect the amount expected in estate transfers with the annual numbers—using the estimates from *Giving USA* of a little more $300 billion—remember that 5 percent, or $15 billion, which is no small amount of money consist of estate transfers, gifts from people who died during the year. If these numbers held for 54 years, from 1998 until 2052, the cutoff date of the Boston College study projections, the total going to charity as a result of estate transfers—simply multiplying $15 billion by 54—would be $810 billion. That's not even close to $6 trillion, the study's low estimate for the amount going to charity. In fact, it's 85 percent less. But because life isn't that static and to put some meat on the matter, let's assume the *Giving USA* number of $15 billion will increase annually by 7.3 percent (as *Giving USA* reports they increased, between 1967 and 2008), and that the portion of the annual amount represented by estate giving stays the same at 5 percent. Based on that, how do the Boston College numbers stack up? They look pretty good, actually. Given those assumptions, the total would be $9 trillion. That's still a far cry from $25 trillion dollars, but it's more than the low estimate of $6 trillion. By the way, to get to $25 trillion, the portion of annual giving represented by estates would have to rise by a rate of 10 percent every year.

The second observation is that the numbers are back-loaded: The report predicts that more will be transferred per year in the later years. The totals are less on average for the first 20 years than they are for the remaining 34. That's good to know because, as of 2006, either deaths or donations were not on schedule. The results during the first years of the study's time period didn't match with the numbers reported out by *Giving USA*. Between 1998 and 2004, $128 billion had been transferred to charities via bequests. That sounds like a lot of money, but it's far less than what a straight-line graph of the low end of wealth-transfer expectations between 1998 and 2017 would show. In fact, on that point, the predictions were off by a whopping 79 percent. The math is this: The study calls for a total of $1.7 trillion over 20 years (for now, forget about 2052). That's an average of $85 billion per year. In 2006, the *Chronicle of Philanthropy* wrote a story that covered the study data through 2004—seven years in. Based on the Boston College projections, by the end of that seventh year, a total of $595 billion would have been collected. But $128 billion is only 21 percent of the predicted amount, which is far too big a discrepancy to be accounted for by annual variations.[24]

So, to hear that the transfer is back-loaded is good. But there's a whole lot of catching up to do. Boston College itself "went on a fundraiser hiring spree" after the study was released.[25] To get even close to the expected totals, annual growth from here (2010) on out is going to have to be far greater than 7.3 percent.

A third point to note, something that actually may have an impact on individual charities, is the project's timeline. Trustees, executive staff, and fundraisers should be imagining what their charities might look like in half a century, after they are no longer working at or volunteering for the organization, after most of them have died. Charities need to believe in their role in society as caretakers of the future. In that sense, they need more than a dose of today's reality—they need to keep looking ahead.

Part of that means not personalizing the big forecast. The most important research a charity can conduct is on its own donors and prospects. If anything, Boston College's intergenerational transfer study should be an impetus for charities to examine their own numbers and project gift expectancies—when donors die and leave charitable bequests—based on their own data. A charity might also try to estimate its share of the annual giving amount— the $300 billion number—and apply that fraction to the projected ranges. While the fraction might seem infinitesimally small, the actual dollar amount that the exercise produces might not be so small. It's been my observation that charities do a poor job of tracking outright gift pledges and deferred gift commitments to when the gifts finally arrive. Perhaps the Boston College study will inspire charities to dig down into their own databases, to see what they've been getting over the years as well as to calculate how deferred gifts compare to the originally expected amounts. There's a whole range of statistically based work that charities could do to help them understand the future.

Why Donors Give

The topic of at least one session at almost every fundraising conference is likely to be why donors make their gifts. There are lots of answers, for donors are not motivated only by one thing or a set of the same things, and so the debate is ongoing as to how to reach out to prospective donors. The Bank of America study found that 81 percent of those who responded to the questionnaire said that their primary motivation was to give back to their communities. Social and political beliefs were high on the list, but so was the response that they give to the same groups every year, indicating that loyalty to an organization, such as a college or a hospital, plays a big role in philanthropic decisions. Of most interest, however, is that, for this group of wealthy people—the study canvassed those with $1 million or more of discretionary assets or at least $200,000 of household income—tax savings did not rank among the 15 categories of charitable motivation.[26]

One motive, appearing about halfway down the list, was something that might seem obvious: they were *asked* to give. This is true for almost every donor and almost every charity almost all the time: People don't give until they are asked. Of course not everyone who is asked does donate, so many charities, blind to the need for an ongoing presence in people's lives, make the fatal error of discontinuing their solicitation activities if they don't get a gift from someone, either because he or she once declined after being asked or because once-regular donations simply stopped. Although it may seem counterintuitive, it actually does pay to stay in touch with people who have not given in a while, and the better fundraising charities do stay in touch.

The corollary to the desire to be asked ought to be obvious too: people will stop giving if they are not asked. As noted earlier, the Bank of America study found that in 2007, many donors—38 percent of high net-worth donors—stopped giving to an organization they had previously supported because they had not been asked again. Twenty percent said they stopped giving to four or more charities. If asked why, people who discontinue giving to a particular organization often say that the primary reason for their decision is that they think the charity forgot about or doesn't care about them. The Bank of America study bears that out in dramatic fashion. Almost 60 percent of respondents who stopped giving to a charity did so because they no longer felt connected to the organization.[27]

The other side of that non-donating coin is that a good chunk of the group—42 percent—also said they were tired of getting so many solicitations. Many groups, once a donor has made a gift, will send additional solicitations as often as every month. This level of persistence is not good and makes people mad. Charities need to be sure to distinguish between helping people feel connected with their cause and mindlessly bombarding them with requests for money without any acknowledgement of past support.

There are other reasons donors stop supporting a cause. Bad press doesn't help matters, but only a small percentage of respondents said the reason was related to mismanaged donations or misleading the public.[28] Apparently, regulators care more about mismanagement than donors do.

A change of in philosophy at a charity can be a problem. More than one alumna was angry when Wheaton College, the women's college in Norton, Massachusetts, decided to admit men in 1987. It didn't help that the announcement was made in the middle of a capital campaign that had given far too little notice to its supporters. Similarly, students at Wells College in New York State said they were misled when that single-gender college decided to admit men. A group of students even filed a lawsuit for fraud and breach of contract to reverse the decision.[29] And a similar story unfolded at Mills College in California when its trustees decided to admit men in 1990. It's not just colleges, either. When WETA, one of two public radio stations in the Washington, D.C., metro listening area, changed its programming format from classical to talk in 2005 and then back to classical again in 2007, listeners were upset. Although these decisions would have been controversial under any circumstances, a common thread running through them was that not enough communication took place before the decisions were made. Charities need to pay a lot of attention to communicating with their current donors and others who have supported them in the past. In particular, they should always be aware of their donors' interest in knowing how the donated money is being used.

Charities do have something indisputable on their side: people can't use their assets after their deaths. A fundraiser at a major college once closed out his speeches to donors by saying: "You know, you can't take it with you. Besides," he said, referring to the school's alumni, "if you could, it would undoubtedly burn."

The Tax Deduction

As already noted, most people rank the tax deductibility of a gift pretty far down on the list of reasons they support charitable causes. Even so, the charitable income tax deduction has quite a history and garners quite a strong defense when it is challenged. The deduction, if for no other reason than that it's an important marketing tool for charities, is very much part of the nonprofit environment.

The deduction comes about to begin with because of the income tax, which became permanent in 1913 with the passage of the Sixteenth Amendment to the Constitution. At the time, rates were low—1 percent for those earning more than $20,000 per year, and rising to a whopping 6 percent for those earning more than $500,000—but there was no charitable deduction. In 1917,

Congress approved the charitable deduction. The dollar value of the deduction is a function of the person's tax bracket. Assume for a moment that a person who earns (adjusted gross income) $100,000 and is, more or less, in the 25 percent tax bracket, gives away $10,000 to charity. Aside from technical issues that might or might not come into play, it is safe to say that he will save $2,500 in federal taxes.

The majority of donors don't mention the deduction first when they are asked why they support charity. A survey conducted in 2008 by the Stelter Company in Iowa, shows that only 21 percent of the donors polled listed tax considerations as an important reason for naming a charity in their wills. They are much more likely to voice such sentiments as "giving back to the community" or "supporting a cause that is close to my heart" as their primary motives.

It's hard to gauge the accuracy of these responses, however. As one skeptical commentator has put it: "It is one thing to enumerate motivating factors, but quite another to put stock in what people say are their actual motivations for doing anything." How sweet altruism feels in the human heart; how nice to think others see us with that capacity. Nevertheless, as that commentator also said, "For argument's sake, let's say that taxes are not a motivation to give, as is almost universally claimed. Could we at least agree that taxes are a *major factor* in decisions regarding large gifts?"[30]

Perhaps. We may never be able to quantify the effect of tax savings on charitable contributions. It is true, though, that some donors, simply want to leave their money in the hands of those who steer the course for a good cause, like

- Clair Adams, a lifelong bachelor, who died at age 95. He lived simply and didn't spend a lot on himself—he was buried in a jacket that cost $9 at Wal-Mart. Yet he died with an estate worth a little more than $1.4 million, which he bequeathed to his parish. It was the largest single gift the parish ever received.[31]
- H. Guy Di Stefano, a retired jewelry-store owner, died leaving a $264million trust to be divided among eight charities: the American Humane Society, Direct Relief International, the Disabled American Veterans Charitable Service Trust, Greenpeace International Inc., the Salvation Army, the Santa Barbara Hospice Foundation, the Santa Barbara Visiting Nurse Association, and the World Wildlife Fund.[32] Di Stefano placed no restrictions on these bequests.

- In 2009 the *Richmond Times-Dispatch* honored celebrated philanthropist Thomas Cannon, a retired postal worker who doled out thousands of dollars to individuals and organizations. The newspaper put up an exhibit at its offices that featured stories about his philanthropy. Cannon died in 2005 at age 79, but he left behind a legacy of giving. His inspiring story and giving spirit was the subject of a number of newspaper articles. Cannon's salary as a postal worker never topped $30,000, but the World War II Navy veteran and his wife believed in living simply so they could give money away. His first donation, when he was 47 years old, went to a woman's club for its work at an elementary school. He usually gave gifts of $1,000 at a time to people of all races, ages, nationalities and incomes. Overall, he gave more than $156,000.[33]

And there are many, many more. Another "poor" donor was Oseola McCarty, a washerwoman from Hattiesburg, Mississippi who, four years before her death, became a benefactor of the University of Southern Mississippi with her gift of $150,000 for scholarships. Oseola was "intelligent, articulate, and straightforward," wrote President Bill Clinton about meeting her at the White House. "She had saved all her life both because she knew the perils of being penniless…" and "wanted young people to have the educational opportunities she'd missed. She was balancing the scales, and that was reward enough."[34]

The Higher Purpose

Larger donors do tend to ask questions about how their money will be used. Warren Buffett asked, and knowing what Gates was trying to accomplish, committed his money to the foundation's coffers. And when Gates set up his foundation, he made sure that he and his wife would maintain control, a point underscored in the first of its 15 Guiding Principles: "This is a family foundation driven by the interests and passions of the Gates family." Another principle, by the way, is, "We demand ethical behavior of ourselves."[35]

The trend for those who give the most to charity—or who at least think of themselves as philanthropic—has been to establish their own foundations, precisely because they can maintain control. Dabbling in this kind of work, however, by those who don't otherwise have a clear philosophy of philanthropy has resulted in less successful efforts.

One mega-philanthropist, David Rockefeller, makes many of his gifts the old-fashioned way—by giving them directly to a charity. When he made a $100 million commitment to Harvard in 2008, he was clear about his objectives for the gift under the university's umbrella. "David Rockefeller's visionary gift," according to the *Harvard Gazette*, "will prompt further exploration of the language and culture that undergraduates experience abroad, while deepening its connection to their academic and extracurricular lives."[36] Rockefeller and others who donate directly to already-established charities make sure their gifts will be used the way they want them used.

The Inherent Satisfaction of Giving

It has been said that donors are happy people. Arthur Brooks, who wrote the section on "Charity and Happiness," based on up-to-date research, in a report called the "Prosperity Index," says flat out: "People who give charitably are happier than people who don't." Citing the research findings, Brooks further declares that "people who give to charity are 12 percentage points more likely than non-givers to say they are very happy people," and that "volunteers are 13 percentage points more likely to be very happy than non-volunteers." He also goes past the correlation by asking if giving causes happiness, and responds that a study of senior citizens in Detroit showed that "a tremendous amount of happiness was attributable to the volunteering experiences..." and that "volunteering during just six months explained increases in morale, self-esteem, and sense of social integration." As for why, he offers up the physiological explanation that "giving affects our brains in pleasurable and beneficial ways—the "helper's high, as he says psychologists put it—and that "charitable giving lowers stress."[37]

Bill Clinton provides anecdotal evidence that seems to support the data. He said of Oseola McCarty, "When I met [her] after she gave her life savings so that young people could have the education she never had, she seemed happy."[38]

*   *   *

All of this donor bonhomie bodes well for the world of nonprofits. But charities would be lazy as well as cynical to depend on people who are simply believers—or, to put it more precisely, to depend on their willingness not to dig too deeply. Believers are so trusting in large part because they take it on faith that the charities they support are doing a good job with their money. Once that trust is broken, it is difficult to earn back.

Dame Stephanie Shirley, the British government's ambassador for philanthropy, says that an important consideration, both in her own giving and in her official position, is to make sure the money is being used efficiently. "It must make a difference to the beneficiaries," she says. As for giving during an economic downturn—a time when charities can seem most desperate—she thinks that, while "the wealthy have an obligation to help with the issues confronting society, charities have an obligation to earn the trust of philanthropists."[39] Yes, that the British government has an ambassador for philanthropy is a step well past where we are in the United States.

What Does All the Money Mean?

We learn from studies that track giving data that not only is a lot of money being given to charitable causes each year, much of it can be accounted for by the biggest individual donors going to the biggest organizations. The national annual pat on the back celebrates the fortunate few charities, while the sector does little to question how the unfortunate many, who receive only the scarcest, most modest morsels of donations, can benefit from the ever-rising tide. We also learn that, from a contextual or even an analytical perspective, we really know very little about the world of philanthropy. Through all the research and statistic-gathering that address some quantifiable questions, a deeper issue emerges: What will all that money mean to society? What happens when donations drop? What happens when they rise?

Mysteriously, costs at charities rise as endowments grow, even when their growth rate exceeds that of inflation. In 2003, Joan Kroc, the widow of McDonald's founder Ray Kroc, died and left National Public Radio $230 million.[40] That's a lot of money for an organization whose budget at the time was around $150 million. The media noted that the extraordinary gift—as did NPR itself, being a big player in the media—would, in a special endowment, "fund activities that provide support for NPR activities independent of other revenue sources."[41] Yet, five years later, when presumably the endowment should have grown, NPR announced that revenue shortfalls were so severe that it would be reducing its work force by 7 percent.[42]

People might wonder how such big gifts can have so little impact on the long-term stability of an organization. It's as if the organization doesn't plan for the future, or that it hoards money in good times and does not use it when times get tough. It's not that simple, of course, but it doesn't help that charities don't explain these things, or explain them well. I once heard the president of a well-endowed major university defend tuition increases that were pacing well ahead of inflation by favorably comparing the per-diem cost of educating a student to the cost of staying one night at the Plaza Hotel in New York City. By saying that, he was inexplicably asking his audience to make the connection between the value of an education and staying at a luxury hotel. There you go.

With so little context, the purpose and promise of the trillions of dollars that are expected to reach charities in the coming years might seem truly incomprehensible. No one says—no one would dare say—for example, that the first $1 trillion of the amount expected to be transferred will be used to shelter all the homeless people in the city of Seattle by 2015, or that the next $2 trillion will cure cancer by 2020, or that another $5 trillion will eliminate carbon emissions by 2030. If *that* were the case, those trillions—even though we still wouldn't have the vaguest idea of where within that variation of 300 percent the country's charitable bequests would end up—could be connected to purpose and promise; we would know how those dollars would matter. Right now, the answers to how the money would be used, as well as about how much money in total will be transferred and which charities will be the beneficiaries of the money, is elusive. It's best not to make too much of statistical projections in the absence of at least some context.

For that matter, not many people are asking how $300 billion is used every year, or what the social impact of nine out of ten households making charitable gifts every year is. It would seem that, although current and expected donation numbers are impressive, it is pointless to celebrate them without an understanding of what those numbers mean. That kind of information, unfortunately, the kind where we get a sense of how much better off we are, is not forthcoming in the same news stories that announce the totals. Comparing one year's totals to the totals of the year before or those of any prior year, actually provides no meaningful context.

It's a little like talking about the national debt. Who really understands the impact of a trillion dollar deficit? Would another couple of billion dollars of national debt mean anything concrete to most people? Who understands the economic impact of illegal immigration? Does hearing that thousands of people illegally cross into the United States each year really mean anything to most people? Who can comprehend that a star is so many millions of light years away from earth? Some people can feel a sense of awe when they hear that the light they see in the sky actually began its journey before they were born—or before Moses was born—but anything more specific is left to that scientific elite that understands what a light year is, and are able to put it into context.

And even though this is closer to our own pocketbooks, who understands what it means that the jobless rate is 9 percent? Or 10 percent? Or 5 percent? Since having a job is a good thing, we understand that not having one is bad and intuit that it is really bad if lots of people don't have a job, but we have no idea how bad.

It's true enough that there are people who know the impact of these otherwise arcane statistics, but, offered up only in easy-to-digest headlines, they provide only a superficial understanding, providing fodder for politicians' screeds and easy in-and-out conversations at cocktail parties.

So it is with charitable giving statistics. What's to talk about when the number $300 billion is tossed into a black hole of understanding? Does it make us think of anything real, even, to further hear that 80 percent of it comes from individuals? Or to learn that education receives about 14 percent of all giving? What can that mean to a particular university? It certainly doesn't alter the strength of its programs, the state of its marketing, or the willingness of its constituency.

What did $230 million do for National Public Radio? Specifically—not just in the general terms of exploring language and culture abroad—how does $100 million make society better?

What we "know" from statistics is only part of what it takes to understand the value of charities. To feel real, the statistics need better context. While the context is wanting in the sense that we have only the broadest measures of where donations come from and where they go, it is positively absent within a far more important framework: how the money is used and whether it does any good.

But if we don't have it, say, in the jobless area—where unemployment benefits can be tracked and analyzed so that we can get a sense of the impact of a jobless rate—we certainly don't have the tools to analyze the impact of philanthropy. We can't yet relate the number of dollars going to charities with a sense of improving the social fabric of society. Therefore, we have no idea how much better things were as a result of the growth in giving from $200 billion to $300 billion, which has been the approximate increase over the past ten years.

Was there an improvement generally in society that $100 billion could describe and measure? What does an improvement of $100 billion look like, anyway? The value of spending $100 billion to build an airport or several urban building projects might be measured in bricks and pavement, results that you can actually feel and see, but how does what is spent on an education or on art, for example, translate to something tangible?

With additional money the food bank might be able to compute an additional number of meals served or a measurably higher quality of food in those meals and the homeless shelter might be able to tell the public it bought more beds or a larger structure to house those beds, and calculate an increase in the people who sleep in them, but, for the most part, we don't know the effect the money has on society. While we have what seems to be an exhaustive supply of statistics relating to charitable giving, we really don't know much about what all the money is doing. How does $60 billion diverted from government spending in the form of deductions compare with how charities used the money they receive? It would require a lot of resources and probably a lot of heated debate to decide what constitutes "results." But it stands to reason that it is in our national interest to know. The nonprofit community should know so that its case to the public can be stronger and more refined, and Congress and the state legislatures should want to know so they can be certain that they are enacting healthy public policy.

But charities have an obligation, both practical and ethical, not to get used to that beneficence. The compact with the public is too important.

*   *   *

With all the talk of giving and megagifts, it's hard not to notice that almost all the studies concentrate on wealthy people and wealthy charities. The Bank of America and other financial organizations that invest the assets of the wealthy, for example, have scant interest in examining the motives of small donors because most of them will never be clients. Most studies look at the wealthy because Americans like to hear about success stories. The poor guy with a nine-to-five job who plods along giving $25 or $50 to his favorite charity every year just isn't part of the picture—unless he turns out to be a washerwoman who saved all that money to make a headline-making gift. But the truth is, just as a strong middle class is what makes capitalism work, those small donors are the backbone of American philanthropy.

Do not get the impression that just because charitable giving is at such a high level and that we hear the most about those who receive the most, that charity itself, across the board, does so well. It doesn't. While the nonprofit world celebrates its successes, there are hundreds of thousands of charities that are practically starving and have no idea how they will last through the year. Donors would be wise to wonder if the person being helped by the Salvation Army is any more deserving than the one being helped by the small-town local food bank that is forced to turn away the hungry because there just isn't enough money. Or whether the student at a well-endowed university is any more deserving of the donated portion of his or her educational costs than the student at a small college with only a modest endowment and disappointing annual giving results. For that matter, it might be well for policymakers and society at large to consider the question of the grand inequalities in the charitable and nonprofit landscape. Perhaps there should be a tax on the charities with the most assets or a sliding scale for tax deductions for different types of charities. Perhaps a stronger charitable ethos that is concerned with really making the world— not just any one charity's piece of it—a stronger and better place. If Warren Buffett, a benefactor, can worry about whole swaths of humanity, then charities, the receivers of benefactions, can worry about humanity as well. Although society ranks the richest people and the richest companies, charities cannot do that, at least not only that, and remain true to their purpose.

Whatever the inequalities, however, each charity must respect— and not simply celebrate—money, and at some basic levels at least, they must respect the bottom line. Their tax-exempt status does not exempt nonprofits from fiscal responsibility. Alongside their efforts to do good deeds for society, charities must, in a real sense, understand that they are businesses. Many of them qualify as big businesses.

Chapter Four

The Perils of Profit-Making in the Nonprofit World

[handwritten: 70% of nonprofits make less than 25k/yr]

Based on the latest information from the IRS, about 300,000 of the more than one million nonprofits classified as 501(c)(3) organizations earn or raise over $25,000 per year. Approximately 100,000 charities own assets of more than $1 million; about 6,000 of them have assets of more than $50 million.[1]

Nongovernment donations account for approximately 13 percent of all revenues at nonprofits; if we include government support, the number increases to about 22 percent. The rest comes from the fees a charity charges the public to use its services, which are generally known as "program service revenue." At universities, this revenue comes from tuition. For charitable organizations that can put money into an endowment, investment income also can play a role in a charity's financial picture. Overall, according to the IRS, investment income represents about 3.5 percent of all revenue at charities. At well-endowed public charities, such as universities, that number is a little higher—closer to 5 percent.[2] *[handwritten: source of most revenue]* *[handwritten: Investment income]*

Much of that investment income is the result of gifts placed into the endowments of those organizations. Because records detailing this information are not kept on a national level, it is almost impossible for anyone—the IRS, Congress, the charitable community, or the public—to know how much of the approximately $300 billion that is donated to charity is earmarked for endowment and how much is used to offset operational costs, but if we consider investment income from securities, and private and government contributions to be the donated part of charitable revenues, then charities can claim to need public support of about 25 percent. It is clear from these numbers that charities rely less on public support than their fundraising letters to potential donors might indicate. Nonetheless, that support is crucial to their success.

While a lot of money flows to charitable organizations every year, a lot flows out too. Donor appeals are based on real needs: covering the costs of funding programs and developing the infrastructure required to implement and sustain them. In its 2009 survey, "the Philanthropy 400," the *Chronicle of Philanthropy* showed that the largest charity, the United Way, had expenses of $4.4 billion; the second largest, the Salvation Army, had expenses of almost $2.9 billion. San Diego State University, which was listed at the bottom of the survey, had expenses that year of about $33 million. San Diego State did well, at least from a balance-sheet perspective, taking in $50 million that year, $17 million more than it spent. The United Way and the Salvation Army, on the other hand, actually took in less than they spent—the United Way with $4.2 billion in and $4.4 billion out, and the Salvation Army with $2 billion in and $2.9 billion out.[3]

Charities must deal with a lot of inflow and outflow, as well as with managing the money they're able to put into the bank. They use their revenues to stay in business, their assets to ensure their futures. Or at least that's the idea. This means that financial matters must be handled well and professionally. All charities must balance the books and run an operating budget to keep their doors open. When the money going out is greater than the money coming in, they often make up the difference by borrowing. The approximately 200,000 or so that have endowments also invest money. The twin tasks of wisely spending and investing require a business mindset that, until recently, many charities were loath to adopt. For some, a dwindling few, the "we're not a business" myth continues as ideas of the past die hard. Charities, after all, serve the public good; nonprofits don't have to concern themselves, at least not very much, with profit.

While the goal isn't so much to make much profit, charities still need to figure out how to stay alive financially. Of the million or so charities that raise money, fewer than 200,000 report assets of more than $100,000. You can be sure that almost all of the rest—800,000—are struggling to make ends meet. Most of them do so with few resources and small budgets; few people on staff get paid anything, and tomorrow always looks bleak. But the 100,000 or so charities with assets of $1 million or more are in a different situation. They, too, must worry about their budgets and the economic climate. But for them, being a nonprofit means ensuring future streams of income from a healthy endowment so that budgeted program services can be provided. Even the larger charities have their problems, however, and those problems tend to bring out the ethical deficit among organizations that should be striving the hardest to make good decisions.

The World of Endowments

Everyone knows about Harvard's large endowment, but many other charities have large endowments too. More than 200 charities in the United States have endowments valued at over $1 billion.[4] And when it comes to endowments, size matters. In fact, endowment assets are the testosterone of charitable organizations. Having a lot of money in the bank and in the markets generates the aura of virility and financial acumen around the charity. A substantial endowment can help to allay some of a charity's inescapable fears about the future. As a result, charities with healthy endowments often feel emboldened.

An endowment can be a measure of how well the charity has adopted the businesslike mindset of wealth; some or much of what it needs is spun off from a permanent, and it is hoped, perpetually growing principal. In that sense, charities with endowments behave much like trust funds; ideally, both generate enough money to cover expenses, and the principal is rarely, if ever, touched. A strong endowment is a significant measure of a financially healthy charity because it means that the organization's program service revenue and annual philanthropic support are not its only sources of revenue.

Endowments are unique to nonprofit organizations; they play an important psychological role in that they help their organizations to feel secure about the future. They also play the financial role of permitting charities the challenge of playing the markets. It's a way for a charity's board members to rub shoulders with those who rule the universe, the money people. Charities can't follow their own stock prices, but placing bets in the markets on entities that are supposed to make a profit and watching endowment value go up—when it goes up—might feel just as good. Although returns fluctuate as the markets go up and down, charities feel they can still count on long-term investment growth.

Of course, some people who work at charities see these market fluctuations as unnecessarily risky, and each dip in stock prices as a warning not to depend on so capricious a source of income. But the reality is that an endowment is and always will be for most charities a far less capricious source than the annual fund or fees.

So if that's the case—if endowment income is such a stabilizer against the vicissitudes of the future—why do so many wealthy charities ask for money every year? One of the apparent contradictions of charitable organizations is that as they grow and become wealthier, or at least more financially stable, they continue to ask for donor support every year. Surprisingly, many donors are not deterred. It may seem counterintuitive, but the charities with the largest endowments are the ones that attract the most annual support. This is often dispiriting to the small charities, the ones with no savings at all, who help the poor and disadvantaged in the most direct ways. These are the charities that struggle to attract even the slimmest support from the public.

Even the wealthy charities ask because they need the money. If you were to examine the books of organizations with large endowments, you would see tight budgets with pretty much everything accounted for. Running a tight ship means allocating the budget items and sticking to your guns. Part of sticking to your guns means abiding by all the complex restrictions that govern the endowment.

While an endowment can be thought of as a great big savings account, in reality it has many components. Usually, there are many small funds within it, and it is often invested in many sectors of the market. In fact, endowments can become so complex that charities need an army of staff to keep track of all the funds and do the accounting, and another group of experts to find the best places to invest the money.

Donors often stipulate that their endowment gifts be used for a specific purpose. That means the staff has to keep track of two things: how much income the investments spin off and whether that income is used properly.

Assessing wealth—as the term is used in connection with endowment size—is therefore a matter of some interpretation. The term "well-endowed" is applied to large organizations with investments of hundreds of millions of dollars and more, but no useful conclusions can be drawn about a charity's wealth that aren't based on an understanding of the budget that the endowment income supports. Because news stories rarely address these issues—the labyrinthine underpinnings of the laws, policies, investment goals, and donor restrictions that affect how endowment income is used—the public has little idea of what endowment values actually represent.

In the next section, we'll see that charities are sometimes careless about staying in touch with donors and abiding by restrictions. Even though the law is not clear—each state has jurisdiction over a charity's need to abide by a donor's wishes and, quite frankly, not very many do a good job—it is generally accepted that charities enter into a legally enforceable obligation to follow the donor's wishes when those wishes are stated in a gift agreement. For example, if a donor who makes an endowment gift to an art museum says she wants the income generated from her gift to pay for a specific program, the museum should, when it accepts the gift, agree to honor her wishes. If it doesn't spend that money on the program as promised, it could be in trouble: the donor can sue the charity and will have a decent chance of winning.

Almost every charity with an endowment has what is called a "spending rule," a policy that dictates how much of the funds invested in the endowment can be spent each year. Typically a charity will agree upon a policy that permits it to spend a certain percentage—5 percent is common—of the assets each year.

[handwritten margin note: often the avg of 3 yrs to limit susceptibility to mkt flux.]

Doing the math, you would think that a charity with an endowment fund worth $10 million could spend $500,000 from that fund in a given year. And you would be almost right. But the math doesn't follow such a straightforward calculation because most charities also apply the allowable percentage to the average value of the endowment over the previous two or three years. This means that if the endowment fund that is valued $11 million today was worth $8 million three years ago, $9 million two years ago, and $10 million last year, the income the charity would apply to the donor's restricted purpose is $450,000—5 percent of the average of those three values. Charities use income averaging for a good reason: to make themselves less susceptible to market fluctuations.

However, while this example makes it all sound simple, it is not. First, put aside any notion that a charity can plan to grow from $8 million to $10 million in such a short time; it happens, of course, but rarely—and it can never be counted upon. More important, when an endowment has hundreds or thousands of funds within, all of varying sizes, individually following and accounting for the values of each is a highly complex task.

Despite the fears of some that investing endowment monies in the stock market is just too risky, the fact is that, for all their ups and downs, in the long run the markets have gone up, not adjusting for inflation. Excluding dividends, the value of the stocks in the Dow Jones Industrial Average has grown by a little less than 5 percent on average each year for the past century.[5] Of course, factoring in dividends is no small matter. Eric Swerdlin, an investment advisor to charitable organizations, says that "approximately one third of total return can be attributed to reinvested dividends," which means that most investors would think of the true stock growth—again, not adjusted for inflation—over that same 100-year period to be closer to a little over 7 percent. Adding in dividends to the equation is not unreasonable. When you think of what you purchase when you buy a stock, to determine the value of that purchase each year you own the stock, you should consider not only the tree but also its fruit.

One thing to keep in mind about endowment investing: there is no time horizon. People who invest for retirement know they will begin to draw down on their retirement accounts someday. This means that the individual investment strategies a person chooses generally depend on his or her age at the time. Younger people can invest more heavily in stocks than older people because the stocks have time to increase in value; older people are generally wise to be more conservative and invest more in stable assets such as high-quality bonds, even though they offer less opportunity for growth. Endowments don't have that concern; generally speaking, endowments are forever.[6]

This means that endowment managers, who, by the way, are among the highest-paid people associated with charities, invest in all kinds of things. It often works this way: Charities hire investment experts to be on staff and also hire outside people who actually make the investment decisions. The investment committee of a charity's board of trustees, usually with the recommendations of the finance staff, decides which outside investment firm to hire. The people at that firm are often the best in the business, meaning that they went to the best colleges and the best business schools and did well at those institutions. They then went on to investing fame by outsmarting the market. That is, they have a track record of returns that that are better than the lackluster 5 percent plus dividends (or whatever the typical benchmark is at any particular period of time) that charities generally expect.

The top on-staff investment expert is typically called the chief investment officer. Although that person generally doesn't earn as much as the outside professionals, he or she does all right. In 2008, four of the five highest-paid employees at large foundations were the chief investment officer or treasurer—each with a salary of more than $1 million.[7]

Together, these entities—the outside investment firm, the board's investment committee, and, if there is one, its chief investment officer and his or her staff—work out broad investing parameters. Investing parameters means the allocation of all the assets, divided into stocks, another portion in bonds, and a little in cash, with several asset classes within each broad category. The outside firm's portfolio managers then execute the strategy on a day-to-day basis.

Even though the whole endowment is put into the care of outside people—and there can be hundreds of them, each with responsibility for different asset classes and sub-asset classes within the endowment—it's the organization's trustees who are legally responsible for the money. As a group, they're not anywhere near as investment savvy as the portfolio managers—the portfolio managers are stars, after all, who make hundreds of thousands of dollars each year—but the trustees are, ultimately, responsible for the sometimes conflicting tasks of ensuring that the money grows while, at the same time, it is kept safe.

They can only anxiously hope that the people they hire can pull it off.

You might never know their level of responsibility, though, if you saw how unengaged some trustees can be when presented with the investment report. You would think the people most accountable for the fiscal health of the organization would scrutinize the report and ask penetrating questions. Yet, too many trustees sit around the table looking at the graphs and supporting numbers as if they'd just had a lobotomy. Their comments might be no more piercing than asking for reassurance that the organization did as well as the stock market, an inexact, almost meaningless comparison. The presenters may be backing up their information with a lot of impressive looking graphs, but graphs can be misleading. What does it tell you that the endowment did as well as a particular stock benchmark? Something, but not enough given the number of asset classes in an endowment and different investment objectives for each.

A general reluctance to get into the details of investing and to ask penetrating questions to ascertain that the charity's fund managers are doing what they should is why things go wrong. Board members, even though most are not as financially sophisticated as the investment managers, must never hesitate to ask questions. They must bring their innate intelligence and intellectual curiosity—traits all board members should have—to discussions of complex matters.

Two major fault lines were identified in 2008. Although they weren't, charities should have been wise to each one.

First up: Bernie Madoff.

Trusting the Investor Who Didn't Invest

Most certainly, Bernie Madoff pulled off the public relations coup of the century. He may not have embraced the marketer's adage that it doesn't matter what you say about the person just as long as you get the name right—his name was not well-known to the public, but he was prominent among investors and regulators—no rock star, professional athlete, or movie icon in our society has ever attained such quick fame. The Ponzi-scheme story came out on Thursday, December 11, 2008, and by that weekend Bernie Madoff was a household name.

Today Madoff is as, if not more, well-known than his famous predecessor, Charles Ponzi who almost a century ago ripped off the public, and profited enormously from the willing ignorance of thousands of investors. But Ponzi himself was out of business after only six months.[8] Madoff managed to pull it off for four decades. Perhaps no one could imagine that a past chairman of the NASDAQ stock exchange and a philanthropist, whose support of lymphoma research in particular was robust, would be capable of such a thing.

Not all of Madoff's victims were individuals. Hundreds of the clients of his brokerage firm were nonprofit organizations: public charities and foundations. During the months following the December revelation, many organizations lost a lot of money. One of the more well-known examples was Yeshiva University in New York City, which lost over $100 million with Madoff. Most of that was "ghost gain"; the loss of actual dollars is estimated to be about $14 million.[9] And over a hundred other public charities and foundations whose managers had invested with Madoff suffered similar losses, including the Jewish Community Foundation of Los Angeles ($18 million); Hadassah, the Women's Zionist Organization of America ($90 million); and the Elie Wiesel Foundation for Humanity ($15 million), which was nearly wiped out.[10] Three foundations with substantial assets had to close their doors. One of them, the Picower Foundation, which in 2008 was ranked as the 71st largest foundation in the United States, lost everything, $1 billion, and went out of business just one week after the Madoff scandal became public.[11]

One of the curiosities of a Ponzi scheme, one of many characteristics that separate it from just a really bad investment, is that the losses are total and immediate. It's not like investors watched their stocks' value drop over time, realizing that their formerly profitable investment was now not going well at all; the people and organizations that invested money with Madoff lost it all instantly. Not only did they not realize gains, which by itself came as quite a shock after years of being told they were doing so well, but they lost their original investments as well.

Not everyone, though. As we focus on the rough journey charities traveled with Madoff and how it came about that so many of them were pulled into his orbit, we shouldn't ignore the fact that some people—and nonprofits—actually realized a profit. This is hardly surprising because the reason Madoff took new money in was to pay it out to clients who wanted some cash, a dividend return on their investment. That not everyone wanted the fruits of his or her investments every year, however, is one of the reasons he was able to pull off the scam for so long. Enough of Madoff's investors were comfortable enough with the bogus reported returns, which were remarkably stable over the years, that his clients simply told him to reinvest whatever income and profits they thought they had earned.

We may wonder why Madoff did it, but we must also wonder why his victims let themselves be victimized. Individuals are in one category, one in which, especially if they did not have an independent financial advisor, they could not be expected to conduct a deep due diligence on Madoff. But for the nonprofits, especially the big ones, it's a different story.

*   *   *

Imagine yourself in the boardroom of a fairly substantial charitable organization. The scene is the quarterly meeting, and the members of the board of directors are listening to a report on the organization's investments during the last year. This part of the meeting is often coupled with the other side of the financial activities of the nonprofit, the budget report. The budget report might come toward the end of all the exciting stuff and by then, after several hours of listening to a financial presentation, people might be a little sleepy. Those who haven't left by the time the endowment is explained may very well be anesthetized, asking few questions. Even if they are fully alert, what would be the point? They're listening to those really smart experts. How could they be wrong? If they say that the Madoff fund earned a magical 12 percent last year, even if some board members know that the overall market grew by only 8 percent, or even lost value no one would think to raise a hand to question it. Madoff was, obviously, one of the smart-investor elite, and he knew things that other people didn't know. Trade confirmations? Madoff provided forgeries of trade confirmations that looked legitimate. But boards don't usually go there. At least they didn't back then.

One board member told me that the concept of due diligence for charity investments has changed fundamentally because of the Madoff scandal. Whereas before, trustees didn't investigate what they thought were small, procedural activities, they now make sure every step of the investment process is audited and accounted for.

We might wonder what took them so long. Even a casual observer might have asked a few questions about the unlikely steadiness of Madoff's returns, especially after 2000 when he continued showing steady positive returns as the stock market dropped, rose, and then fell again.

But if the investors are the stars, the auditors are the back-room people, doing their work without fanfare. It wouldn't be going too far out on a limb to suggest that not many people, certainly not the investors and the fundraisers at charities, think of them as terribly social. Of course, many auditors are perfectly social, but when they are doing their work, examining the books of a nonprofit, they are all business. That business is akin to accounting forensics. They come in, generally once a year, to measure the inflow and outflow of money, prepare the balance sheet, and ascertain whether the charity is telling the truth about its financial affairs. They get down to the details, and in the process, manage to annoy almost everyone.

Regardless of the size of the gift, no matter how small, the auditors will insist on proof of every transaction. For example, because credit-card gifts, modest ones anyway, are now common at charities, auditors insist on examining the receipts, both the charity's, which show that a donor actually parted with some money, and those of the company that processes the transactions, which show that the money made it into the charity's account. Similarly, if the development director makes a cross-country trip to visit a prospective donor, the auditors want to see receipts for all expenditures. And they may question a receipt; for example if a flight wasn't in coach class. Some really exacting auditors might also ask when the ticket was purchased and whether the fare was in fact the lowest available at the time—could the charity have saved some money by purchasing the ticket two weeks earlier? Do the purchasing decisions, such as whether a director is permitted to fly business class or first class, conform to the charity's policies? Even if the answer is yes, the auditor may still want to see a copy of the charity's rules on such matters.

Deferred or planned gifts, which are promised but will be received sometime in the future, are very common at many charities. These future commitments, the irrevocable ones, must be valued as part of the charity's assets. One of the primary questions that must be decided is the discount rate the charity should use to calculate the present value of the gift. The charity may think the gift is worth million dollars right now, but an auditor may insist on a different discount rate that might lower the value to far less. And in addition to agreeing on a valuation methodology, the auditor wants to see proof that the gift is irrevocably assigned to the charity.

Those kinds of things drive the staff at charities nuts. Most everyone at a charity wants the books to be accurate, but auditors can, it seems, find the smallest, most insignificant nits to pick. So, it would be quite a surprise to see those auditors make such a sharp turn away from all that persnicketiness.

But in Madoff's case, apparently they did.

It is hard to imagine how people whose training and personalities guide them to track down the smallest detail didn't question that the Madoff funds in charitable endowments continued to rise significantly or remained so steady for so long while everyone else was experiencing the jarring vicissitudes characteristic of real investments. But if they had any doubts, they didn't mention them. It's as if Madoff had a pass. It's as if even the auditors thought that Madoff must really have known his stuff, and so was beyond scrutiny. No board members asked why the funds were doing so well. No one asked for confirmation of any transactions. No one wondered why his reports looked a little odd because they were typed up the old-fashioned way, like they were put together in the 1970s, even though other funds issued computer-generated reports. Auditors didn't see in the Madoff reports a modern professionalism, and they didn't comment on the fact that the reports were clearly discordant with how the rest of the investment industry had developed client reports. But it didn't seem to matter. They apparently didn't even ask to see the trading confirmations, proof of transactions. Yet, all the while, those same auditors would often drill down on the reports from other asset managers.

The auditors were silent and they were inattentive. While it could be that the people at the charity who would look good if the investments did well would have little incentive to look very deeply under the hood, the question that remains to this day is why the auditors also didn't do their job.

The auditors' silence and inattentiveness were their complicity. Charity board members then abetted the problem with their lack of oversight of the auditors.

Yeshiva University

Ezra Merkin, who along with Madoff was on the board of Yeshiva University, was a hedge fund investor who funneled a lot of money Madoff's way.[12] Merkin did that, by the way, in his capacity as chairman of the university's investment committee. The conflict-of-interest issue was acute, but there it was, *ex vi termini*, unaddressed, or, at least, addressed inadequately: While holding Yeshiva's assets in trust—that's what board members at charities do—he made recommendations and influenced decisions that lined his and Madoff's pockets. That is, Yeshiva's trustees invested a great deal of money with Bernie Madoff on the advice of Ezra Merkin. It didn't matter that everyone at the time thought Madoff was a genius. The fundamental violation of the conflict-of-interest rules was that Merkin's and Madoff's interest were in conflict with Yeshiva's.

Avoiding conflicts of interest is important at charities. Charities should remove the potential to undermine impartiality among those who make the decisions. Unfortunately, the concept has not been codified in all states as it relates to charities, nor is it fully enforced when it is. Conflict-of-interest issues are most likely to be a concern at the level of board members and key employees. They have the most power and influence in a nonprofit organization, and so they must be most diligent about not violating the rules.[13]

What's to keep a board member, for example, from using the charity's treasury to take out a personal loan at below-market interest rates? Or from making a loan at higher-than-market rates? What's to keep a board member who has given a lot of money to the charity from strong-arming the rest of the board to grant his company a construction project?

Some states have strict guidelines—New York is one[14]—requiring board members to disclose potential conflicts of interest. Today, more charities are asking for such disclosure as part of the "entrance exam" for board candidates. But that doesn't mean the person won't become a board member; it just alerts the rest of the group to possible conflicts. But a policy, written by the charity, should spell out its definition of conflict of interest as well as what is acceptable and what is not. Not all conflicts are unacceptable, but all board members should know the facts of a person's situation so that they can determine if there is a substantive conflict and whether to prevent that person from benefitting from the decision.

Lesson: While the world of investing is exciting, and aggressive investing can result in great returns, the trustees of a nonprofit should always pay attention at meetings, ask the hard questions (even if they think it will make them appear foolish and uneducated), and never put their friends in a place where they can destroy the position.

Alternative Investments

In 1997, Emory University reported that its endowment had grown by a truly stunning 35 percent during its 1996 fiscal year. At that time the endowment was valued at $3 billion. This was fantastic news, of course. The Dow Jones Industrial Average, which saw gains of more than 15 percent, excluding dividends, during the high-flying 1990s, didn't come close to that, to say nothing of the returns of other nonprofit endowments that invested in a relatively safe mix of stocks and bonds that would mitigate against such high returns. The news release from Emory provided the explanation: Coca-Cola. According to the report, as of June 30, 1996, Emory held $1.8 billion of Coca-Cola stock—roughly two-thirds of its assets—which made it one of the company's largest private shareholders.[15]

Lost in the excitement was the examination of a question that no one seemed to ask: Is it prudent for a university, or any other entity for that matter, to invest almost two-thirds of its assets in a single stock?

No, it is not. If the stock was donated, it would not have been a good idea to keep it. Sometimes donors want to restrict the sale of stock they give to charity, but the wise charity will almost never acquiesce. Even if there were a legal restriction against selling the Coca-Cola stock, wording in a trust document, for example, it would have been unwise to accept the gift with that condition. And if the stock was purchased by Emory's investment managers, it was an equally bad idea.

You may wonder: Bad idea? How can anything that generates so much value be a bad idea? This is why: Charities are bound by the standards put forth in the legal doctrine known as the Prudent Investor Rule and can be held to those standards in a court of law. One of the Rule's five bedrock principles speaks to diversification: "Diversification is a basic tenet of risk management, without which investment portfolios would tend to be more volatile than necessary while having similar long-term expected returns."[16]

The Rule is not meant to guarantee or even suggest a result or a level of performance, but it does provide guidance in making decisions. If you are the beneficiary of a trust and your income drops a lot because the trustee didn't diversify assets, you may have a case in court.

Putting two-thirds of a $3 billion endowment into one stock— not one class of stocks, and not one mutual fund, but one single stock—is hardly an example of adhering to the principles or spirit of the Prudent Investor Rule. But no one complained because the value went up, and, of course, up is good.

While investing in one stock or just a few stocks usually exposes the weakness with a lack of diversification, diversification is not about being complicated. It's about balancing stocks, bonds and other assets to best address a person's or organization's propensity for risk and reward. If anything, Emory's investment strategy was too simple. Complicated, in the way nonprofits were affected during the market and economic downturn in 2008, came later. But when "complicated" arrived, it arrived most prominently in the form of alternative investments, and, within the world of alternative, or nontraditional, investments, it arrived most perniciously in the name of private equity. Alternative investments can include rare stamps, coins, oil and gas partnerships, even wine; they can be found by themselves or in hedge funds or venture capital projects, like privately held companies that have the possibility of growing quickly but also have a good chance of failing miserably. While being complicated is part of legitimate financial life these days for large portfolios, when it came about through the schemes of alternative investment strategies—at least in the way those schemes were unfolding in the late 2000s—complicated became destructive.

*   *   *

Until the late 1990s, investing by charitable endowments was not the horse race it has become. Consider the headline of this September 27, 2007 *New York Times* article, "Yale Endowment Grows 28%, Topping $22 Billion." The article lauded the savvy of Yale's investment managers during the period from July 2006 to June 2007. It went on to say that "the endowment...outperformed all its competitors," and then explained that Yale's average annual growth over the prior ten years was 17.8 percent. The growth rate, excluding dividends of the Dow Jones Industrial Average during that same time, was less than 6 percent.[17] The *Times* also reported that Yale's annualized performance over the decade bettered Harvard's by 2.8 percent and Princeton's by 1.6 percent.[18] Many other large endowments grew quickly as well.

And remember that the first decade of the twenty-first century was the worst decade in stock-market history. The *Wall Street Journal* reported in December 2009, "In nearly 200 years of recorded stock-market history, no calendar decade has seen such a dismal performance as the 2000s."[19] During that same time the Dow Jones Industrials experienced an annualized growth, excluding dividends, of less than 1 percent.

Most people might think that endowments are invested in the stock and bond markets. They may understand that not all the money is in a savings account or in treasury bonds—they know that such large sums ought to be invested where they can be expected to grow—but they are almost certainly not aware of just how intricate the investments can be. It's not just a matter of determining that one company or another—based on, say, its price-earnings ratio—has good prospects for growth. Nor is it just a matter of making sure that only the highest quality bonds—none of that junk in *our* portfolio, please—will make the cut. It is something altogether different.

Several of the larger endowments began to earn those record gains in the first decade of the century by going outside the conventional asset classes. By 2005, organizations with the largest endowments, including all the Ivy League universities, increased their allocation in alternative investments to 25 percent, up from 5 percent in 1991.[20] In addition to the Ivy League, Purdue, Stanford and the University of Virginia all bought heavily into alternative investments. Instead of dividing their portfolio in the usual ways to look something like this: 58 percent in stocks, 38 percent in bonds, and the remaining 4 percent in cash and cash equivalents, they began to invest in alternatives investment classes and with private-equity firms. Although these larger endowments started small, investing in alternatives cautiously at first, it didn't take long for endowment managers to get frisky and make more daring investments. It involved a game of a massive swapping of assets that were all going further and further into debt. Debt was the new equity, after all: so cheap when the prospects were so good. But it was only a new twist and the revitalization of a disgraced investment philosophy from an earlier era. In its 2009 survey, the National Association of College and University Business Officers reported that 842 institutions of higher learning that participated in the survey had, on average, 51 percent of their investments in alternative strategies. While alternative investments fall into the category of stocks, domestic equities, the bread and butter of equity investments, totaled only 18 percent.[21]

The new financial bible was alluring, and playing the market by a whole new set of rules was fun.

*   *   *

As already noted, not many people complain when things are good. Nobody complained about Emory in 1997, and nobody complained about any of the other fast-growing university endowments in the 2000s. Very few people complain when investments do well but not in a disciplined manner. Whereas to most people a 5 percent rise in part of an investment seems acceptable, those who know the nuances of the market and how similar stocks or funds performed may have reason to think that it should have gone up more—or down even. The public may not see any red flags, but an expert should be able to read the signs that a stock or fund is not performing as well as it could be. The opposite is also true: A stock or fund's drop in value does not necessarily signal that things are bad when examined through the lens of investment discipline.

Although this growth spurt was not about investing too much money in a single stock, as happened at Emory University, it was about universities, as well as other charities, investing imprudently. As we know, the euphoria ended when it all came crashing down in the stock market drop beginning in late 2007. In December 2008, Yale reported that in the first four months of its fiscal year—July through October—the school's endowment lost 13.4 percent. Yale's president, Richard Levin, wrote to his faculty and staff that the school's operating budget would see a shortfall of as much as $100 million the following year.[22] As of June 30, 2009, mirroring the worldwide market decline, as well as many other university endowments, Harvard's endowment shrunk by $8 billion, from $37 billion to $29 billion.

The game universities and others played throughout the last years of the twentieth century and the better part of the first decade of the twenty-first wasn't about investing in stocks that would grow because the companies would sell more products or run more efficiently; that is, because they would actually make a legitimate profit. Instead, it was about betting on the future while still trying to squeeze the life out of any possibility that might make the future real. Why look to the future, which is so far away, when the future—or at least its economic benefits—might be had for a scam right now?

This is not to suggest that the people running university endowments are bad people. Far from it. Because it is their job to generate returns, they became part of the larger picture. All investing is a gamble: Even investing in an old matron like General Electric is a gamble. But it's a safer gamble than investing in private equity. This is how it works: A company buys a failing company, leverages it with borrowings to pay off its stockholders and executives—leaving the workers at the failing purchased company in the dark—and then sells those companies off to investors, some of whom are the endowment managers of universities. As bad as that practice seems, however, it can be a legitimate investment strategy for some venues that play the high gamble, like hedge funds, that go for the gold. That's the roller coaster ride of high-stakes investing: When you win, you win big, and when you lose, it can be equally dramatic. For a long time, most of the players were winning more than they were losing.

But the piper is paid big time when those who are in debt cannot pay. Many of those funds were in debt to the endowments at Harvard, Yale, Princeton, Stanford and other big money places. And the kicker is: private equity locks up an organization's money even when it hasn't yet invested in the private equity fund. The deal goes something like this: The private-equity firm says it will invest in opportunities that will generate profits of 25 to 50 percent—or more. The endowment managers sign a contract for, say, $100 million, to be invested over the next two years. Initially, the fund might ask for only $25 million because it has no place to put the rest of the money; it doesn't have the right investment opportunity to expect a large return. That doesn't free up the $75 million for the charity, however. It needs to keep that in reserve because it may have to hand the money over at any time. The moment the private-equity firm asks for the money, the charity must pay. That's why, in 2009, when liquidity was scarce and the value of private-equity properties was nose-diving, places like Stanford, Harvard, and the University of Virginia wanted to sell chunks of their stake in private equity.[23]

Let's go back to Harvard for a moment, although many charities were in the same boat. In a well-managed portfolio, it might be prudent to put between 5 and 10 percent into alternative investments—investments that are illiquid and risky; even a charity ought to take some advantage of market upswings in unusual places. But, according to one analysis written in 2009, because of its legal commitments to private-equity firms, Harvard's illiquid assets would get to 30 percent by 2010 and to over 40 percent by 2012.[24]

*   *   *

While the general market crash is distinct from alternative investments doing poorly, those organizations invested heavily in alternative investments did worse than those only with traditional investments. While the value of pretty much everything went down, what made it worse for charities was the lack of liquidity. Remember the "spending rule" concept? One might wonder why a charity would run into so much difficulty so quickly when its spending is limited to a percentage of the average value of assets over three years. Averaging means that if an endowment drops by 30 percent in one year, the income from it should drop by only 10 percent. But if much of that value isn't liquid, the lost income has to be made up from the liquid side of the endowment. This is how Bloomberg.com put it in a news story on July 22, 2009: "While the Standard & Poor's 500 Index has increased 41 percent from its low in March [2009], endowments have been weighed down by holdings of private equity, real estate and commodities, which haven't recovered as fast. These assets are also harder to sell, making it more difficult for schools to raise cash."[25]

Combine that with rules that prohibit funds within an endowment from spending any money if they drop below their original individual values, and with the overall and sudden drop in the value of the already illiquid alternative investments—and you have what some might call a perfect storm.

The Invesment Philosophy Triangle

Charities began investing in the 1990s and in the first decade of the 2000s, not for solid gains and a reasonable measure of safety, but for the stars. In a rising market people fear that if they're not doing as well they are falling behind. True enough, relatively speaking—and the pressure to stay abreast is enormous—but heavy alternative investing shattered the idea of financial security in an endowment.

It has often been said that otherwise intelligent people leave their brains at the door of the nonprofit boardroom. Eric Swerdlin, the investment manager for charities, says that we might think of the dangers as three points of a triangle, each of which lives closely, but uncomfortably, in contrast to the other two.

The first danger point is fraud, as shown by the Madoff scandal. "There absolutely must be a policy at charities that prevents the custodian from being the same entity as the investment manager," Swerdlin says. "That way, charities are able to ensure that trades are actually taking place when the investment manager says they are taking place." Of course, that's not the only outlet for fraud; there are many others, and trustees need to be on the watch and carefully craft all policies with preventing fraud in mind.

Another corner of danger, according to Swerdlin, is the mind-set that is too risk-averse. "People who volunteer their time, who are not paid to make good decisions," he says, "have no personal financial upside while they have a lot of reputational downside." This leads trustees to be too conservative. A 1987 *Fortune* magazine article took Laurence Tisch to task for being too conservative when he was on the board of directors at New York University. "Few institutions offer a more dramatic lesson in how not to run an endowment than New York University," the article began, noting that NYU's "star-studded board of trustees is led by CBS Chief Executive Laurence Tisch. Theirs is the only university in the country with an endowment of over $3 million that owns no stocks whatever. For the past six years, the NYU trustees have watched the bull market of a lifetime from the sidelines." *Fortune* estimated that NYU could have added between $200 million and $500 million to its endowment over the prior ten years with a more traditional allocation of 60 percent in stocks and 40 percent in bonds.[26] Reputational risk with no personal profit upside often keeps trustees from being bold enough in their investment decisions.

Here's the thing, though. This is why we invoke hindsight so often, and why predicting anything relating to investments is a fool's errand. The *Fortune* article was dated October 26, 1987, and so may house one of the greater ironies in all the writings of the investment world. Magazines date themselves a week or so into the future, and the articles themselves are written months in advance. *Fortune*, therefore, can be excused for missing what must have been a sigh of relief at NYU's board—on the morning after the stock-market crash of October 19, 1987.

And then there's the third danger point of the triangle, the focus of all the miserable endowment news at big universities in 2009.

"It's an exciting world and these people have no skin in the game," Swerdlin says. "Some of these larger entities feel they are sophisticated enough to get into exotic investments, stuff they don't fully understand."[27] Everyone on the board should understand what the organization's investments are all about. The investment discussion is not the time to drift off.

Trustees need to be in the middle of that triangle, and not on any of its points. And the quest for diversification, which is a primary goal when it comes to investing, must include liquidity. Sacrificing liquidity to growth is simply not smart.

The question is: Has irresponsible investing shattered the idea of what a charity is all about? While the original perfect storm was created by the wrath of Mother Nature, the perfect storm of investments was created by people who may have thought they were smarter than everyone else. But they weren't.

Believing so deeply in the false promise of quick profits was a mindset that threw the Prudent Investor Rule in the garbage in the quest for what could be called immoral gains: immoral in this case because the cost of buying companies with debt and turning them around in the most efficient manner is often, as it is particularly likely when the economy is otherwise failing, the loss of thousands and thousands of jobs. Truly, college endowments began betting not on the health of companies, but on their illnesses.

Well-endowed universities, organizations that make up a significant portion of the nonprofit world, which exist to serve and improve society, made their headlines and their investment managers rich by betting on, even being responsible for, lost jobs.

Where do such decisions fall in the ethical landscape? For, even though money managers and boards may understand investments as primarily about money, they are not. They are primarily about nonquantifiable decisions, only in the wake of which end up being financial. If Laurence Tisch can be reprimanded for being too conservative, just where is the fulcrum between risk and safety? If liquidity is expensive, as Yale's chief investment officer, David Swensen, contends,[28] then how costly is its absence when students or other clients at a charity do not have access to its services because there's no money, the kind people can spend?

Is there really a place for the mindset of the masters of the universe in the nonprofit world?

Section III

Perceptions and Money: Their Fragile Compact with Good Deeds

Chapter Five

Do Some Charities Want Too Much?

In his will, Hector Guy Di Stefano, who died at the age of 90 in the State of Washington in July 2006, left $264 million to eight charities equally, amounting to $33 million each. It was one of the largest charitable gifts in the United States that year.

Di Stefano's wife, who died a year before he did, had inherited a fortune in UPS stock from her father, who early on had been a manager at UPS and later an executive. The couple had three children, but Hector had disinherited them[1]; hence the bonanza for eight fortunate charities: Greenpeace, the Salvation Army, Direct Relief International, the Santa Barbara Hospice Foundation, the Santa Barbara Visiting Nurse Association, the American Humane Society, the Disabled American Veterans Charitable Service Trust, and the World Wildlife Fund.[2]

Nothing is more exciting for an executive director or a development professional than to receive a phone call or a letter from an executor, usually an attorney or a financial institution, informing the charity that it is the beneficiary of someone's will. When the amount is over $100,000 smiles emerge; when it's over a million dollars, it's an oh-my-God moment; when it's in the range of $30 million, it can be transformational. Simply putting the money into an endowment that would generate a 5 percent annual return would mean an annual increase in the charitable organization's operating budget more than $1.6 million. And that's just the beginning.

The way these things usually things go, when a will lists several charities as beneficiaries, each one generally knows who else is on the list. Not always, but often. Depending on the size of the bequest to each, this may elicit pleasant surprise; responses like, "Wow; we're getting so much more than the other guys." Or, it might prompt a little soul searching: "We really do need to step up our marketing efforts. That other charity doesn't do nearly as much as we do." But when more than one charity is named as a beneficiary, each charity is glad for all of the others. That's part of the nonprofit ethos: no one wishes another any ill will.

At least, that's the case most of the time.

The Salvation Army versus Greenpeace

Di Stefano's will had been prepared in 1991, and it named a group called Greenpeace International, part of Greenpeace, Inc. as one of the charitable beneficiaries. Some months before Di Stefano died, however, Greenpeace International was absorbed into the Greenpeace Fund, which was also under the umbrella of Greenpeace, Inc. When Bank of America, the trustee for the estate, discovered the change, it asked a court in King County, Washington, how it should proceed. The bank wasn't trying to create problems; it was simply trying to "clarify its duties" and make the right decision about where at Greenpeace the money should go.[3]

However, the Salvation Army got wind of the bank's request and decided to challenge the bequest designation. The aforementioned charitable ethos crumbled more than just a little when the organization asked the court to cut out Greenpeace altogether and divide its share among the remaining seven charities, which would have provided them with about $4.7 million more each.

Reacting to the move, John Passacantando, Greenpeace's executive director, commented wryly, "First you get the best news of all time, and then you get the most bizarre news of all time." But he also expressed disbelief. "I'm mystified why anyone, let alone the Salvation Army, would oppose Greenpeace receiving this generous donation...It's obvious that the donor's intent was for Greenpeace to benefit from this."[4] His surprise most certainly was born of the suddenly apparent discord: charities just don't behave that way, he must have thought; they just aren't that greedy or small-minded.

The Western Territory of the Salvation Army chose not to see the donor's intentions the same way Greenpeace did. It contended that Di Stefano didn't want the gift to go to the Greenpeace Fund, arguing that if he had wanted the money to go there, he would have updated his will.[5] Michael Woodruff, the general counsel for the Salvation Army's Western Territory, said the Salvation Army was "only trying to honor Mr. Di Stefano's intent." He put it this way: "The donor's intent was specific. If a corporation or charity named in the trust does not qualify, that gift lapses, and he [Di Stefano] specifically named Greenpeace International."[6]

Greenpeace insisted that the name change was just a technicality, that, in fact, the IRS had suggested the change to reduce the amount of paperwork, and that, for all intents and purposes, the missions of the two groups—Greenpeace International and the Greenpeace Fund—were virtually identical. The Greenpeace lawyers also argued that Di Stefano wouldn't have cared about the change. The *New York Times* reported that "Thomas W. Wetterer, the general counsel for Greenpeace, said Charles W. Willey, the lawyer who drew up the trust document for Mr. Di Stefano, testified in a deposition that he had pulled the name 'Greenpeace International' off an Internal Revenue Service publication after his client had mentioned wanting to give to 'Greenpeace.' "

Furthermore, attorneys whom I have spoken to over the years say it is common to take into account the concept of "successor-in-interest," which permits successor organizations, when things are not completely clear, to be the recipient of gifts.

The case was settled out of court and left Greenpeace with $27 million. Why it was less than the intended amount—and I have to believe the donor intended Greenpeace to get its full share—is anyone's guess, and the principals to the settlement aren't talking.

Ironically, there was a question of whether the Salvation Army's Western Territory should have gotten the money. The will named "The Salvation Army & its Components" and lists the charity's location as New York, which, under the Salvation Army's policies, means the money would go to the Eastern Territory, headquartered in New York. The Western region claimed the bequest because the donor lived in Washington State.[7] We'll probably never know if that issue would have been played out in court, however, because the terms of the settlement required everyone close to the case to remain forever silent on the details.

It would be speculation to think that the other charitable beneficiaries saw the case the same way the Salvation Army did. Christopher Clay, general counsel and planned giving director at Disabled American Veterans, said, "In my 10 years as a legal counsel here, we have never gotten involved in a dispute over donor intent, and we certainly have had the opportunity. For a national charity to get out there in this kind of a case would take a compelling reason, and I don't think there's a compelling reason here."[8]

*   *   *

Many donors, like Di Stefano, include charitable intentions in their estate plans without telling the charities about those plans in advance. They may do this because they don't want the publicity, or they may want to be able to change their minds. Whatever the reason, charities receive far more in estate giving—general estimates are by a factor of four or five—than they are led to expect by their donors. When they are not involved in the planning process, however, charities do not have the opportunity to inform donors of organization changes or other information that may be relevant to the bequest.

The Red Cross encounters this issue all the time. Each chapter of the Red Cross is its own separate legal entity, and many people who leave money to the Red Cross really intend to leave it for the benefit of a local organization. The national organization receives a lot too, of course, but people, as with their politics, generally think of their charity as local. The problem arises when a will is so loosely drafted that the donor's intentions are unclear. Does the person in Nevada, whose will says she is leaving $10,000 to the Red Cross mean the Nevada chapter or the national organization? Other large organizations with local chapters face this difficulty, and they must do more to find ways to let their donors know how to leave them money.

Lesson: While it is true that development offices need to stay in touch with their donors—especially when natural heirs are disinherited—the trickier issue is staying in touch with people they are not aware of as possible donors. The best thing a charity can do is to reiterate how people can name the charity in their will—in its written publications and prominently on its website—which should include the charity's legal name, its current address, and its IRS identification number.

And, as the Salvation Army story should be used as a lesson, after all that, a charity still should not trust other charities to see things its way. Of the confusing will designations that name a charity as a beneficiary, most are actually not as clear as Di Stefano's was.

The National Heritage Foundation

Most people, if they gave it any thought at all, wouldn't think of the National Heritage Foundation (NHF) as a charity; or, even, although it is structured as one, a foundation.

NHF isn't the type of place that actually serves people. It doesn't behave as, say, a university or a museum or a religious organization or a homeless shelter does. Instead, it can best be described as a collection of accounts, established by people who say they want to use those accounts to serve society.

The donor first puts money into an account, and, since NHF is a tax-exempt entity, the contribution to it is tax deductible. The account is established when the money is transferred. The donor later determines what end-use charity or charities should get the money. Sometimes the distributed money is just the interest of the gift and sometimes it includes part or all or the principal. In the meantime, the money is parked, doing nothing.

Structurally, this is the way real foundations work. In fact, the parking-lot feature is what distinguishes a foundation from a public charity, an organization that serves people directly. Both are considered charitable entities by the IRS—both are 501(c)(3) organizations—but, in the broader sense of establishing a foundation to serve a higher good, NHF isn't a foundation and neither are its accounts.

One reason is that a large part of NHF's goal is to help people figure out how not to pay taxes. Dr. J.T. Dock Houk, the founder of NHF, writes much on his website about the hardships the tax laws impose on what he calls "charity entrepreneurship."

Of the most important tax bill passed in the last half century affecting the nonprofit world, the Tax Act of 1969, he says, "I reckoned that while it was aimed at curbing real abuses among charities, it was a bad thing. Before 1969, charity entrepreneurship was easy. Or relatively so. You could set up a charity, donate to it, then begin your charitable program and take a salary and expenses to do so."[9] The part about "taking a salary" is a dominant theme throughout his descriptions of the joys of establishing a charity, or accounts at NHF. Almost anyone who has studied and respects the world of nonprofits would infer from those words that the defining cause of NHF is to help people avoid paying taxes, and not, as he gives lip-service to, helping society.

Houk told the *Los Angeles Times* in 1999, that his "clients had repaired a Buddhist temple in Tibet, fed the hungry in Cairo and operated a soup kitchen in Philadelphia." But NHF also advised donors that they could legally use their tax-exempt money to pay salaries to themselves and family members who managed their charitable giving.[10]

The IRS closed National Heritage in 1983 for alleged tax violations, but the foundation bounced back after successfully suing the IRS in the U.S. Court of Claims. In 1999, it ranked 63rd in the Philanthropy 400. Houk wasn't surprised at beating the IRS, and implies that more charities ought to embrace a more businesslike perspective. "A lot of the so-called outrage comes from charities that are feeling the pressure of competition, which is long overdue in the charitable sector."[11]

Perhaps it is that love of competition in a sector that tries to establish its identity apart from the for-profit world that prompts most of the criticism of NHF. In the summer of 2005, an article written by Jeff Krehely, "National Heritage Foundation: Pushing the Tax Laws to the Limit," in *Responsive Philanthropy*, starts out by asserting:

> A careful study of the National Heritage Foundation's website at www.nhf.org should be required of members of Congress and leaders of the nonprofit and philanthropic sectors who question the need for additional and tougher government oversight of nonprofit organizations and foundations. After just a few clicks through the site, it becomes clear how easy it is to use the non-profit sector for personal enrichment and benefit under current laws and regulations.[12]

As far as Houk is concerned, the spirit of charitable entrepreneurship dominates, or should dominate, the process of giving. What that is exactly, no one is quite sure, except that it has to do with avoiding taxes and otherwise finding a way around regulations. Acknowledged nonprofit experts heralded the 1969 Tax Reform Act as a good thing because it did curb abuses and did establish regulations that helped to ensure that when donors took a tax deduction for a charitable gift the money would actually go the charity. On the NHF website, however, Houk adds to his view of why that legislation was so bad. Before 1969 setting up a charity:

> was time consuming. Or relatively so. You could set up a charity, donate to it, then begin. It was time consuming, expensive, and filled with *administrivia*, but at least you could begin relating to the concerns that motivated you.

After the '69 Tax Reform Act, that opportunity was gone. The lawmakers created a new category of charity called the Private Foundation, which had so many regulations, strictures, and penalty teeth, I thought that the new law would be the death knell of charitable entrepreneurship.

He then implied why a place like NHF would be necessary:

I concluded that if a charity was set up whose charitable purpose included the "restoration, maintenance and extension of our national heritage," project by project, we could encourage private sector charitable entrepreneurship.[13]

Apparently, the "entrepreneurship" part of charitable entrepreneurship was in trouble. Already known as a rebel and buoyed by his success in fighting the IRS, Houk developed an organization that became the antithesis of what charities are all about. NHF's controversies can be summarized through the lens of two schemes: "donor-advised funds" (DAFs) and "charitable split-dollar life insurance."

Donor-Advised Funds

Conceptually, DAFs are simple. A donor establishes and puts money into the fund. The transfer is considered a tax-deductible charitable donation. Any charity—and some organizations that are not charities, such as banks—can house the fund.[14] The donor has control over the distributions from the fund to one or more public charities. NHF is essentially a collection of DAFs. Each fund has its own separate identity, its own tax exemption. NHF claims to have established 10,000 of them since 1968.[15]

Many charity professionals—such as those who work at community foundations—feel there is no need for DAFs and that, worse, the potential for abuse is high. Only in the name of donor control—more and more an influencing part of the philanthropic landscape—have DAFs become popular. There are no rules in the IRS Code explicitly prohibiting them, so the IRS does nothing about them, giving them its tacit approval.

In general, the sections of the tax code that govern the tax-exempt world have one goal: to ensure that the amount donors deduct for their charitable gifts is used for the public good. While there are many ways deductions are correlated with the gifts to which they are attached—the complicated but exacting process for determining the charitable portion of split-interest gifts is an example—the donor's reward of a lesser tax bill is to be commensurate with the value of the public good that derives from the gift.

The law, however, is often not clear. And Houk's philosophy on doing the right thing goes something like this: "The envelope needs pushing."[16] Houk pushed the envelope when it came to DAFs, and claimed for several years that donors funding their own foundation at NHF (for the purposes of this chapter, think of "foundation" and "donor-advised fund" as pretty much the same thing) could pay themselves with the money they received via the income tax deduction by setting up the foundation. In an article written in 2000 the *New York Times* reported finding this on the NHF website: "We would strive to bring your salary up to private industry standards."[17] Houk was speaking to all would be like-minded individuals who want to pay less in taxes by flouting the intention of Congress.

Also on the NHF website at the time was the following:

> One of the most fundamental principles behind the National Heritage Foundation (NHF) is that you can set up and then work for your own foundation receiving taxable income—even if the only donations are those you provided. Think of the retirement planning implications. Put money in a "Foundation at NHF" where it grows tax free. Then during retirement, recover these funds as taxable income and nontaxable expenses for bona fide charitable activities.

Houk also pushed the envelope by advising potential donors in the United States how to circumvent the regulations preventing claiming a tax deduction on to foreign charities:

> As you know, a person seeking a deduction of a contribution to a charity or charitable project in another country, must make that donation to a U. S.-based charity like the National Heritage Foundation. A gift directly to the project is not deductible.
>
> One of the objectives of NHF is to "touch lives in other countries". We support our "Foundations at NHF" when they desire to do so. 1. They may support charitable organizations in other countries, and 2. They may support charitable projects in other countries.[18]

From the Krehely article in *Responsive Philanthropy*: NHF is "a slick organization that knows how to push nonprofit tax law to the limit, while generating hundreds of thousands of dollars in profits for the Houk family and the cadre of 'investors' involved with the organization."

When the envelope gets pushed too far—and that can happen when people in the nonprofit world think they're running a business and the pursuit of a dollar is their primary aim—the system fails. In 2006, Congress got wise and passed the Pension Protection Act (PPA), which made it illegal for donors to be paid for their services as directors of their DAFs. At the Senate Finance Committee, Senator Charles Grassley was adamant and vocal about charity abuse, and he saw DAFs as Exhibit A. The PPA devotes 140 pages to the nonprofit sector, much of that to DAFs, so much in fact, that it has inspired some people to call the PPA "the Anti-NHF Act of 2006."[19]

In her testimony before the Senate Finance Committee in 2004, J.J. McNab, a financial planner and insurance analyst in Bethesda, Maryland, summarized the National Heritage Foundation, and others similar to it, this way: "The abuses in this field are too numerous to list. Family vacations, school tuition, Olympic size swimming pools, deferred compensation plans are all being funded through accommodation charities who are willing to often bend and sometimes break the rules."[20]

Life Insurance Misused

Shoddy donor-advised funds weren't the only problem at the National Heritage Foundation. It was also recklessly promoting a complex life-insurance strategy called "split-dollar." This is an arrangement in which an employer and an employee split the premium payments on the policy. The proceeds from the death benefit are also split between the company and the employee's beneficiaries. This is cheaper for each entity than for either to pay for the policy individually, and can make good business sense under the right circumstances. Employers often want insurance protection on their key employees and the employees can save money. The critical consideration is that the employer has an "insurable interest" in the employee; that is, the employer stands to lose economically if the employee dies, and therefore has an interest in the employee being insured. A good deal of imagination, however, is required to think that a charity can claim economic hardship if a person who otherwise isn't already donating dies. A stunning absence of donative intent—a desire to help a charitable cause— was often a major characteristic of people on whom these policies were written. Although NHF wasn't the first charitable organization to market split-dollar life insurance, it certainly became the national poster child for endorsing it.

As it did with DAFs, the NHF aggressively marketed the policies, promoting benefits that would never pass the scrutiny of any lawmaker who cared. Typically, the insurance premium would be deducted as a charitable gift on the tax return of the "donor," while much of the death benefit would go to the donor's family members.

The reason given as to why the premium would be deductible was that the owner and beneficiary of the policy would be NHF; the donor transferred money to NHF—it would be characterized as a gift—and then NHF bought the policy insuring the donor's life. NHF would then make sure the proper allocation between personal and charitable interests was made. NHF charged a fee to the donor of 4.5 percent of the death benefit.

*   *   *

In December 1997, Juan Mancillas, a doctor in Cameron County, Texas, and his wife, Sylvia, took out three life-insurance policies whose death benefits totaled $7 million. The bulk of the benefits, $5 million, was to be placed in a trust whose beneficiary was their adult brain-damaged son. The remaining $2 million was to be placed into a family foundation, housed at the National Heritage Foundation, to ultimately benefit the Sisters of the Incarnate Word, a charity in Brownsville. The policy was a second-to-die policy, which means that the death benefits are paid after the second person dies. The annual premiums were approximately $85,000.

Like the DAFs, the split-dollar insurance scheme, which married charities and donors who claimed to want to make a charitable gift but who were at the same time intent on parting with as little money as possible, was also a form of abuse-in-waiting. It never made sense in the charitable arena because so little of the substance of the transaction was motivated by a desire to help charity—so little donative intent. Promoters of the scheme, like NHF, argued that the charity was under no legal obligation to buy the insurance or maintain it once it was purchased, and so, technically, the gift to the charity should be deductible. For years, the IRS had its doubts about the scheme, but it couldn't put its finger on exactly what was wrong with it.

But the IRS always knew that its guiding tax principle was that a gift should ensure that the benefit to charity would be commensurate with what being deducted. The IRS finally figured it out by parsing the "substance over form" argument: "The Service is not required to respect the form of a taxpayer's transaction when to do so would yield a result that is inconsistent with the substance of the transaction."[21] The substance of these transactions, it had been shown over the course of many analyses the IRS conducted, was a sham. In 1999, the IRS officially ruled that the premiums in charitable split-dollar policies were not deductible.

For six years after the IRS nixed the plan, the Mancillases, not knowing that the law had changed, continued to pay the premiums—which totaled $550,000 between 1999 and 2005—still believing that their son would receive the money in the event of their deaths. NHF, of course, knew the law had changed but didn't tell the couple and, also without informing them, changed the terms of the policies so that the foundation was the sole beneficiary. This was possible because NHF was the owner of the policies. When the Mancillases found out that the policies had been changed, they sued, claiming that NHF "failed to carry out" their "financial plans or charitable intent."[22] A 12-person jury issued a guilty verdict in September 2008 and recommended a payment of $9 million. The judge then lowered the award to $6.5 million. The couple's lawyer, Albert Garcia, said, "I can't help but wonder how many of the other 600 families with charitable split-dollar life-insurance plans with NHF have also had their children removed as beneficiaries just so that NHF could be the sole beneficiary. NHF said nothing to the Mancillases, so why wouldn't they pull the same stunt with these 600 other families." Garcia estimated the fees collected by NHF in connection to split-dollar policies to be "between $25 and $90 million."[23]

* * *

The NHF is alive today, but just barely. In January 2009 NHF filed for bankruptcy protection. On its 2008 990, NHF reported that donations had decreased from $65 million in 2004 to a little more than $17 million in 2008. That's a drop of almost 75 percent. Also, during that year, NHF saw its asset base shrinking. Total assets fell during 2008 from $232 million to $170 million, a 27 percent drop.[24]

NHF filed for bankruptcy protection in January 2009, and it appears that what prompted the move was a court order two days earlier requiring the organization to identify its assets. On that day NHF, saying it was "unable to meet its obligations," wired $1 million to an affiliate charity, and, temporarily anyway, out of reach of its creditors.[25] Prior to the bankruptcy, a senior financial analyst for the firm, Julia Weltmann, was deposed as part of Garcia's search for NHF's assets. Her testimony showed how unstable the foundation really was. She said that $25 million had been placed in a private investment scheme, a mutual fund that was not the type registered with federal regulators. She also explained that NHF had loaned $14 million to a software company, Stellar/McKim in Stroudsburg, Pennsylvania, headed by Ian Scott-Dunn, who also served as NHF's investment banker and investment advisor. Scott-Dunn was not licensed as an investment professional, however, and Stellar/McKim hadn't made any loan payments for three years. Asked why she thought he would have been named the foundation's investment advisor, Weltmann said, "I have no answer for that."[26] Later, Weltmann admitted that no credit analysis had been performed of the company to which the foundation lent so many millions of dollars because Scott-Dunn was a friend of the NHF board president.[27]

* * *

Charitable gift annuities were also imperiled. The Planned Giving Design Center, an online planned giving resource, said in 2009, "Of particular concern is the fact that, according to Weltmann, the $14 million loaned to Stellar came from donations made to NHF by numerous donors in exchange for charitable gift annuities which require NHF to make fixed annuity payments to annuitants for their lifetimes. Weltmann expressed further concerns regarding NHF's ability to recover its principal."[28] Most donor money is typically invested so that there is a pool from which to make annuity payments. But here, too, NHF was misleading donors, telling them that that their money would be invested conservatively. Weltmann testified that the money had instead been put into private placements, a riskier investment strategy and one that was not paying off.[29]

Wanting Too Much for a Charity

The stories in this chapter don't define the world of nonprofits—although they are certainly not the only such stories; tomorrow will no doubt bring new headlines—but they do illustrate the questions that charities must deal with regularly. What oversight a board of directors has over the organization and what the board's relationship is with the executive director, how to protect a donor's interests while at the same time allowing a charity to make its own decisions about growing into the future, ensuring that donors' wishes are honored even after they die, identifying charities that don't act much like charities, at least not in the altruistic way we typically think of charitable work...these and other issues are growing in society's collective consciousness as we are beginning to realize that our nation's nonprofit sector long ago grew out of its stage of innocence into something much more corporate than it has ever been before.

It's a different world for nonprofits from the one of only a generation ago, to say nothing of the way charities worked in the middle of the last century and before that. The questions have become enormous. Not an insignificant number of lawyers make their living representing charities or otherwise working on issues relating to nonprofits. But, the legal questions—as is evident not only with the nonprofit sector, but in all three sectors of society—are not the only questions. While they must be answered, answering only those will not move us forward.

What will it take to move us forward? It will take a mindset that may not yet exist—one that combines the best of the mind and the heart, one that acknowledges and honors the words on a written legal document while at the same time—mustering all the reserves of common sense, dignity and respect for others—giving *equal weight* to the complexities of context and human emotion and desires. Right now the legal standing of an issue is its only standing. And that must change.

Chapter Six

How Long Does the Dead Hand Live?

The idea of making gifts to charities is so fundamental that we've come to take our understanding of it for granted. It is this obvious: When you send a check, transfer stock, or convey any of a number of other assets, the charity uses it as wisely as possible in furthering its mission. How complicated can it be? I give you money. Use it well.

Good Intentions

Charities have in the past decade or so begun to offer donors categories of activity—meals for the homeless, scholarships, or faculty salaries at a university—so that the appeal from the charity has more appeal to the prospective donor. Nonetheless, to follow an actual gift through the charity's accounting labyrinth is nearly impossible, and once donors feel that the charity will use the gift well, they often don't care about the details.

At least that's true for modest gifts. Donors of gifts in the million-dollar-and-up category often take a different view, which has garnered more and more support from the attorney general's office in many states. The is the view that a gift is no longer a mere transfer of money that gives a charity complete control over how to spend it. The justification for this shift in attitude was illustrated most dramatically at the Red Cross after 9/11. The Red Cross collected money to aid the survivors but then used or saved the money for other purposes. Those purposes were legitimately within the scope of the mission of the Red Cross, but they had nothing to do with 9/11 victims. The public cried foul. People had given money in response to a specific appeal—as emotionally charged as any in history—and they naturally felt cheated when it wasn't used in the way they were led to believe it would be spent. The Red Cross had established the Liberty Disaster Fund, whose purpose was to help the victims of 9/11.

But the fund ended up with too much money to be used that way and so the Red Cross, unilaterally and without telling the public, decided it would use the money for other purposes. Donors who thought they were lending a helping hand to the victims of the gravest tragedy on American soil since the Civil War were upset. The *New York Times* in November 2001 wrote, "The reserve fund had provoked intense criticism from victim families and lawmakers, who accused the agency of misleading many of its donors about how their money would be spent."[1]

Since then, the courts and state officials have made it clear that putting a purpose to a gift is not merely a quaint marketing idea. Donors have a right to expect that their money will be used the way the charity says it will be used. In charity parlance this concept is known as *donative intent* or *donors' rights*. When these intentions are clearly spelled out, there is usually a written agreement in which the donor stipulates how the charity must use the money, as well as a variety other conditions, such as when financial reports are to be sent. One generous donor I know routinely has his attorney draft charitable gift agreements that are typically over 20 pages long, and sometimes as long as 50 pages. To him, these agreements provide assurance that the charity will do as he wishes with his money. "When I give my money," he says, "I want to be sure the charity does exactly what I want them to with it."

Some charities take a slightly different view. They think that a gift is just that: It belongs to the recipient, to use it however it wants. There should be no restrictions, certainly no legal ones, on how the money is spent, as long as it is used well by the charity.[2] One headmaster at a private school once told me that he would never allow a donor to dictate his budget. It does happen, however, that donors explain their preferences, and the charity takes the money having agreed to those preferences, and this can lead to problems.

One complication in such cases is that budgets are fungible; money can be moved around underneath the published numbers. For example, a charity can say that money earmarked for scholarships went to scholarships even if it didn't. A charity might agree that a donor's $100,000 gift will go to scholarships. If the school's scholarship fund is $1 million, the donor may think—if she is aware of the budget amount—that thanks to her gift, next year it will be to $1,100,000. (For the sake of simplicity, let's not factor in inflation.) But even though the gift goes into the scholarship budget, the total may stay at $1 million, while $100,000 that *was* in the scholarship budget is taken out to be used elsewhere. True, the donated money became part of the scholarship line, but the benefit to economically disadvantaged students did not increase. However, the charity can, without being dishonest, claim that it used the gift for the stated purpose. That's fungibility. After all, the donor didn't specify that the scholarship budget had to increase by $100,000. This flexibility is what the headmaster wants to protect. The idea of fungibility even holds for endowment gifts in which only the revenues the endowment generates or a certain percentage of the assets can be used each year.

A donor may not care that her gift will not increase the budget of a program she says she wants to support, but she deserves to know whether it will or not. Donors are not likely to initiate this conversation because they normally do not think of such technicalities, so charities have the obligation to let them know. In not engaging in a discussion of budgeting, the typical charity does not intend to mislead; it's just that life is easier if the conversation never takes place. Think of how this might sound like an intrusion on the decision-making process: "Will my gift will *add* to the money available for a program or will it, because you can shift money around, simply replace other expenditures in the charity's budget? I prefer—I demand—that it add to the budget of the program I'm supporting." From the charity's perspective, that may sound like an ultimatum. And it is. But nothing is wrong with it. (Quite frankly, too many charities haven't given the issue enough thought to even develop a policy on whether such a conversation should take place.) If they are ethically secure, charities will explain these kinds of things to their prospective donors without worrying that they will hijack the budgeting process. Charities should be aggressively honest about how donated money is used.

What happens, then, when the donor alleges that the money wasn't used in the way it should have been used? Complaints like this have been made, and donors or their heirs have taken their claims to the courts. This happened at no less a prestigious place than Princeton University, an Ivy League school whose reputation for integrity has been over 250 years in the making.

The Robertson Gift

In July 1961, Marie Robertson donated to Princeton 700,000 shares of A&P, the grocery store giant. The gift, which was commonly understood to be made by both Marie and her husband Charles, was valued at $35 million. At the time, the gift was the largest Princeton had ever received and the largest anonymous gift in the history of higher education,[3] although the gift didn't stay anonymous for long. Its purpose was to benefit the already-existing graduate program at Princeton's prestigious Woodrow Wilson School of Public and International Affairs. The school had been founded in 1930 and renamed in 1948 to honor alumnus and former Princeton president Woodrow Wilson, the former United States president. This was a heady time of American intellectual export. During his presidential campaign, John Kennedy challenged college students to devote two years of their post-graduate lives abroad to make the world a better place.[4] Three months after he took office, Kennedy created the Peace Corp. Three months after that, the Robertsons made their gift.

The idea behind the gift, which was consistent with the Wilson School's mission, was to encourage students to enter careers in government, particularly in "international relations and affairs."[5] The Robertson agreement read, in part, the "objective is to strengthen the Government of the United States and increase its ability and determination to defend and extend freedom throughout the world by improving the facilities for the training and education of men and women for government service."[6] Marie Robertson knew she wanted to do something for society. Her husband Charles served in World War II. His admiration for the civil service of Eisenhower and Churchill prompted him and his wife to think about doing something big on the world stage. Their gift to Princeton was to be an expression of that admiration.

The Robertson Foundation

Most donors who want to establish an endowed fund do so simply by giving directly to a charitable organization; the money is accounted for separately to be certain it funds the right program, but the gift is still under the overall umbrella of the organization; that is, the money is an asset of the charity and the charity controls how it is invested. When large donors—those in a wholly different category of wealth—want complete assurance that their money will be used as they intend, they will often set up a private or a family foundation, which permits them to direct money to any charitable organizations they choose. But that isn't the way the Robertson Foundation worked. It was tied to one charity: Princeton.

Back in 1961, the tax laws were not written as they are today. Major changes in the way foundations work were approved in the Tax Act of 1969,[7] and so, as a result, the Robertson Foundation became a Type I Supporting Organization. This is the way the IRS describes a supporting organization:

> Supporting organizations are charities that carry out their exempt purposes by supporting other exempt organizations, usually other public charities. The classification is important because it is one means by which a charity can avoid classification as a private foundation, a status that is subject to a much more restrictive regulatory regime. The key feature of a supporting organization is a strong relationship with an organization it supports. The strong relationship enables the supported organization to oversee the operations of the supporting organization. Therefore, the supporting organization is classified as a public charity, even though it may be funded by a small number of persons in a manner similar to a private foundation.[8]

Accordingly, the Robertson Foundation had its own board of directors, separate from the Princeton board. Princeton controlled four of the seven seats on the board, and the Robertson family determined who the other three would be. William Robertson was one of the three. The Robertson voice would always be in the minority, but that's because a key characteristic of a supporting organization is that the board is structured so that the organization it supports is in control. The board made investment and other decisions relating to the foundation's expenditures, all of which were technically and in reality distinct from the decisions made by Princeton's trustees. The foundation didn't make money grants, but it reimbursed the university for the funds attributed to the Wilson School expenditures each year. Because the Robertson Foundation was prohibited from spending money on anything other than the Woodrow Wilson School—the foundation's sole purpose was to support the Wilson School—Princeton correctly counted the foundation's money as its own; the university's endowment values included the foundation's assets. The concept is a little confusing. One entity exists to serve another, and the one has its own level of autonomy but its assets are included in those of the other.

The IRS's phrase in its description of a supporting organization, about a "strong relationship with an organization it supports," would become the central concept in the dispute that divided William Robertson, the son of Charles and Marie, and Princeton, a dispute that led to the biggest legal unraveling in the history of American charity.

The Lawsuit

The perspective of Robertson, the plaintiff: Princeton did not honor the written wishes of the donor. The perspective of Princeton, the defendant: We did what the donor wanted us to do.

In a sporting event, both sides know at the end who won and who lost. One side doesn't like it, but the outcome is clear. Both sides respect it and move on. But that's not the way it is in nonathletic competition, in real life. Not today, when hundreds of millions of dollars are at stake, much of the time at the mercy of subjective interpretation. That was the aftermath of the Princeton case. The lawsuit was settled out of court, and the issues that brought the dispute into the courtroom are today not fully settled. The search for clarity in its lessons, therefore, may be in vain, although the drama demands everyone connected to the nonprofit world to pause and think about donors' rights, financial accounting in accordance with the terms of an agreement, and just how strong a dead hand continues to be.

*   *   *

The two sides lined up the way the foundation board was divided: the descendants of Charles and Marie Robertson and the foundation's family-designated trustees against Princeton University and the university-designated trustees. William Robertson was the lead plaintiff and he accused Princeton of not using the foundation's assets properly.

The complaint had three components: (1) the Princeton wing of the board used its influence to wrongfully change investment managers, (2) the foundation wrongfully used its income on expenses unrelated to the Wilson school—keep in mind that Princeton controlled the foundation, and (3) the university ignored the donor's original intentions by not ensuring that the school's graduates entered public service at the proper rate. Princeton's perspective was that the charges were unwarranted.

Also, since at least the early 1970s, well before he died, Charles Robertson, according to his son,[9] had been concerned that

Princeton wasn't fully living up to the spirit of the gift. Although no legal account of the case will include it, this gnawing, anxious undercurrent fed William Robertson's suspicions to such a degree that it became the driving force behind his desire to dissolve the foundation.

The Investment Issue

The Foundation's endowment was large. By the middle of 2008 the foundation's endowment had grown from the original $35 million to more than $900 million. By the early 2000s the foundation's three-person investment committee, which consisted of William Robertson and two people from Princeton's faction of the board, began to think about changing the way investment decisions were made. Prior to that time, the investment committee itself had been making important and technical decisions. By 2003 the Princeton contingent of the group felt that the investment world had gotten so sophisticated and complicated and that the foundation had grown so large, that professional investment managers were needed. On January 1, 2004, after interviewing several candidates, the board decided by a vote of 4 to 3 to employ the Princeton University Investment Company (PRINCO), which was in charge of investing the university's endowment, to make its investment decisions. William Robertson and the other two members of the board representing the family opposed the decision.

*   *   *

The relevant wording from the Certificate of Incorporation relating to investments is this: "The Board of Trustees shall have the full power to manage the affairs of the corporation..." William Robertson's position was that this meant that it was wrong to hire an outside management firm. Princeton's position was that "full power" means just that, including the power to use professionals. That is, although hiring outside professionals was not explicitly permitted, the Certificate of Incorporation did not disallow it. While hiring PRINCO might have been an obvious move—the much smaller supporting organization hiring the same firm that the larger, supported organization was using—it can also be argued that PRINCO did an extraordinary job for the Robertson Foundation. Between January 1, 2004, when PRINCO took over the foundation's investments, and June 30, 2008, the average annual growth of the Dow Jones Industrial Average was approximately 1.8 percent. Over that same period, the foundation grew from $561 million to more than $900 million, a net annualized growth, minus certain small expenditures to support the program, of more than 10 percent.

Robertson did not dispute that the foundation board had the authority to look to other managers, but he did question Princeton's motives for making the change, pointing out that for years prior to the change, the foundation's investments actually did better than Princeton's; in fact, they did so well, he said, that Princeton was a little "embarrassed" by the results. His question was simply this: Knowing that his parents wanted to keep the foundation separate from Princeton, why did the university trustees want to make the change? He contended that it was a way for Princeton to muddy the distinction between the Wilson School and Princeton, as well as a way to separate the Robertsons from the school. In effect, he said, Princeton didn't like him and wanted to get rid of him.[10] The way Princeton tells it, changing the investment philosophy and deciding to hire a professional firm were why Robertson initiated the lawsuit.

The Expenditures Issue

Robertson denied that, however, saying that while he opposed the decision to hire new investment managers, that was not the reason for the lawsuit.[11] He said that Princeton had been misusing the foundation's assets for a long time by spending money on things that were unrelated to the mission of the foundation. An example of the kind of expenditure Robertson objected to was the use of faculty from other divisions at the university to teach Wilson School students topics that he felt were not relevant to his parents' goals. Princeton took the view that the goals of Charles and Marie Robertson included broad academic objectives, and not, as they put it, "a kind of vocational program."[12]

Without going into the detail of years of accounting, it is fair to say that university programs often draw on outside resources—outside the program but within the university—to enrich the learning experience. While it was true that faculty not directly employed by the Wilson school were hired to teach some classes, Robertson and Princeton saw the issue from opposite views. One of the strengths of the Wilson School, at the time of the gift and since, has been that it is able to call upon other Princeton faculty to provide a robust education for its students. In a university setting, expenses relating to an educational enterprise are, by their nature, subject to the university's evaluation of what it needs to create the best possible program. The school felt it could not possibly delegate its academic oversight to anyone less knowledgeable about what it takes to prepare someone for public service. Furthermore, Princeton argued that how expenses were to be allocated was outlined in a formula that everyone on the foundation board had agreed on. Only after Robertson brought the lawsuit, according to Princeton, did he pursue the issue of expense allocation.

Even so, in hindsight it can be argued that Princeton made a few mistakes. From Robertson's perspective, and, according to sources close to the case,[13] supported by a detailed analysis by PricewaterhouseCoopers, Princeton made some costly mistakes—to the tune of $207 million. Robertson said in a statement, "Princeton has been caught with its hand in the Foundation's cookie jar."[14] Today the value of that amount—this is aside from the endowment growth—would be approximately $500 million. At the time the case was settled, Princeton was in the process of preparing its own detailed explanation of all the expenses.

Even expenditures that the plaintiffs acknowledged as legitimate were, from their perspective, inefficient. Robertson claimed that between 1990 and 2003, Princeton spent $195 million to educate 886 graduate students, yet, only 86 of those students took jobs with the government after graduation. He calculated that the school had therefore spent $2.3 million per student.

Donative Intent

As it happened, the nonprofit world was experiencing, concurrent with the Princeton lawsuit, an upsurge in donors' queries about how their gifts were being used. That upsurge has become what may be a permanent plateau of donor concern. States' attorneys general began showing more interest in the donors' rights issue, and charitable organizations were feeling the heat. One of the more notable cases outside of Princeton was that of Newcomb College, the women's undergraduate school at Tulane University in New Orleans. Tulane closed Newcomb, rolling it into the men's undergraduate division, in the wake of the financial hardship brought on by Hurricane Katrina in 2005. Descendants of Josephine Newcomb sued Tulane, claiming the terms of the original gift in 1886 did not allow Tulane to close the school.

The issue that received the most publicity in the Robertson lawsuit was donor intent or donor's rights. The *Wall Street Journal* said, "*Robertson v. Princeton* may be the most important case higher education has faced over the question of honoring the wishes of a donor."[15] Today, in editorials and board rooms, many words are expended on the topic of donor rights. But it's easy to talk of the rights of donors and how important they are to charities. The difficulty comes in making decisions actually honoring donors, as well as whatever rights they may have—an issue far from decided on a state or federal level—and many people in fundraising offices across the country were waiting for some guidance on the issue in the Princeton case.

Because the issue of protecting a donor's intentions was catching and holding the anxious attention of the nonprofit world, it is important to refer to the relevant wording from the Robertson Foundation's Certificate of Incorporation:

> Its [the foundation's] objective is to strengthen the Government of the United States and increase its ability and determination to defend and extend freedom throughout the world by improving the facilities for the training and education of men and women for government service.

The money generated from the fund was:

> To establish or maintain and support at Princeton University, and as part of the Woodrow Wilson School, a Graduate School, where men and women dedicated to public service may prepare themselves for careers in government service, with particular emphasis on the education of such persons for careers in those areas of the Federal Government that are concerned with international relations and affairs.[16]

Whether or not the Wilson School ought to have graduated more people into direct government service, and particularly into foreign affairs, is central to the donative-intent issue. Princeton argued that it has no control over what its graduates do. Besides, the original document made no mention of a specific number of people who should go into public service. (The word "objective," as opposed to "requirement" is used, for example, and "may," not "must.") Princeton felt that Robertson wanted to "narrow the Foundation mission from the one agreed to...in 1961."[17] Robert Durkee, the university's vice president and secretary, said that the question raised about *intent* was in fact precisely the reverse of what was alleged. From Princeton's point of view, the salient issue was "whether the descendants of a donor can overturn the donor's intent." That is, Princeton said that it *honors* the ideal of donor intent and had been doing so for almost 50 years. It claimed that it had fully adhered to the terms of the donor agreement, which it said was written in intentionally broad language precisely so as not to put the university into an academic strait jacket.[18] Furthermore, on the matter of donor intent, in addition to being "the best damned foreign service school in the world," as one person told me, Princeton said that "Mrs. Robertson's clear intent was to donate the $35 million to Princeton—not to leave it in the control of her children."[19]

William Robertson, tired of what he thought was stonewalling on the part of the university, wanted to call it quits; he wanted to dissolve the foundation and he wanted all the money back, not for himself or any other private purpose, but to establish a foreign service school at another university. He wanted $1.4 billion from Princeton—the $900 million in the endowment and the inflation-adjusted $500 million of wrongful expenses—to start another foundation. According to the *Chronicle of Philanthropy*, as early as 2007, Robertson began approaching other universities. "He has approached more than ten universities," according to the *Chronicle*, "to discuss how they could put the money to work. He says the institutions have welcomed his interest, and he is evaluating which programs are best so that he can prepare a plan to show Judge Shuster [the judge in the case] about how he would use the Robertson money."

Princeton was stunned to learn this. To quote again from the *Chronicle* article, Cass Cliatt, a Princeton spokesperson, said, "If these approaches have been made, they reflect a shocking disregard by Bill Robertson for his fiduciary duties as a trustee of the Robertson Foundation, as well as a profound miscalculation of his likelihood of success in the litigation." Princeton officials also said, apparently in response to all this, that Robertson was "unfit to serve as trustee" of the foundation.[20]

The question, according to Princeton, boiled down to how narrowly a gift agreement should be read. Charities that care about their donors, present as well as past, do what they can in a world of changing circumstances to best honor what they thought their donors wanted—and would want into the future. How that gets played out over time is where the question is hinged. Unfortunately, because the case was settled before the commencement of a trial, and the relevant court papers are forever sealed, we will never know all the nuances of the arguments or how the court might have decided.

*   *   *

It was said that Robertson was running out of money. Princeton had a great deal of money in its pocket; the Wilson School endowment, even as its value was hovering just above $900 million, represented only about 6 percent of Princeton's entire endowment. The Robertson side was being funded by another foundation, the Banbury Fund, which is headed by Robertson. (In 2007, Robertson's salary for his work at the Banbury Fund was $150,000.[21]) He claimed, however, that he was not running out of money, that Princeton underestimated not only his resolve but also his financial ability to take the case all the way through. "If Princeton thought I or Banbury would soon run out of money," Robertson said, "they were wrong." Not only was he not running out of money, he was also prepared to spend it.[22]

*   *   *

As an aside to this case—although it is an important issue—Princeton's position was that it was inappropriate for the legal costs to be born by another foundation because the money at foundations is not meant to be spent on legal bills that have nothing to do with protecting itself or its mission. That is, charities shouldn't be spending money on things that don't concern them. Victoria Bjorklund, an attorney who worked on behalf of Princeton and a former chair of the IRS's Tax Exempt Advisory Committee, said that Robertson, by using the Banbury Fund's money to pay for his legal expenses, may have been engaged in "self-dealing"—using charity money for personal use—which is prohibited.[23] This meant, as Princeton saw it, that Robertson really didn't have any skin in the game; there would be no financial loss to him, no matter the outcome of the lawsuit. As time went along, because of legal and public relations costs, Banbury's assets diminished from approximately $50 million to $20 million.

The Settlement

The settlement was reached on December 8, 2008. It called for Princeton to pay $50 million between 2012 and 2018 from the foundation's assets to a new charitable foundation, the Robertson Foundation for Government. In addition, Princeton paid $40 million the Robertson's defense costs, as well as its own. In total, it would cost Princeton about $100 million to be free and clear of Robertson.

*   *   *

The headline of the Robertson news release after the unraveling: "Princeton to pay more than $100 million to settle lawsuit alleging misuse of donated funds." If that doesn't clarify the Robertson perspective, this, from the body of the announcement, does: "This settlement is more than a slap on the wrist. This settlement came only when Princeton officials realized they underestimated us and miscalculated our resolve, and would soon face a terribly embarrassing trial."[24]

Robertson also had this to say after the settlement:

> The money "will carry out my parents' dream of helping our country by preparing America's best and brightest students for government careers with an emphasis on federal jobs in international relations and affairs." And: "For many decades, university officials refused to honor their commitments to my parents, thereby dooming a powerful and patriotic program."[25]

The headline from Princeton, as you might imagine, draws a different slant: "Settlement retains Princeton's control, use of Robertson funds." And Princeton's perspective: "This settlement achieves the university's highest priorities in this lawsuit, which were to ensure that Marie Robertson's gift will continue to support the graduate program of the Woodrow Wilson School and that the University would have full authority to make academic judgments about how these funds are to be used."[26]

Princeton also had this to say:

> The case lasted 76 months, and the plaintiffs attempted to examine almost every spending decision of the Robertson Foundation for the past 47 years. To deal with these and other matters, Princeton engaged nine expert witnesses, while the Robertsons engaged seven. There were 29 reports prepared by these experts, totaling 2,098 pages. In the six and a half years of the pre-trial discovery phase of the case, the university produced almost half a million pages of electronic and print documents; there were more than 80 depositions of fact and expert witnesses covering more than 25,000 transcript pages; complex motions required more than 3,000 pages of briefing; 124 witnesses were listed to testify at trial; and more

than 5,000 trial exhibits were identified. Pursuant to the settlement agreement, the university's defense costs, to the extent they
are not covered by insurance, will be reimbursed by the Robertson
Foundation.[27]

Each side is convinced that had the case gone to trial it would
have won. Both sides made this observation: had there been no
lawsuit, what was spent on legal fees could have been used for
charitable purposes. Both sides claimed to protect the idea of
donor intent. In terms of the settlement, each side thinks it did
win. That's telling all by itself.

*   *   *

Even if honorable people can quibble about the meaning of the
words as they are interpreted through the lens of original intent,
what went so terribly wrong at the Wilson School that would justify a legal action of this scope? What basis did the plaintiffs have
for making their allegations relating to donor intent? Why would
Robertson want to hinder Princeton's academic flexibility? After
all, for decades no one publicly complained about the investments
or the program. Looking at the chronology of events, remember
that what started the public dispute was the proposed change in
the foundation's investment oversight. And that issue, as it turned
out—demonstrably so, well before the lawsuit was scheduled to
go to trial—just didn't stand; the foundation's endowment grew
well—both before and after PRINCO took over.

Is it possible that something else was going on?

Robert Durkee's personal theory goes like this: William
Robertson had no other professional identity, "He never had a real
role in life," said Durkee. "He clung to his work as a member of
the foundation investment committee. When that role was taken
away, and as the fund balance continued to grow," according to
Durkee, "Robertson grew more bitter." Robertson's only other line
of attack was to challenge whether the university was adhering to
the original purpose of the gift—honoring donative intent—and
that's when he "took on a new identity as the poster child for the
donative intent cause."[28] That's why there were charges relating
to where the school's graduates were employed in their first year
out of the school. The words from the founding document make
no mention of who goes where. In fact, no school—whether it is
a business school, a law school, or a truck-driving school—can
guarantee what its graduates will do.

Despite the *Wall Street Journal* article, and there were several others on the topic, and a growing awareness of donor's rights and honoring donative intent, Princeton insists that the case was not, in fact, about protecting the wishes of donors. The wishes of Charles and Marie Robertson were being protected. The words written by their hands, although now long dead, would be obeyed.

While Robertson conceded that the wording in the incorporation document neither prevented a different investment approach nor specified that a certain number of students had to enter government service right after graduation, he continued to maintain that the school was not respecting his parents' wishes. He said he had letters, written by his father, proving that he was concerned about the way Princeton was spending the foundation's money as early as the early 1970s. As far as the son was concerned, not only was there a problem when the father was alive, it was important that Princeton abide by the spirit of the gift from two people who, he said, were "the most philanthropic and the most altruistic he'd ever known or had even ever heard of."

In the end, for William Robertson—and for his two sisters who supported him in all this—it was about a personal commitment to his parents' memory and dream. Far from being unfit as a trustee, he thought he was the very model of protecting his parents' wishes. He scoffed at the assertion that his driving force was that he had no other role in life. He said he was busy with many things—including running a successful business, as well as managing a foundation—and didn't need to sue Princeton to express an act of self-actualization.[29]

Victoria Bjorklund, the attorney, said that "this case has given me pause about allowing [her client] charities to participate in Type I Supporting Organizations that go beyond the donor generation." You see, she said, in the Princeton case, there "was no problem when the father was alive."[30]

William Robertson said there were plenty of problems. The problems were personal, however, and, as legitimate as they may have been, his father signed a document in 1961, a document that he and his attorneys labored over—whose words became, as they must become as time passes—the guiding vision. The letters outside the document would have had no legal effect.

But this is where the real problem lies: the legal issue, regardless of all the posturing of attorneys in a case, is not the only issue for donors or charities, and it's surprisingly often not even the most important issue. Understanding where people are coming from is often a far better barometer than words on paper. But as words on paper are often all we have, those words ought to reflect where someone is coming from.

In 2007, by which time things had gotten wildly out of control, Robertson said that it was too late for amends, that he wanted a "divorce." He got one. But, as is the case in most divorces, both sides lost a lot.

Princeton has its school unencumbered by Robertson, but with every intention, it says, of honoring the founding document's idea of educating and preparing students to enter the world of public service, regardless of how that might happen. Robertson has established another foundation, this one a family foundation—no more supporting organizations for him—and plans to grant annual gifts to universities and perhaps to other types of organizations that will honor his wishes. And he won't have to take anyone to court if any of the recipients use the money in a way he does not approve of. If that happens, he can simply stop supporting them.

The Dead Hand

To get a sense of how the Princeton problem can be avoided by other charities, we need to look to the past. Founded in 1911, the Carnegie Corporation of New York is one of the largest and most effective foundations in the United States, doing work that is wide ranging and well regarded. In making his gift, Andrew Carnegie, in his way, addressed the dangers of a dead hand.

It can be said that Carnegie started his own charity. Because his fortune wasn't going to an already established charity, he may not have felt secure about the future worthiness of his gift. He understood that times change and later generations would make the important decisions about how the money would be spent. The following, which was written by Carnegie in 1911 would, if it represented donors' sentiments, be a charity's dream. Major donors today generally don't think in these terms—their advisors tell them not to, and the scandals of late have created an environment that cautions against it—but more charities should conduct frank discussions about how times change and that a dead hand can only grip so much as time passes into the distant and unknowable future.

Conditions upon the earth inevitably change; hence, no wise man will bind Trustees forever to certain paths, causes or institutions... I

give my trustees full authority to change policy or causes hitherto
aided, from time to time, when this, in their opinion, has become
necessary or desirable. They shall best conform to my wishes by
using their own judgment...[31]

Anyone deciding to make a large donation must balance her
own sense of what is important against the needs the charity itself
has identified, knowing that future generations—both those running the charity and those using its services—will almost certainly
have different needs.

One charity, an independent school to which a donor I know
has made several significant gifts, insists upon being able to
change the purpose of his endowed gift for just that reason. The
donor wanted one of his gifts to endow a chair in the English
department. The school responded that there might come a day,
in the far distant future, when English was no longer taught at the
school—or at any school—because no one would be speaking it.
It was perhaps an extreme caution, but the school was making the
point that it had to have the flexibility to change the purpose of
the endowed gifts at some future time if circumstances dictated
such a change.

It's not that donors cannot or should not impose restrictions
on their gifts, but the question is about how much restriction and
for how long it should be imposed. That is not a legal question so
much as it is an ethical one—one in which one party promises to
make good on an agreement but at the same time wants the flexibility to do what is necessary into the future.

The question may then become, Is it too much to ask that a
charity abide by the restrictions forever? It may be. But whatever
the decision is, both donors and charities need to give the question
a lot more thought than they have so far.

Chapter Seven

Why Good Governance Matters

Sometimes executives at charitable organizations begin to view them as their own personal fiefdoms. It is as if they feel like entrepreneurs, who started the business with their own money and therefore have the right to make or delegate all the decisions—and also to dip into the checking account when it's convenient. There have been numerous instances of leaders of small charities who have done exactly this kind of thing. Because there's often a lack of a formal bureaucracy in charitable organizations, the person may just began to feel that the board does not need to be consulted. Even at the largest charities, the controls are not always what they should be, and charismatic executives have been known to engage in more individual decision-making than is healthy for the organization. Almost always, when things go bad it's because the board's oversight isn't what it should be.

That was what happened at both the Smithsonian in Washington, D.C., and Stevens Institute of Technology in New Jersey.

The Smithsonian

"The Nation's Attic," as the Smithsonian is commonly called, is the country's premier museum and the biggest tourist attraction in Washington, D.C. It was founded in 1826, after James Smithson, a British scientist, named the United States as a contingent beneficiary of the bulk of his estate. The contingency was that his nephew die before producing "a child or children, legitimate or illegitimate..." It was an exceptionally generous gift, but it seemed unlikely that the museum would ever see any of it because, at the time, the nephew was only in his 20s. But six years after Smithson died in 1829, his nephew died—childless. The gift was valued at approximately $508,000. Initially, Congress couldn't decide if the government was within its rights to accept the money, but it did accept it in 1836. This didn't preclude the usual Capitol Hill bickering. No one could agree on what to do with the money—establish a university, a research laboratory, a library, a museum? The provision in the will said only the United States was "to found at Washington, under the name of the Smithsonian Institution, an establishment for the increase and diffusion of knowledge among men." Given that kind of latitude, it's a wonder Congress ever made up its mind. But eight years later, in 1846, the Smithsonian was born, and today it is the world's largest museum and research complex.[1]

No one knows why Smithson made such an extraordinary gift. He had never visited the United States and didn't know anyone here. He was a chemist who was the youngest elected member of the Royal Society, England's national academy of science, but much of what we would otherwise know of his life was destroyed when his papers and diaries were burned in a fire at the museum in 1865. There is speculation that part of his motive for making the contingent gift—on the condition that his nephew died without heirs—was that, because he was born illegitimately, he felt the pressures of a rigid and unaccepting societal structure, as England's was at the time.

Whatever his motivation, he did make the gift and as a result has earned a place in our country's history. In 1904, after it was learned that the cemetery in Genoa, Italy, where Smithson was buried, was to be demolished, Alexander Graham Bell, a Smithsonian regent at the time (Smithsonian trustees are called "regents") personally traveled to Italy and escorted Smithson's remains to Washington.[2] The museum's great benefactor was reinterred at its headquarters, affectionately known as the Castle, on the National Mall, that strip of land that extends from the Capitol Building through the Washington Monument and to the Lincoln Memorial, along the Potomac River.

Today, the Smithsonian employs about 4,500 people and operates on an annual budget of more than $1 billion. The federal government funds about 60 percent of that; the rest is provided by corporations, foundations, and individual donors, all of whom the Smithsonian aggressively cultivates.[3]

As with any organization with a large budget and staff, running the Smithsonian is a tough job. The regents must have felt they found just the right man when in 2000 they selected Lawrence Small to be its chief executive, a position that at the Smithsonian carries the title of "secretary." For the previous nine years, Small had been the president and chief operating officer of Fannie Mae.

For many years before that, he was at Citicorp. He was one of Washington's leading cultural lights, volunteering his time as a trustee at the National Gallery of Art and the Woodrow Wilson International Center for Scholars. On paper, and probably in many tangible ways as well, he impressed the regents as an excellent candidate. It turned out, however, that his on-paper qualifications did not fully qualify him for a leadership role at a charitable institution—even a large one—and so his harsh and sudden downfall seven years later—with not a little rancor, Small submitted his resignation in March 2007—took the city of Washington by surprise and left the nonprofit world wondering how things could have gone so wrong at one of the world's greatest and most prestigious museum complexes.

The Smithsonian's Board of Regents established the Independent Review Committee (IRC) to investigate reports of financial irregularities, and on June 17, 2007, the committee issued a 108-page report that summarized the issues relating to Small's leadership. The three principal authors of the report were Charles Bowsher, Stephen Potts, and A. W. "Pete" Smith. Bowsher was a former Comptroller General of the United States; Potts had been the chair of the Ethics Resource Center in Washington; and Smith was a highly regarded businessman and consultant who advised corporations around the world on executive compensation and benefits. None of these men was inclined to hyperbole, which made the severity of the report's reprimand all the more shocking; it would be difficult to imagine anything more critical. Among other things, the report said that: Small's excessive compensation was "not fully disclosed to the board"; contributions declined during his tenure; his expenses were not reviewed for "reasonableness"; he was absent from the job for "substantial periods"; and his disposition was "ill suited" for the position.[4]

Executive Compensation

Before Small arrived, the Smithsonian paid its secretaries approximately what the heads of other large museums on average were being paid. But in 2000, after a tough negotiation over Small's contract, the board set Small's incoming compensation package at $536,100, more than 40 percent higher than what his predecessor was paid. By the time he left the Smithsonian in 2007, Small's total annual compensation package was scheduled to be more than $900,000.[5] After Small arrived, but before he personally became controversial, some people in Congress wanted to know why he was being paid so much more than the president of the United States—on the face of it, 168 percent more in 2000 and 125 percent more by 2007. It was a valid question, and the answer requires a valid comparison.

The cash salary of the president of the United States in 2000 was $200,000. Of his total compensation package, Small's actual salary in 2000 was $330,000 (65, not 168, percent more than the president's). By 2007, Congress had doubled the president's salary to $400,000. By then, Small's actual cash salary grew to $617,672 (54, not 125, percent more than the president's). Still, during his tenure at the Smithsonian, Small made substantially more than either President Clinton or President Bush.

The Mortgage Allowance

Small's total compensation package included a pension contribution and a housing allowance. People at the Smithsonian were quick to point out that the president, unlike the head of the Smithsonian, has Air Force One, a large, personal airplane that flies at the whim of one person, at his disposal. And this is true. Like the presidency, however, the Smithsonian job does come with an official residence. But Small, who lived in Washington, didn't need the house, so he instead received a housing allowance of $150,000 per year. These monies were meant to reimburse Small for certain expenses, including cleaning, maintenance, and utilities, and for Smithsonian-related functions, called "official Smithsonian hospitality" in Small's contract.[6] That is, he would be reimbursed for the costs he incurred entertaining donors and other people important to the institution.

It turns out, however, that Small didn't use the home for official Smithsonian hospitality very often. The *Washington Post* reported in April 2007 that Small had used his home only four times for official business since 2003, and not once after 2005, a fact that troubled Senator Charles Grassley, who had been investigating abuses at charities. The senator was not pleased to learn that in the entire year of 2005, by which time Small's annual housing allowance had climbed to almost $180,000, the secretary hosted only one dinner, for 10 people. He said, "The American taxpayers will be pleased to hear on the day after filing their taxes that they helped underwrite a dinner that cost over $18,000 a plate."[7]

Small responded to that observation with a verbal sleight of hand: "Given the exciting new museums and modernized exhibits which opened over the last several years, it became overwhelmingly clear that it was far more compelling and cost-effective to entertain donors in the Smithsonian's unique settings than in a private home."[8] The Smithsonian did have a lot of "exciting" and "new" places, words which could have been meant to connect all that progress with Small. The term "cost-effective" showed that the secretary was budget-minded, looking out for the Smithsonian's best financial interests. But the explanation was really a distraction. It didn't address the issue of why the housing allowance remained so large.

In addition to reimbursing Small for his cost-of-living expenses, such as mortgage payments, insurance, and taxes, the employment agreement's housing allowance provided that the Smithsonian would reimburse Small for what were referred to as "equivalent costs of home ownership" up to 50 percent of actual costs and upon receipt of proper documentation. For example, when the bank sent a copy of a mortgage bill, Small was to keep a record of that, along with his payment, and submit the bill or a copy of it to the Smithsonian.[9] Anyone in business who has ever fronted a business expense for his or her employer is familiar with the drill.

After just a few months, though, Small decided that, "for administrative ease," he would no longer go to the trouble of providing expense documentation.[10] He didn't have to ask anyone's permission. He was the boss, after all. Of course, he, too, had bosses, but the regents weren't paying attention. Since the maximum amount was already determined, it appears that Small just took a monthly allotment of that total, regardless of his actual expenses. No for-profit business would ever permit such a thing, even if the expenses were legitimate. And in Small's case, they weren't.

As president and chief operating officer of Fannie Mae, Small was compensated to the tune of $4.2 million a year, exclusive of bonuses. Larry Small owned his home free and clear. He had no mortgage and therefore no mortgage interest rate. What Small did was truly ingenious, and full of moxy: He calculated his housing expense using a *hypothetical* interest rate. He claimed a mortgage of $4 million—perhaps because that's what the house was valued at—and used a rate of 8.5 percent for a 30-year fixed "virtual mortgage."[11] When the questions about Small's spending habits arose, the inspector general analyzed Small's expenses and saw that the average comparable interest rate in 2000 was 8.05 percent.

It dropped over the following years, and by 2005 the average rate for a fixed 30-year mortgage was 5.87 percent. Even though it was high to begin with, Small maintained the 8.5 percent rate. The higher assumed interest rate, of course, generated a higher "bill" for the Smithsonian to pay Small. Yet, it seems that the forest was missed for the trees: in a letter to the Smithsonian's board, the acting inspector general, by dickering about the difference in the hypothetical rates—should Small have claimed something other than 8.5 percent?—lost sight of the fact that Small shouldn't have claimed anything at all for a mortgage: there was no mortgage. When the regents learned of the inspector general's report, they not only disregarded the recommendation that Small do more record keeping, they endorsed the "no-receipts" arrangement and then increased the housing allowance to $193,000 for 2007.[12]

Small's Other Problems

The authors of the IRC report said that a person familiar with Small's initial contract negotiations told them that "the language of the contract was misleading and that the housing allowance was, in fact, a 'packaging device' for delivering to Mr. Small additional compensation in a manner that would conceal the true size of his pay."[13]

The publicity was apparently too much. Under pressure from some of the people on the Smithsonian board, four days after Senator Grassley had persuaded the Senate to freeze a $17 million increase in the Smithsonian's financing, singling out what was called "out-of-control" spending,[14] Small resigned. He claimed, in his defense, that he had raised a good deal of money for the Smithsonian. Roger Sant, the chairman of the Smithsonian's executive committee, said that there were "some regrets" because of Small's "long and outstanding service."[15] One aspect of that service, or so it was widely believed, was Small's fundraising success. In his resignation letter, Small claimed that he had raised "$1.1 billion from the private sector, an amount far surpassing anything in the past."[16] Even his detractors begrudgingly acknowledged his fundraising abilities. That and other accomplishments, according to Sant, had to be "weighed against the current contrary feelings among some people in the community."

But the facts didn't bear out Small's claims. The IRC report said, "There is a perception...Mr. Small succeeded in those efforts [to increase private fundraising]." It goes on to say, however, "private funds raised annually from donors have actually declined over the course of Mr. Small's tenure. Funds contributed by private sources peaked in 2000, and thereafter the amount of private funds committed to the Smithsonian began to decline, reaching a low of $88 million in 2003. Although Mr. Small was involved in finalizing a gift of $80 million from The Behring Foundation in 2000, and gifts of $30 million and $45 million from the Donald Reynolds Foundations in 2001 and 2005, respectively, those donations originated from the work of others. Private funds raised in 2006 improved to $132 million, but that figure is about ten percent lower than the amount raised in 1999, the year before Mr. Small took over." Addressing the argument in this post–9/11 world, that charitable gifts were declining everywhere, the report said that "the evidence collected by the Committee regarding comparable nonprofits does not show a similar decline in fundraising over the same period."[17] However, even stellar fundraising should mean nothing, by way of justification, in response to the question of improper spending. That it was even brought up as a justification should tell us something of Small's ethics.

In hiring Small, the regents wanted a person with business experience, someone with the brains and the assertiveness to take the Smithsonian into a new era of fiscal growth. But the IRC report said of Small, "it is clear...that his attitude and disposition were ill-suited to public service...The mismatch between Mr. Small and the Institution appeared as early as the initial negotiations...when he made it clear that if he and his wife were not allowed to travel in first class, it would be a 'deal breaker.'" If not Air Force One, the Smithsonian, with over half its budget provided for by public money, would be contractually obligated to provide the next best thing. Then, the IRC turned the spotlight on the Smithsonian's governing body: "Over the years, Mr. Small placed too much emphasis on his compensation and expenses. Rather than seeing this as an indication of the need for careful oversight, the Regents involved in Mr. Small's compensation, to the contrary, became complicit in Mr. Small's desire to maximize his personal income and have the Smithsonian pay his expenses." Ultimately, Small's unauthorized expenses totaled $90,000, including private jet travel and gifts.

In 2004, during his tenure, Small pleaded guilty to a federal misdemeanor count of possessing and importing Amazonian artifacts made of feathers and other parts of endangered birds, for which he was sentenced to two years of probation and 100 hours of community service. And there's more: Small's executive assistant, James Hobbins, resigned in August 2007 after it was learned that he had destroyed a transcript of a meeting where Small's compensation package was discussed. A spokeswoman said that destroying initial transcripts—documents from which formal meetings minute are prepared—had been routine. Nonetheless, the general council had recently sent a memo to employees instructing them to retain the documents.[18]

There were also questionable gifts from an oil company for an ocean initiative, the controversial departure of the head of Smithsonian Business Ventures, and questionable for-profit deals that had executives, including Small, earning significant amounts by serving on corporate boards, and more. On the eve of the IRC report, the Smithsonian's second-ranking official, Sheila Burke, the deputy secretary and chief operating officer, resigned.

In the first half of 2007 the Nation's Attic was a mess. A significant reason was that the oversight activities of the board were not being addressed.

Stevens Institute of Technology

One newsletter said it "could turn out to be the nonprofit case of the year."[19] The year was 2009, and in September, the New Jersey attorney general, Anne Milgram, filed a broad and sweeping 16-count civil complaint in the state's Superior Court against the trustees of the Stevens Institute of Technology, specifically naming President Harold Raveche and board Chair Lawrence Babbio, and alleging "financial mismanagement, excessive spending of endowment gains, improper handling of specific endowments and investments, failure to properly maintain records and accounts, and excessive compensation of the school's president." In addition to asking that the school's procedures be cleaned up, the complaint called for the removal of Raveche and Babbio.[20]

This came as quite a shock to the institute's alumni and other friends, as well as to the citizens of New Jersey. Located in Hoboken, across the Hudson River from Manhattan, the Stevens Institute has a solid reputation as a good engineering school, and its peers rank it respectably among other colleges of its type. Nonetheless, anyone who had first learned of Stevens by way of Milgram's complaint might be excused for thinking that the place was filled with deceit, arrogance, and incompetence.

After a three-year investigation, the attorney general claimed that "beginning in 1999 annual financial reports misstated the school's assets." Outside auditors repeatedly warned the school to shape up, and, when it didn't, PricewaterhouseCoopers, the school's independent accountant from 2000 to 2005, fired the school due to the "high risk the school posed to the accounting company." The next auditor, Grant Thornton, continued to find problems, and it, too, issued repeated warnings about how badly the place was run. According to the attorney general, investigators were told that the board was kept in the dark about many important financial decisions, including the president's salary.[21]

Perhaps the general growing concern over what charities pay their executives is overblown—of the million charities that raise money from the public, most people would agree that very few are overpaid and that most are underpaid—but the Stevens case, like so many others before it (and, no doubt, after), only fanned the flame of suspicion that donations are sometimes used more for perks than for programs.

Raveche's Salary

President Harold Raveche's salary climbed from $362,458 in 1999 to just over $1 million by 2008. In addition, he received loans at below-market rates totaling $1.8 million, half of which, according to his 2007 employment agreement, would be forgiven. Among the other complaints, the attorney general said that the board did not have the authority, under New Jersey law, to forgive the loans.

A salary increase of over 200 percent in just under a decade might be by itself enough to raise eyebrows, but to understand the attorney general's rationale for including the president's wages in the complaint, we must also look at the policy known as "comparables," deciding how much to pay a top executive by looking at the salaries of other top executives in similar positions; in this case, finding out what universities similar to Stevens were paying their presidents.

After Raveche's high salary became common knowledge, an unidentified Stevens trustee sent an e-mail to a professor in 2003 saying that "the key figure in all this is Larry Babbio who...is the one who organizes the compensation committee and OKs these salaries and perks. The board never saw any of the details during my time. If you asked you got some but not all the details. It is a complicated web and needs to be audited in detail." Another trustee said about the president's salary, "It was news to me." Another stated that "the board never voted on, approved, or was shown comparability analyses relating to [the president's] compensation."[22]

The attorney general was quite clear: "In 1999 Trustee-Defendant Babbio falsely represented that the Compensation Committee had procured a report concluding that the 'president's compensation...was in line with those of comparable schools.'" No such process had taken place. In 2002, the president "misrepresented to the board that benchmarking 'was done last year and will be done next year,'" when it hadn't been and wouldn't be. In December 2002, the president's salary was increased "to $375,000 with a $220,000 bonus, without any benchmarking or analysis of comparability beyond Raveche's own submissions describing his accomplishments.'" It was not until the following year that Stevens hired an executive compensation consultant.[23] Then, things got really botched up.

The consultant didn't do a very good job, according to the attorney general, and a few years later another group, Towers Perrin (now Towers Watson), was hired. Towers Perrin recommended a review of similar organizations, but Stevens wanted to include larger and more prestigious organizations so that a higher salary could be justified. Towers Perrin responded, "Size-based criteria, and particularly revenue operating budget, typically best predict compensation levels...That explains why Carnegie Mellon, MIT, and CalTech are not appropriate schools to include in the peer group."[24]

Stevens didn't like that perspective very much. It fired Towers Perrin and hired another group, which did not conduct as comprehensive an analysis as Towers Perrin did. Stevens pressured the new group to include in its report the larger schools that Towers Perrin had said should not be included. The attorney general did not mince words in her complaint: "Raveche has been excessively compensated." What she meant was that he was being paid too much for the size and the quality of the school he was running. Raveche's 2008 base salary of $1,089,789 did not include a housing allowance ($54,000); a tuition allowance ($24,000); an automobile allowance ($12,777); the school's contributions to Raveche's retirement plan ($29,905 in 2008); or the below-market loans he had received.

On top of all that, the attorney general said that the president's compensation had not been properly disclosed on the school's 990.

The Taylor Trusts

Stevens had two trusts that constituted 30 percent of the entire endowment. The trusts were funded by a donor, Robert Taylor, who imposed restrictions on each, which Stevens accepted. One was that only the income from the investments could be spent. In 2008, Stevens' whole endowment was valued at $150 million, and the restricted portion of that—the income that was designated for specific purposes—was $106 million. The Taylor trusts were valued at a little over $46 million, or about 43 percent of the unrestricted endowment.

Probably because the rest of the endowment was invested for total return and the spending rate was a percentage of the whole value, Stevens decided to treat the Taylor trusts the same way. In January 2009, the Finance and Investment Committee decided that "the assets of the Taylor trusts...are unrestricted." The problem was that treating the trust assets in the same way as the rest of the endowment was a violation of the agreement between Stevens and Taylor, and the trustees did not have the authority to overrule the donor's restrictions. The attorney general maintained that Stevens violated its fiduciary duties by pooling the Taylor trusts with the rest of the endowment.[25]

Related to the investment issue was that of asset diversification, a philosophy that, as we saw in chapter four, is often violated in the desire to make a quick buck. Besides the violation of the Taylor trust restrictions, Milgram saw that trouble was brewing in the Stevens investment portfolio. In her complaint, she said, "The board failed to monitor and diversify the endowment portfolio in violation of its fiduciary duties and UMIFA."[26] UMIFA is the Uniform Management of Institutional Funds Act,[27] and it is designed to provide investment guidelines for charitable endowments. Within the context of UMIFA, business care and prudence are the touchstones of the guidelines, and Stevens violated both. As we saw in chapter four, charities with endowments have investment policies that point to optimum ranges within each asset class. Over a 20-year period, from 1990 to 2009, charities, particularly those with large endowments, invested increasingly heavily in alternative, or nontraditional, investments. Stevens' policy in 2005 called for a maximum of 15 percent for such investments, but that year, they made up 27 percent of the investments, and by 2008, they constituted over 60 percent.

As a result of the nation's financial crisis, much of what was in alternative investments was either lost or, for a time, rendered illiquid. The New Jersey attorney general said that the Stevens endowment was worth less than $120 million in 2008—eight years earlier it had been valued at $158 million—and that $38 million, because most of it was in private equity, was illiquid.

The Settlement

In January 2010, Stevens and New Jersey reached an out-of-court settlement. The board got most of the attention because, much like the problems the Smithsonian faced with its top executive, the violations outlined in the attorney general's complaint don't happen without an absence of board oversight. Board members now cannot serve more than 12 years and not later than when they reach 72 years of age. The chair and the vice-chair are held to 15-year terms. In practice, these rules are not all that confining—most charities have shorter terms than 15 years for their board members—but it is telling, because the school's governance was apparently so devoid of any meaningful policies at all, that even those liberal guidelines are new and restrictive at Stevens. The settlement also required that the entire Stevens board must approve the president's contract and annual compensation and the salaries of the five other highest-paid employees, and must review all financial results at every board meeting. The president is no longer a voting member of the board.

The school is required to hire outside consultants to review board governance and auditing policies. A consultant must be hired to establish compensation policies and performance metrics for the president and the next five highest-paid employees to make sure they're doing a good job. The investment committee must hire a professional to review the school's asset allocation policies. Loans to executives are no longer permitted. The outstanding mortgage for the prior president must be satisfied by July 2014, which gave him four and a half years to pay the money back. In what might be the most comprehensive effort at forced transparency ever, consolidated financial statements, the 990, reports from credit ratings agencies, the investment performance of the endowment portfolio, key governance documents, and a donor's bill of rights must be posted on the school's website. Stevens also must approve a gift acceptance policy.

This may seem like a lot, and one might imagine that the Stevens employees would not be happy about all the extra work, but I would bet, based on what I know of the people in the development and finance offices at Stevens, that they welcomed this initiative. Stevens is one of those places that, but for the behavior of the board, would have flourished. But that's the effect a board has on an organization—it's huge—and that's why boards need to work so hard to do their jobs well.

Some people think the attorney general caved by settling because the case was so airtight, to say nothing of principle. The thinking behind this hard-line attitude is that Stevens screwed up, and they should have to pay the price so that a clear message is sent to other boards that they can't ignore or play fast and loose with the rules. I take it on faith that the state of New Jersey's allegations against the school were accurate. That's admittedly a reach, given that the allegations weren't tested in a trial, but here's why: the complaint was so detailed, the attorney general had to know the specifics; also someone (unimpeachable to me) on campus close to the case said she knew for "for a fact" that the complaint was substantively true in all its aspects. Perhaps a few things were miscalculated or exaggerated, but the case was strong.

On the other hand, a new attorney general would soon be sworn in under a new administration of a different party. Could it be that the settlement came just in time before the lawsuit would be dropped? No one but a few people in the attorney general's office close to the decision-making process, a process that will probably never be fully known to the public, know for certain, but there are some in government who mistakenly feel that charities, especially universities with substantial endowments, are beyond reproach and that ensuring that they follow arcane laws whose violations in effect harm no one is a waste of time. The attorney general clearly spent a lot of time and political capital taking the case to the public, so was it better to simply end it when the terms might be most favorable to the public? After all, the president would resign soon afterward and several board members would also resign. The reasons for the decision not to wait for a new administration with perhaps different priorities were not made available to the public.

Parties to a lawsuit can become amazingly pragmatic, even when high-level politics don't interfere. Out-of-court settlements are often useful because of the time and money they save. No arbitration took place; the two parties simply decided that it would be better to avoid a trial. More than one person, both on and off campus, close to the case put it this way: the attorney general's job is to protect charitable assets for the public good. Looking into the future, she might have seen the ongoing waste of those assets as they went to attorneys' fees. And what good would that accomplish? Perhaps, in an enlightened self-interest sort of way, the New Jersey attorney general weighed two negative outcomes—missing an opportunity to fully prosecute what she must have thought was a solid case, and potentially spending, and forcing Stevens to spend, millions of dollars—and made her choice.

Milgram might also have felt that she would be outgunned. Not only would the case be expensive to take to its end, there was no certainty it would end well for New Jersey. "Right" doesn't always win in court, and the defense may have planned to gum up the process with technical roadblocks to draw things out as much as possible. I was told that New Jersey offered up a couple of inexperienced attorneys to do battle with a handful of well-paid legal firms. In the end, it might have been difficult to actually prove that the president was being paid too much or that certain expenses out of the endowment or the charitable trusts were in absolute violation of the law. This is where the subjectivity of the language we use to grease the gears of society can do harm.

A Word of Advice to Charities

All charities would be wise to review the directives in the Stevens settlement. While some organizations, although not enough, have addressed the board-member-term issue and have policies in place to prevent board members from serving indefinitely, the overriding effort in the settlement was to get Stevens to adopt practices to ensure proper oversight, transparency, accountability, and disclosure of conflicts of interest. These practices, as will be discussed in the next chapter, constitute the backbone of ethical behavior at charities, and not enough charities have taken them on. It may be that Stevens's bad governance was blatant and that New Jersey's attorney general was unusually on the ball—most state attorneys general really don't do much in the way of nonprofit oversight—so this may simply be a bullet some charities are glad they missed. They may feel the safety of poor oversight. But they would be wrong, and at the least irresponsible, to count on it. The goal for charities should never be to dodge the bullet. The goal ought to be to ensure that the bullet never gets fired in the first place. Why, then, is one of the most important lessons from the Stevens case about the board? A board that refreshes itself every so often can be better assured that bad practices won't become ingrained in the organizational culture. Of those that have instituted policies addressing the issue of term limits, the average seems to be either three or five years with the potential to renew for a second term.

Another provision of the Stevens' settlement called for a competent consultant to conduct research and make recommendations relating to the salary of the president, as well as that of other key employees. Why this isn't done as a matter of course everywhere is a mystery. So far, based on conversations with consultants I've had over the years, it would seem that there are no standardized guidelines for determining what a charity's chief executive should be paid. Those that do exist are not usually well thought out. In fact, they often have had the effect of increasing salaries beyond reason. The pressure brought to bear at Stevens by its president and his sympathizers, while extreme, is not, at its root, unusual: everyone wants to think the place he or she works at is special, and every chief executive wants more money than he or she is actually getting. It is not so surprising that Stevens wanted its president to be paid on par with the president of MIT, CalTech, and other large and prestigious organizations. Rationalizing is so much a part of being human that charities need to establish real and strong systems to overcome the instinct to justify excessively high salaries. Boards need to guard against telling themselves, for example, that any particular president has had such a hard time of it that he or she deserves more, and the normal rules don't apply. And it's really an up-in-the-air process when no one knows what the normal rules are—because there aren't any.

Some people think consultants are never needed. But as we see from the Stevens agreement, some consulting activity was required. This brings up the issues of not only the willingness to hire a good consultant and the fortitude to follow the consultant's advice, but also to candidly assess whether the consultant does a good job and provides an intelligent and objective critique. A consultant who tells the board, the fundraising staff, or the executive staff at an organization what it wants to hear is probably not doing a very good job. Good consultants are frank about the shortcomings in the areas they have been hired to review, and they make recommendations. Governance is a key issue at all charities. More than most board members and charity employees realize—to say nothing of the general public—many boards at charitable organizations are in need of a governance overhaul, an introspective process that requires the asking of tough questions about commitment and competence. These questions are that much tougher to ask and answer when an outside perspective is absent, and tougher still to address when no one on the board is getting paid to do the job.

The primary lesson learned from the Stevens case, as well as from the Smithsonian, is that a nonprofit must always be looking inward and stripping away any pretense that it is somehow better than other organizations. It seems counterintuitive, but part of actually being good is not assuming you are better than others. I see it time and again as I travel to different organizations—large and small, well-known and not—the ones who are really on top of their work are also those who are the most humble about their successes.

It takes a good charity to ask simple questions. It takes a healthy sense of self-confidence to look within. Charities aren't by nature bad places, but the people who run them, who often may not be perfect in the way they look at their management and oversight responsibilities, sometimes get their priorities confused. When that happens, they stop asking the right questions and start asking the wrong ones. Instead of asking the investment managers about how to get the best return, they should be asking whether the "price" of getting the best return will be worth it in the long run. They should not decide to invade an endowed gift's corpus without asking whether they have the right to do that or what consequences there will be to the agreement both the donor and the charity signed.

There is no road map for charities to asking the right questions and making the right decisions. Besides, what's right at one charity may not necessarily be right at another. The quest is to intelligently and compassionately address the myriad issues facing any modern nonprofit, with all their attendant complexities. To do this well, charity officials need to reach past the technical and legal issues, while absorbing all of them, and grasp a higher, ethical dimension. They must do this on their own. And they must do so soon. Otherwise charities will surrender their ethical responsibilities to the regulators, who—wrong as they may be—are already prone to think that almost every answer of consequence can be found in a courtroom.

Section IV

The Ethical Sector

Chapter Eight

The Four Pillars: The Backbone
of Ethics at Nonprofits

Four concepts form the backbone of ethics at nonprofit organizations: disclosure, transparency, avoidance of conflict of interest, and oversight.

Actually charities would do well to structure all of their activities around these practices. Every decision should be begin by searching for a fidelity to those words. The people making decisions should ask themselves whether they would do the same thing if knew their actions would be disclosed to the public. To ignore the growing level of interest the public and the regulators have in charities, or, worse, to fight them, is a loser idea, akin to automobile manufacturers fighting the requirement to install airbags in all cars.

But how can charities ensure fidelity to the words? Words are subjective; they can mean what people want them to mean. There is no clear line that divides transparency from secrecy; disclosure from silence; conflict of interest from objectivity; oversight from unhealthy meddling. The meaning of these terms can be relative, depending on circumstances; defining where on the spectrum one thing becomes another can be tricky.

If nonprofits are to reflect the best of our ethical culture, they need to understand that, although these words can be hard to define, it is important to try to define them and act on them. Vigorous intellectual effort must be applied here precisely because no one can agree about their everyday application to the way charities ought to be run.

It behooves us therefore to assign some meaning to these words and to tie them to specific practices. Instead of marginalizing them because we don't completely understand them, let's try to put some flesh on them. After all, you know when something smells wrong, so why not try to find out, as precisely as possible, just where the bad smell is coming from?

Disclosure

The noun "disclosure," usually preceded by the adjective "full," has legal connotations and is often used in connection with a commercial or business transaction, The idea is that each party ought to make known to the other all the relevant information it needs to accurately assess what it is getting out of the deal. This helps each determine whether the potential price is fair. Sometimes, the information that must be disclosed is straightforward: Does the car you are selling have 30,000 miles on it, or is it closer to 100,000? Does the basement of the house you just put on the market flood? But often it's not so straightforward. How does the fine print of the insurance policy read? How does the charitable gift annuity operate? The goal, whether the information is clear-cut or whether what is chosen to be disclosed is subjective, is to make sure that the other person understands the significant facts about the transaction. Not only do you want to know what the other person thinks is significant, you want the other party to know what you think is important. Sometimes facts that aren't so significant to the one person are very significant to the other.

But how could it be otherwise? People who think the law is black and white might be surprised to learn of how many key legal concepts require interpretation: "In due course," "reasonable doubt," and "separate but equal" are phrases that resonate in our system of jurisprudence. These terms—and many more like them that are meant to guide social behavior—have meanings that are often open to subjective interpretation. And when the meaning of a concept can be construed in different ways, it doesn't really clarify much when imprecise adjectives like "full," "relevant," or "material" are attached to it. Even the IRS uses subjective terms, defining "fair market value" as: "the price at which the property would change hands between a willing buyer and a willing seller, neither being under any compulsion to buy or to sell and both having reasonable knowledge of relevant facts."[1]

One of the key provisions of the Philanthropy Protection Act in 1995 was that it required charities to disclose important information to donors when their gifts were commingled with the gifts of other donors in a planned giving program or in a charity's endowment. The PPA was hailed as a great victory for charities because it meant that they don't have to register with the SEC, despite the fact that they buy and sell stocks and bonds and in many other ways act like broker-dealers and investment companies. In effect, prior to

1995 the SEC gave a wink and a nod to charities that were investing gift assets—the regulatory agency had bigger fish to fry and,
besides, it didn't appear that charities were doing anything harm-
ful to donors. Although the SEC provided its own guidance about
questions involving charities and investments, the federal law on
the subject remained benignly unclear for decades. It took a massive
lawsuit in Texas—Ozee v. American Council on Gift Annuities—to
focus the charitable community and Congress on clearing up a few
things. The PPA, assuming certain provisions were followed, gave
charities the green light to invest assets. One of those provisions
addressed disclosure: "Each fund...shall provide, to each donor
to such fund, at the time of the donation...written information
describing the material terms of the operation of such fund."[2]

Therein lay the rub. The PPA did not specify what the material
terms were. After testifying for the bill before a House subcommittee,[3]
I called Barry Barbash, the head of the SEC's division of investment
management, who had also testified in its favor, to ask what information would have to be disclosed. And what did "material" mean?
Barbash said that he didn't know. Nor should he, he said; because
the requirements would not be the same for all charities; the specifics
would be left to each organization. But he did add, "If an 85-year-old
person who is financially unsophisticated cannot understand your
disclosure statement, then you haven't disclosed anything."

That's a crucial point.

If the range of possibilities is wide in the rarefied world of
planned giving, and the disclosure statement must be comprehen-
sible to ordinary folks, think of how wide that range could be
when the idea of disclosure is applied to all of the activities at a
charitable organization.

Eighty years earlier, in his book, *Other People's Money and
How the Bankers Use It*, Supreme Court Justice Louis Brandeis,
commented on the issue of disclosure when he criticized the secrecy
within the banking industry. He said, "Sunlight is said to be the
best of disinfectants."[4] The book, published in 1914, was about
large banks that colluded with business moguls to create trusts
that protected big business interests and did nothing to help ordinary people. In fact, "Brandeis felt that not only did trusts stifle
competition, they also became so large that they couldn't operate
efficiently."[5] Brandeis addressed what he called "real disclosure"
as it relates to the investment world:

> But the disclosure must be real. And it must be a disclosure to
> the investor. It will not suffice to require merely the filing of a

statement of facts with the Commissioner of Corporations. To be effective, knowledge of the facts must be actually brought home to the investor, and this can best be done by requiring the facts to be stated in good, large type in every notice, circular, letter and advertisement inviting the investor to purchase. Compliance with this requirement should also be obligatory, and not something which the investor could waive. For the whole public is interested in putting an end to the bankers' exactions.[6]

Brandeis's concept of full disclosure seems very akin to Barbash's call for clarity and simplicity. Apparently, we haven't come very far in the better part of a century. Read the disclosure statements of some big organizations, from the Red Cross to Exxon, and you will likely find the vast majority of them confusing, if not incomprehensible. What does this actual statement about gift annuities disclose?

> Your federal income tax charitable deduction is based on your age and a certain Internal Revenue Service interest rate (the "discount rate"), which changes monthly. The higher the discount rate, the higher your deduction. You may elect to use the discount rate for either of the two months preceding the month you establish your annuity. The election is made by filing a certain form with your tax return. Check with your tax adviser for details.

Do you think a financially unsophisticated person has any idea what that might mean, or why it might be important information in deciding to make a gift to a charity?

Would that more people shared Warren Buffett's philosophy about disclosure: "Our guideline is to tell you the business facts that we would want to know if our positions were reversed. We owe you no less."[7]

* * *

Some charities knowingly choose to keep important information secret. One charity, the Center for Consumer Freedom, has on its website this exchange:

Q: Who funds you guys? How about some "full disclosure?"

A: The Center for Consumer Freedom is supported by restaurants, food companies and thousands of individual consumers. From farm to fork, from urban to rural, our friends and supporters include businesses, their employees, and their customers. The Center is a nonprofit 501(c)(3) organization. We file regular statements with the Internal Revenue Service, which are open to public inspection. Many of the companies and individuals who support the Center financially have indicated that they want anonymity as contributors. They are reasonably apprehensive about privacy and safety in light of the violence and other forms of aggression some activists have adopted as a "game plan" to impose their views, so we respect their wishes.[8]

It's that part that boasts about filing regular statements with the IRS, documents that are open to public inspection, that falls into the category of deceitfulness. This group does nothing more than it must—and calls it disclosure. Then, invoking confidentiality it stays pointedly quiet about who funds the charity.

doing what is necessary + disclosure

The absence of disclosure does not have to be as pernicious as the kind of misleading material put forth by the National Heritage Foundation, as described in chapter five, or the Center for Consumer Freedom. Many charities don't disclose important financial information, such as the audited report—which is not the same as a Form 990—or important but unflattering news, such as the theft of money, about a board member or a key staff employee.

Transparency

Ambiguity, at least for most organizations that try to be transparent, is as present a challenge in transparency as it is in disclosure: Not many people know what the word "transparency" means as a practical matter. Looking at a few dictionaries you would see that something transparent is "fine or sheer enough to be seen through, free from pretense or deceit, easily detected or seen through, readily understood, and characterized by visibility or accessibility of information especially concerning business practices." Synonyms include frank, obvious, and clear.

So, how to apply all that to the work of nonprofits? Let's return for a moment to the phrase "self-dealing," an act prohibited by law at charities. A charity cannot lend money to a "disqualified" person; that is, a person close to the charity, like its executive director or a board member. The 990 asks about this.

A disqualified person, if he or she is on the staff, cannot be paid too much either. Such pay restrictions are couched in language such as "excessive compensation," but the issue in transparency is not so much the amount a person is being paid—almost always, we're talking about the head of the charity—but the process by which the salary is determined.

In the case of Stevens Institute of Technology (chapter 7), Harold Raveche was paid a lot, but the bigger problem was that neither the process nor the amount of his salary was made clear to the school's community. While much discussion centers on how much a person is being paid, far too little attention is paid to why that is. Usually, the question as to *why* comes about because of a severe lack of transparency.

While it is good to be thought highly of by others, the numbers on a 990—or their ratings agency derivatives—do not equal transparency. Transparency means openness and communicating that openness. It doesn't mean that other people think you're great. It means figuring out what's important that's going on in your organization, and intelligently and fully telling people what that is.

The Nature Conservancy (TNC), the world's largest environmental organization, provides some insight. An excellent organization by almost any measure, in 2003 it, too, endured its own transparency problems,[9] TNC's main issue then was that the charity put together inside deals for its trustees around the country to buy land at reduced prices, the reductions the result of placing permanent conservation easements on property it had acquired. An easement protects the property from development and reduces its value. (See the discussion in chapter 2 of easements relating to the Kiva Dunes defense of an IRS deduction challenge.) The Nature Conservancy then made the properties at the reduced price available to selected individuals. While nothing was technically wrong with the arrangement, it smacked of benefitting insiders to the organization.[10]

Since then, TNC has done much to not only stop that practice but to tell the public what its policies are. Its pages on governance and transparency are a model for other organizations—the result of taking seriously the public outcry in 2003.

Still, TNC is quick to associate the issues of transparency and leadership with how well the organization ranks in the various ratings agencies. One of its website pages has the headline, "Accountability and Transparency of The Nature Conservancy," but immediately suggests evidence of its commitment to both by saying that it is "highly rated by charity watchdog organizations." Only after that is the reader linked to the far more comprehensive information on its governance policies.[11]

Can charities be a lot more transparent than they are now? Sure they can.

Here are a couple of ideas.

What about a charity putting its financial information on its website? It's way past dawn when it comes to making 990s easily and quickly available to the public. GuideStar[12] has seen to that. Since the late 1990s, GuideStar has made 990s available and today has an easily searchable database of reports on 1.8 million non-profits. But if you're a charity, why not save people the trouble of searching through GuideStar and put a link to your 990s—all of them; not just the IRS-mandated most recent three years—on the your own site? For that matter, the charity could post its audited financial statements, and any comments or letters the auditors may have written that would qualify the results. Remember, this level of disclosure and transparency was a requirement in the Stevens settlement.

[handwritten margin note: detailed results]

And that capital campaign the charity just finished? The one that was so successful? Why not detail the results? Capital campaigns are a mix of past gifts, current outright donations and pledges, and future irrevocable and revocable commitments. None of that breakdown is ever found on a charity's website, but it makes a difference if the campaign for scholarships or the new building is declared to be a success, even though much of the money won't be available for many years.

The effort to be transparent can follow many paths, some or all of which might be appropriate for any one charity. Is the organization that details only some things any worse than another that details more? Not necessarily. Each organization and its board must make these decisions for themselves. It is not a legal requirement to reveal the information described in the suggestions above, but keep in mind that the law sets the bar pretty low; proper refuge cannot be found there.

Are Disclosure and Transparency the Same Thing?

Not quite. But they are close to each other. Let's agree that transparency is the mindset of openness and being free from deceit, and disclosure is the process of using that mindset of openness to communicate important things to the public. *[handwritten margin mark: ✳]* Another way of saying it is that transparency is the process of permitting people to see what you're doing, and disclosure is the process of affirmatively telling them what you're doing.

Real disclosure depends on transparency.

Let us understand two things, however. In the real world the two words are used almost interchangeably, and without a lot of thought given to the distinction between the two. But this too must change. Disclosure, as we have been exposed to it from charities, is rarely helpful.

One way to distinguish the two concepts: disclosure is the act of pro-actively telling people what you are doing and transparency is the process of intentionally calling their attention to what you are doing.

Before we get to how the nonprofit world should intersect with disclosure and transparency, one more thought on history. Most people are familiar with Santayana's quote, "Those who cannot remember the past are condemned to repeat it." Fewer know the phrase just preceding it: "When experience is not retained, as among savages, infancy is perpetual."[13] It is the obligation of charities to adhere to the meanings of disclosure and transparency, and to search out ways they can employ the concepts in their everyday world when they make decisions and take actions.

Avoidance of Conflict of Interest

If disclosure and transparency are difficult to define, conflict of interest is easier to get a handle on. Intuitively, we know what it means: an interest in one thing that could potentially corrupt an interest in another. In chapter four, we looked at Yeshiva University, where Ezra Merkin was an investment adviser who tossed a lot of business to Bernie Madoff's firm. Both men sat on the board of directors and so both had an interest, a potentially corrupting interest in sending Yeshiva's money to the Madoff funds. As an investment manager, Merkin made money by sending assets to Madoff. But we should not dwell on Merkin or Madoff to make this point. Clearly, the inherent conflict of interest that arises when a board member is able to send a charity's money to his own firm is not good and must be avoided. That's not to say the investment adviser is doing a bad job—but that a person, with something to gain in a position to make or influence a decision about an organization's money is not in a good place. Not for the organization, anyway.

As it happens, Merkin also served on the board of United Jewish Appeal Federation of New York. But the conflict-of-interest issue was seen differently. This, from the *Commentator*, the student newspaper at Yeshiva: "The UJA-Federation of New York, where Mr. Merkin had formerly served on the board's investment committee, did not lose money with Ascot Capital because a conflict-of-interest policy prevented Mr. Merkin from directing their endowment towards his own funds, according to their recent statement."[14]

But is it possible to be too unbending? Is the existence of a potential conflict-of-interest evidence of wrongdoing?

No. It is not. That's why thoughtful policies need to be developed. Most charity experts agree that inherent in the concept of *duty of loyalty*, which is one of the benchmarks of service on a charity's board of trustees, is the disclosure of potential conflicts. As the New York State Charities Bureau describes it: The "duty of loyalty requires that any conflict of interest, real or possible, be disclosed to the board. Board members must avoid transactions in which they or their family members benefit personally to the detriment of the organization."[15]

From the section titled "Duty of Loyalty" in the booklet, "Good Governance Practices," published by the IRS:

> The board of directors should adopt and regularly evaluate an effective conflict-of-interest policy that: requires directors and staff to act solely in the interests of the charity without regard for personal interests; includes written procedures for determining whether a relationship, financial interest, or business affiliation results in conflict of interest; and prescribes a certain course of action in the event a conflict of interest is identified.
>
> Directors and staff should be required to disclose annually in writing any known financial interest that the individual, or a member of the individual's family, has in any business entity that transacts business with the charity. Instructions to Form 1023 contain a sample conflict-of-interest policy.[16]

The problem is that the kind of people you want on a board are often prominent, and they tend to be involved in services or products that a charity might need. There is certainly no requirement that the charity forego quality. The board member may very well be, for example, the best general contractor to take charge of building the new science center or steeple. The issue is one of disclosing a potential conflict of interest, not that there can be no conflict. This is why boards must be careful in writing their policies.

The worst scenario is when everyone on the board knows of a conflict but conscientiously ignores its seriousness.

Some charities have policies that do prohibit any conflict of interest, and act upon that even if it means pursuing people or services that are of a lesser quality than what a board member could provide. That is, a policy might address conflicts of interest but not prevent them. In that case, the type of conflict should be reviewed. It is the smaller charity, typically in a smaller town, where it is more likely to need people on the board who also have a legitimate potential conflict of interest. In that situation, however, the board member must still disclose the conflict and the charity should have a formal mechanism that permits him or her to make the disclosure.

But New York is not a small town. Yeshiva could hardly have argued that there weren't very many investment managers in the city. That's why, if a poll were taken, the prevailing opinion of experts in charitable governance would conclude that a blanket rule in that situation is exactly what *was* needed, and would have been needed even if Madoff turned out to be the most brilliant and honest investor ever. Jack Siegel, an attorney and accountant who writes extensively on charity governance, mainly in at his site, *Charity Governance*, said in April 2010 that Yeshiva "got religion."

Ten years earlier, Yeshiva may have been given the green light to enact a policy that led to losing so much money to Madoff. A January 1, 2009 article in Bloomberg.com, referencing a letter from a prominent attorney, said:

> Ira M. Millstein, a corporate-governance specialist for four decades, helped clear the way for Yeshiva University's millions of dollars in losses in a fund with ties to the Madoff scandal.
>
> Millstein, a senior partner of Weil, Gotshal & Manges, said in a letter seen by Bloomberg News that Yeshiva had "followed procedures adequate to prevent either the appearance or the reality of a conflict of interest." The September 2000 opinion cleared financier J. Ezra Merkin to continue to accept Yeshiva as an investor as long as Merkin's role was disclosed, according to a person familiar with the matter. Merkin was a trustee who served on the investment committee at the New York school.
>
> Yeshiva invested in Merkin's Ascot Partners LP, which channeled money to Bernard Madoff, the man now accused of defrauding multiple investors of $50 billion. Madoff served as a Yeshiva trustee at the time of Millstein's letter. It generally isn't wise for a school to do business with its own advisers, said Alice Handy, founder of Investure LLC, which manages about $5 billion for 10 schools and foundations.

"It's preferable never to have a business relationship with a board member," said Handy, whose company is based in Charlottesville, Virginia, in a Dec. 30 interview. "Under any circumstances, it needs to be fully disclosed. Often you inherit that position when a person becomes a board member. You should always have somebody neutral overseeing that investment."[17]

After criticizing the Millstein letter, Jack Siegel opined that the prevailing attitude about conflict-of-interest issues among so many board members is seriously wanting:

Real men can manage conflicts of interest so they need not be bothered with the niceties that good governance wimps advocate. And then we have the Three-Mile Island meltdown. All of a sudden the wimps don't look so wimpy and the macho men find religion. Everybody would be far better off if boards would skip the meltdown stage and just adopt tough conflicts-of-interest policies from the outset.[18]

Of the four pillars, the concept of conflict of interest may well be the most defied. Evidence of that just might be how often the phrase is beginning to emerge in state statutes, such as in New York, that define the issue.

Oversight

The fourth pillar of ethics at charities is oversight. The IRS says, "Boards should be composed of persons who are informed and active in overseeing a charity's operations and finances."[19] This couldn't be more straightforward, but charities still have problems complying. The most obvious problem is the board member who just doesn't care. A part of the group that doesn't care very much are the trophy names brought into the fold, where there is no expectation of actually doing or overseeing anything. I've sat in on and presented at hundreds of board meetings in my career and the most likely no-show is the "star." "Oh, she never actually comes to meetings," I am, for example, likely to be told. Very often these big names are regarded as window dressing, people whose status and prestige give the organization a higher profile. Yet that person, like all the other board members, is responsible for oversight. But it's not just the high-profile people who tend to think board attendance is optional. The other part of the no-show group consists of the people who aren't famous but who still don't care.

No one keeps data on charity board absenteeism nationwide, but it's far too high. Just because it's a volunteer job doesn't mean it's not important. The number of members who regularly don't show up for board meetings reminds me of a meeting of charity executives I attended a few years ago where it was posited that of the nine million charity board seats in America, half are empty. The comment was made to inspire the meeting's participants to work harder at getting more board members at their charities. Still, when it comes to oversight, it's not all about showing up. Board members who never miss a meeting can be just as ineffective and clueless to their oversight responsibilities.

The orbit of oversight, however, does not mean that board members must examine every minute detail. Oversight does not mean, for example, requiring a report on the office supplies purchased, although it does mean requiring a report on consolidated expenses. It does not mean worrying about every investment transaction, although it does mean requiring the auditors to certify that they have done everything they should to ensure transactions were executed properly.

Trustees often don't want to ask what they think is a stupid question. The problem is that some trustees bog down discussions with questions relating to administrative or other trivia. Determining what is trivial is, of course, subjective, but intelligent board member must be able to discern the difference between the pedantic and the fundamental. Generally speaking, understanding financial matters is not trivial. Board members need to become knowledgeable about the finances at the charity they are charged to oversee. If they don't know much about the numbers or don't read the reports, they waste everyone's time by asking basic questions that are already covered or whose answers should be known. A question, for example, about what a footnote refers to when the footnote explains that a transfer of money was made is one thing, whereas a question as to why the transfer was made—the kind of question that should be put to the auditors—is altogether different. The difference will often be a function of the circumstances of the moment and the level of detail into which a particular board discussion has delved.

In its most obvious application, although by no means the one most executed, oversight means that the board treats the paid head of a charity as an employee and not as a god. Almost every charity scandal involving an organization's executive director or president has its roots in the lack of board oversight when it comes to the organization's executive director or president.

A Few More Examples of Ethical Lapses

Ethical considerations, or the lack of them, permeates everyday decisions. In almost every situation where something goes wrong, the board has not dealt squarely with the concepts discussed in this chapter, as in the three examples that follow:

- Florida State University

  (From the *Miami Herald,* January 12, 2010):

  Florida State University's new president will have a larger salary than his predecessor, T.K. Wetherell, and stands to make even more in bonuses as a reward for big-time fundraising. FSU trustees chairman Jim Smith confirmed Monday that Eric Barron has signed a contract that includes a base salary of $395,000 a year in state and private dollars, plus the chance to earn annual bonuses of $100,000 for every $100 million in private donations raised.[20]

  The university's president? Beyond the obvious unseemliness of the idea, every ethics code in the nonprofit world prohibits commission-based fundraising. Yet one supporter of the bogus bonus plan defended it this way:

  In a world where state governments are abdicating their responsibilities to fund public colleges and universities, yet wish to claim them as "state universities" and set tuition rates and name the trustees, new models of fund raising are necessary.... It will be easier to recruit presidents with the "carrot" of bonuses based upon success in the new model than compensation schemes that are not tied to these explicit new job goals.[21]

  Commissions are scorned in the charitable world because if the person asking for money stands to gain personally by bringing in as much as possible, donors would rightly get the idea that he or she may have dual motives, not to mention that money that could be spent on programs and operations would go into paying commissions. As a practical matter, commissions don't work when gifts are pledges and deferred commitments. The last thing a charity should want, aside from paying any commission at all, is to pay a commission on money that is not in the bank.

- The Museum of Modern Art (New York City)

  (From the *New York Times,* February 16, 2007)

  Glenn D. Lowry, director of the Museum of Modern Art for nearly 12 years, has long been one of the highest-paid museum officials in the country, with salary, bonus and benefits total-ing $1.28 million in the year that ended June 30, 2005...Yet for more than eight years, his income was even higher than the museum reported in its tax forms, thanks to a trust created by two of the museum's wealthiest trustees...The trust used the money to make payments to Mr. Lowry. Between 1995 and 2003, that trust paid him a total of $5.35 million—in amounts ranging from $35,800 to $3.5 million a year—aside from the compensa-tion supplied by the museum...Former state and federal regula-tors said the system of payments by the trust was unorthodox and raised many questions, ranging from the completeness of the trust's and the museum's tax reporting to whether the I.R.S. was fully aware of the trust's purpose when it granted it a tax exemp-tion...Marcus S. Owens, who formerly headed the division of the Internal Revenue Service that oversees nonprofits, said he did not consider the recent filing...as adequate. "They've essentially admitted...that more compensation was paid than has been reported," Mr. Owens said.[22]

Although the museum filed the information in what it called a supplemental document, the problem here was a lack of disclosure. Regardless of the explanation, the public was led to believe something about the director's pay that was not accurate. One person close to the museum told me, "It wouldn't look good if the public knew that the director was being paid more than $1 million."

• Hackensack University Medical Center
  (From *NorthJersey.com,* November 20, 2009)

Board members at Hackensack University Medical Center, among New Jersey's most powerful contractors and businesspeople, won't be permitted to do business with the hospital under sweep-ing reforms adopted this week to clean up the damage from a brib-ery scandal this year. "Too many" board members have conflicts, said J. Fletcher Creamer Jr., chairman of the hospital's board of governors. Creamer has made millions—he says less than $30 mil-lion—from construction projects at the hospital, but said in the future "I will not do business with the hospital. Going forward, board members will have no business dealings with Hackensack University Medical Center." In a dramatic break with the corpo-rate culture created by former chief executive John P. Ferguson, who was forced into retirement in May, the 60-member board voted "overwhelmingly" to adopt all but one of the recommenda-tions made by outside governance experts.

The $952,000 report was commissioned during the federal corruption trial of former state Sen. Joseph Coniglio, who began serving a 2 1/2-year sentence this month after his conviction on charges that he used his office to steer millions in grants to the medical center. The hospital paid Coniglio $103,000 to serve as what prosecutors called a "sham consultant" from May 2004 to February 2006.[23]

There's a reason the law generally requires a person who stole a loaf of bread to pay for his actions by doing something more than merely returning the bread. It makes the dirty deed more than just a gamble without consequence. While the board acknowledged a wrong, which was a good thing, the board chair's self-congratulatory tone in making what the public was apparently meant to think was a revelation wasn't, even though his company earned less than $30 million. Ethical decision making is about more than an after-the-fact acknowledgement of wrongdoing, especially when the person knew that what he or she was doing was wrong. Conflict-of-interest issues should be addressed before the conflict becomes an issue.

But there are a couple of other points to ponder in this story. How many people of the 60-member board do you really think knew what was going on? And do you think it is significant that the person identified as the "executive in charge of fundraising"[24] at Hackensack University Medical Center was being paid over $850,000 as of two years prior to the scandal? Or that the medical center reported spending zero dollars—nothing at all—on fundraising while raising $22 million in 2007?[25] I found it just a little odd that, at the least, the chief fundraiser was paid the better part of a million dollars while none of that was attributed to fundraising costs.

Combining the Pillars

Part of the problem, I'm convinced, is that the four terms discussed in this chapter, in addition to being subject to interpretation, all get mixed together in the vernacular of articles, memos, and board dialogues. While the words are all multi-syllabic and sound substantive off the tongue, they lend themselves to corporate-speak— meaningful-sounding pronouncements that actually mean very little. As we have seen, in this chapter and earlier ones, when words mean little, it is hard to act on them.

What they need is context, a way for people to be clear about what these practices mean. They need to know what disclosure, transparency, conflict of interest, and oversight are, and that, precisely because they are both important and not defined in law, they are very much part of the ethical structure of an organization.

But the idea of ethical underpinnings goes even to places where those who run charities, who are thoughtful and caring about not only these concepts but of how they should be applied to good charitable governance, are not explicit about the role of ethics—when in fact, ethics is the whole game, the underpinning of good governance.

Figure 8.1 shows that ethics informs the concepts I've been describing in this chapter, and how those concepts are connected through ethics.

Now imagine that emerging from the area of ethics—already incorporating disclosure, transparency, avoiding conflicts of interest, and oversight—is the idea of good governance. That is, governance, whether the goal is to describe the way a board should behave or how it should lead, is informed primarily by ethical decision making.

Good governance is also an elusive concept, although it's the subject of many articles and not a few books. In its mission statement, BoardSource, the nonprofit that is perhaps most on top of governance issues, says it is "dedicated to advancing the public

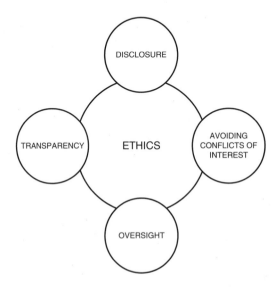

Figure 8.1   The four pillars of ethics.

good by building exceptional nonprofit boards and inspiring board service."[26] In *Governance as Leadership*, Richard Chait, William Ryan, and Barbara Taylor describe what they call the three modes of governance: fiduciary, strategic, and generative. In what they call "triple helix" issues,[27] they contend that leadership uses not only facts and data, which form the basis of fiduciary governance, or even a logical reasoning process, the basis for strategic planning, but something they call "sense-making," a mindset that allows "ideas and plans to take shape in organizations."[28]

That third level is the place to be. To be sure, you can't get there without mastering the first two, and all three must be acted upon together, but charities are wanting without arriving at the generative level. It's not a luxury, but a necessity.

To illustrate what generative thinking is, the authors describe a situation faced some years ago by the Boston Museum of Fine Arts, which had to decide whether to loan 21 Monet masterpieces to the Bellagio in Las Vegas. The casino had asked to borrow them for a while, perhaps to give a little class to the famous Strip, otherwise known for its schmaltzy glitz. On the fiduciary level, the questions would be along the lines of whether the pieces were travel-worthy and how much the Bellagio should pay for the privilege. The strategic questions would be about the effect an association with the casino might have on the museum's reputation. The generative level of thinking brought forth questions about the implications on the museum's mission of loaning art to the highest bidder and and displaying it in a pop culture, for-profit venue.[29]

The generative level is the essence of ethical decision making. As you might imagine, the board was divided—although ultimately there was no dissent—and the issue was not so much whether or not the museum actually went ahead with the loan, but the process by which the decision was made. In the end, after adding up all the pros and cons, after confronting and evaluating the values forced into the open by frank discussions, the board made its decision: in return for a fee of more than $1 million the Monets found their way to Las Vegas.

The decision was not without controversy. Selma Holo, an authority on museums and a professor at the University of Southern California, said, "I will not buy that this is about non-elitism. This is about desperation and about making money, and nothing else." *Newsweek*, in an article entitled, "Show Me the Monet," questioned the ethics behind the arrangement and the *Los Angeles*

Times critic Christopher Knight said the museum "ought to be ashamed of itself."

The museum's director, Malcolm Rogers, had this riposte: "Museums have always been very conservative institutions and we're trying to make them less conservative by revealing beauty in unexpected places. Las Vegas is an unexpected place. Let us send beautiful things there. Let us send them art."[30] People may disagree with the decision, but the reasons for it were thought out.

Now apply that construct to Stevens Institute of Technology, where the board was accused of ignoring the most fundamental issues of being a university for the momentary satisfaction of its president. Or to Harvard and other universities with big endowments that sacrificed liquidity, needed to serve its students, for larger paper gains.

Chapter Nine

Inside a Good Charity

It is time to look at a charity that embraces the four pillars of ethical behavior at nonprofits. This may be risky because you never know when a once-venerated charity or leader of a charity might be exposed in the press, having been implicated in the latest scandal to rock the nonprofit world. Gateway to a Cure comes immediately to mind in this regard. Established in the 1990s to support spinal cord research, in 2007 its reputation was turned completely around—the wrong way. The charity was started by Lou Sengheiser to support spinal cord research after his son was severely injured in a fall. The story was so compelling that the Missouri chapter of Blacktie, a group that connects "nonprofits and the people who support them,"[1] wrote an adulatory story about Gateway for a Cure in its magazine. "By giving something back to participants," Blacktie wrote, the founder "makes charitable giving an active, two-way relationship."[2] The only problem was that the charity wasn't really doing very much to raise money for spinal cord research, and then it was learned the founder had been running a bogus auction—at $1,000 per ticket—to win a mansion on a golf course that personally benefited him.[3]

Unfortunately, broken promises litter the charitable landscape, and because we could be wrong, we cautiously hand out praise. Yet, not to make the effort is to risk succumbing to cynicism. I'd prefer to take the chance of being wrong than becoming so calloused as to be immune to the wonderful work that so many charities do. Besides, the praise that follows doesn't come from simply rewriting a charity's press releases. It's the result of looking deep inside a group that takes itself seriously, absent pretension. It's the result of joining ideal ethical guidelines with generally agreed-upon business practices, and applying those ideals and business practices to an evaluation of the way one charity operates.

The four pillars of ethical behavior are evident in this story, but they don't stand alone, as if each were a silo. One of the realities of the behavior of any nonprofit is that it comprises characteristics that blend into one another, permeating the culture of the organization and influencing its activity in a way that is not easily measured. Applying ethical standards to a charity, as opposed to simply looking at the numbers, makes the evaluation difficult and in some ways subjective, but it also speaks to the perspective that ought to drive the public's perception of charitable work.

So, while some people, and charities themselves, may find comfort in doing the math, a real evaluation means also integrating values.

So Others Might Eat

The charity So Others Might Eat (SOME) in Washington, D.C., is an interfaith, community-based organization that provides food, clothing, and health care to the city's poor and homeless. Their goal is to "break the cycle of homelessness by offering services, such as affordable housing, job training, addiction treatment, and counseling to the poor, the elderly, and individuals with mental illness."[4] The food line is only the first step for many of the poor, not all of them homeless, and almost everyone who uses the charity's other services is introduced to them by being served a balanced hot meal.

One of the days I went to SOME, to interview employees and clients, and to take in a personal feel for the organization, was during the heavy snows of the winter of 2010. As I trudged the fifteen blocks to SOME from my office—from a tony northwest neighborhood of Washington to a far seedier one near Capitol Hill—I realized how different the world is for some people. When it snows too much, hungry, homeless people don't complain about having to stock up at the grocery store, and they don't worry about shoveling anything. Many simply endure the cold all night long. They don't shop and they don't shovel. Some die because of the cold.

The first thing you notice on its website is that SOME knows who it is. That is to say, the organization knows it is not primarily a *what,* but a *who,* filled with people who go there for food and services, whose lives are affected by what the people who work there, and the people who volunteer there, do. SOME's mission statement and its values are prominently featured. It is clear and complete about its history, from its humble beginnings in 1970, when its founder, Father Horace McKenna, decided to do what he could to help feed the city's destitute citizens, through the addition of services over the decades to accomplishments today.

After a few years, SOME began offering meals with an eye on nutrition, as opposed to simply food that would fill stomachs; in the 1980s SOME opened its medical clinic; in the late 1980s, the charity created the first affordable housing program for homeless single adults; and in the 1990s SOME launched a job training program.[5] A visitor to the dining room or the health facilities is confronted with a strong and unapologetic pride of purpose. Every day SOME serves over 400 people a hot meal, and the staff there told me that it has never turned anyone away. The website is impressive not because it is glossy but because it is both extensive and modest.

As it seemed to me that many people come each day to eat and take advantage of the medical services, I asked them to back up the claim that they never turn anyone away. "Don't you ever run out of food," I asked. "What about if you have a particularly large group of people because of cold weather or it's the time of the month when a lot of people are close to being paid but haven't been and so have run out of money?" I was taken to a large room filled with provisions. "I won't say it can't happen," I was told while being shown rows and rows of cans of soup and other long-lasting food. "I *can* say it never has and that our goal is to never turn anyone away because we've run out of food." I was informed that food donors are aware that they may be called upon in a pinch to either buy or bring over food in an emergency.

Anyone can ask the same question I did and be shown—not only told—how the organization has stocked up food. Of course I had to ask—no organization can anticipate everyone's questions—but the answer was quick, honest, and demonstrable. That's not the entire definition of disclosure or transparency, but it was a pretty good start. This is important because many charities are not so forthcoming.

The organization's website does not emanate anonymously: the executive director; well-known individuals, such as Maya Angelou; the president of the board of directors; its first board chair; and Father John Adams, the heart and soul of SOME, all explain why they think the organization is special and plays a vital role in the community.

*   *   *

In addition to what can be found on its website, SOME has many physical materials—brochures and other handouts, as well as a

40th anniversary book—each piece of which describes what the organization does.

That's my recommendation as a first stop for potential donors: the information the organization has on its website and its written materials. What does the charity say about itself and *how* does it say it? Is its mission clear and upfront, or is it vague and general?

The reason the quality of the writing is important is that it reflects the quality of the thinking at the organization, and the quality of the thinking leads its activities. And while competent communication is important, the material should not be a slave to stiff, grammatically correct precision at the expense of clear ideas about what the organization is all about. SOME writes of its values this way: "We value empowering the people we serve by respecting their human dignity and by helping them to restore faith in their lives."

Then, of course, you must determine if the message resonates with you. Many people are drawn to different causes and, even if the message is competently put forth, it still may not be the right cause for you to support—but you won't know that unless the message is clear about who and what the organization is.

* * *

But while that's all good—and the materials at SOME did have the air of competent assurance—what can we know of a charity by looking only at the materials?

As it's easy to search anything that's ever been written, either for a traditional newspaper or on the Internet, or put on a television or radio program, you should also search for stories about the charity that were written or broadcast about the charity. As it happens, SOME has a few—many came up in newspaper accounts and many also came up under Youtube's site; several of those were television reports—and they were all positive. There was no indication that anyone had ever complained about the charity and there were plenty of signs that it is a good one.

* * *

In my letter to Father John Adams, the president of SOME, I asked to talk with him, the finance director, the development director, one or two donors, one or two current clients, one or two past clients, the board chair and another board member. I said I'd like to meet everyone in person. I told him that I wanted to get a sense of how decisions are made, what his vision for SOME is, and his reason for being there. I wanted to review the finances—not just the 990, but also audited reports and other relevant documents containing information that are not required by the IRS. I wanted to speak with donors. "For the purposes of this project," I wrote, "think of me as a combination of your most important private donor, your most important government funder, your most exacting auditor, the District of Columbia Attorney General, the IRS, and the chair of the Senate Finance Committee. Only think of it as much more fun."

I got a lot in return. Transparency and disclosure, I learned, are not mere abstracts at SOME. Everyone to whom I spoke was cooperative and did not hesitate to open the books. "You want this report? You may have it." I was able to review every document I wanted to see. But at SOME, as is the case with most charities, its vitality is seen in its people—the employees who work on the front lines and the people they serve. At a university, that might be a professor and a student; at a museum, that might be a curator and a patron; at a hospital, that may be a doctor and a patient. The most important thing I wanted to be able to do at SOME was to talk to an employee and to a client. Neither was chosen specially; each just happened to be available on the day I showed up.

Harvest House Supervisor: Bonnie McDonald

Bonnie McDonald is the program supervisor at Harvest House, the program at SOME that provides transitional housing for women. Bonnie is also a recovering "all-aholic," as she says it. "You name it, I did it," she says. She started using when she was 12 years old. "I guess I didn't have a good role model," she says. I asked her how she lived. She had no job and the life of an addict is expensive.

"Addiction is a 'feeling' disease," Bonnie said. She meant that everything she had been doing was to make her feel good—only temporarily perhaps, but that's all the window any addict needs to trade a life. When you begin your journey to nowhere when you're only 12, as Bonnie was when, in her way, she was first tempted to cure the feeling disease, short-term satisfaction is the only thing that counts. No matter what.

Even with all her challenges—the type that most people cannot imagine confronting, let alone enduring and overcoming—Bonnie has found the temperamental sweet spot: she is neither angry nor submissive. She speaks of her past as a fact, regrettable no doubt but in a way that today reflects her appreciation of others, as well as of herself. Her humanity, which shines sincerely through her eyes, her words, and her gestures, is evidence of the strength she brings to her job to help others who are very much like she used to be. Been there, done that—but without the dismissive, condescending attitude that usually helps define that phrase.

*   *   *

As saintly as people like Father John and his staff are, they are everyday tested, immersed in the hopelessness of the destitute; the people who seek help from SOME come from an ugly, sordid world. That world has almost nothing to do with ethics. Ethics as a way of thinking, to the people who come to SOME, is as foreign a concept as living the life of a millionaire. Yet the people who use the services at this charity are not necessarily unethical. Somewhere inside many of them, even if it isn't conscious, is a moral code, a sense of right and wrong. A sense of wanting to do the right thing. The challenge is for SOME to conscientiously exercise its values and translate that effort to an ethical code so it can best help its people in need. One example is treating everyone else fairly and not making a special case of yourself, a principal tenet in the application of ethics. SOME conveys this tenet marvelously in the way its people do their everyday work. To ensure that the idea is conveyed so that all its clients understand that they too should treat others in the same way—as well as to teach them to expect that kind of treatment from others—is an ongoing challenge.

The charity's employees are aware of the pressures and temptations of the dark side. The life of the streets is harsh and easy bargains with unscrupulous people are made all the time. Yet the people at SOME don't judge; not judging is a key component in ethics. SOME does not have a religious requirement and, more important, there is no sense that anyone—on the food line or in treatment—must live up to anyone else's standards but his or her own.

Bonnie McDonald stumbled across SOME because she was drunkenly following a guy with a bottle, and she wanted a taste. He happened to be on this way there for a reason she didn't comprehend, and when she was standing in the office waiting for him to come out so they could retrieve another bottle—or so she assumed—a woman behind the desk asked her if she could help her. "Me? No way," she answered. The woman behind the desk said, "That's okay. We're here if you need us." It took a while, but

Bonnie eventually figured out that she needed help after her four children were taken from her because she was such a mess. That was 14 years earlier.

In that time, she accepted all the help SOME could give and then, straight and determined to be a mother again, she decided she wanted to give something back. After a rigorous application process and ongoing evaluations, Bonnie now heads the home where others who are in the same place she was come for help. Three months after my visit with Bonnie, she was awarded her bachelor's degree in social services from Catholic University. Her children are now grown and healthy. She proudly talked about them all and how often she sees them—she so wants to be the role model that she never had—but I most acutely remember her telling me that her daughter, 28, was gladly risking her life for her country as a Marine in Iraq. She now helps out and cares for her grandchildren in a way she was not able to do for her children.

Bonnie is now happily married. The Friday before I visited with her, she and her husband celebrated their fifth wedding anniversary.

It's been a long journey from where she hung out as an addict just a few blocks away from SOME to where she is today, and it will continue, she says, because it's never over. She will never forget, she says of the women she helps at Harvest House "that I am them—the women who are here."

While Bonnie told me her wonderful story, she talked of the person responsible for the crucial turning point in her drama—the staff person in the SOME office that night who asked Bonnie if she could be of help. Bonnie said that without her, she would never have gotten straight. She didn't take the woman up on her offer right off, but the question stuck in her mind, and some months later, perhaps as an act of desperation, she returned—drunk, disorderly, and wasted—and asked for help. I asked Father John about that and he told me that it's part of the organization's ethos. "We don't judge," he said. "All our employees are taught that."

Where within the four pillars of ethical behavior does that directive fit? Oversight. Part of a board's oversight function is to hire people as heads of the organizations and executive directors whose values are already in line with the organization's, and to be clear about how they think the staff ought to be managed. In this case, both Father John and SOME's executive director, Richard Gerlach, have seen many board members come and go, so they must also independently exercise an ethics code. And they do. No one can remember who that employee was so many years ago, the one that made the crucial difference in Bonnie's life, but her calm acceptance reflected the nonjudgmental culture at SOME.

A Client: Vanessa Herndon

Vanessa Herndon wants to be like Bonnie someday—but she's not there yet. Vanessa started with SOME three months before I met her in early 2010, and she too had been in a real mess. She actually had a bit more on the ball during her troubled years than Bonnie did because she was at least trying to get into SOME. "I tried for three years but they wouldn't accept me. They let me eat, but they said I had to stop using and I just couldn't."

One of the rules at SOME is that if you're going to be given treatment, you have to be serious about wanting it. The food line is open to anyone with no questions asked, but treatment comes with a price: a desire to get better. And it took a while: "I tried for three years but they wouldn't accept me."

Vanessa wanted to get better, but she says her prayers to stop using just weren't being answered. It's understandable that her desire was strong. "I was never married," she said when I asked. Any children? "No. I had a child, but it died in childbirth because I was so drunk. See? I just gave up on myself."

Today Vanessa says that she is grateful—"I can't tell you how grateful"—that she had enough fortitude to stop taking drugs, and she credits SOME with giving her the strength to stay off them. "I had a hard heart, and they taught me how to cry. When that happened I saw a different person inside of me."

For many people, it is likely difficult to connect to this kind of reality. How must it feel to give up on yourself? After a point, it must feel normal—that being anything other than despondent isn't possible, so it becomes your frame of reference. How difficult it must be to overcome that. How important to the healing process it is that the people at SOME don't judge. If you have given up on yourself, you need more than anything to be around people who won't give up on you.

Indeed, as both Bonnie and Vanessa said without hesitation, when I asked where they would be if it weren't for SOME, "Dead. Literally. Dead." No doubt about SOME's living up to its mission there. In the quest to define and exercise ethical behavior of charities, we must remember that it informs how charities act out their mission.

Beyond the Numbers

As much as the stories like Bonnie's and Vanessa's at the same time break your heart and resurrect your hope for humanity—an organization that serves the poor does so with money. SOME's annual budget is around $17 million. Their need is staggering, which means that the place has to be run with brains as well as heart.

How many people do you know who are in charge of a charity's finances and who prefer the language of mission over the language of accounting? I am convinced that a critical piece of the ethical construct at SOME is Emily van Loon. I asked her and the director of development, Linda Parisi, how they got along. It's been my experience that the development and finance offices at charities don't always play well in the sandbox. The vernacular is different in each office, and the goals can often seem different. One wants to promise the world to donors, while the other wants to nail down commitments and protect the bottom line. "We have 'robust' conversations all the time," Linda and Emily said, "but we respect each other and we know we both want the same thing." Emily said that "it's a safe environment for disagreement."

Then she outlined what I think is a crucial component to SOME's success. "I look at the process of reporting out to our president, our staff, the board, and the public as an ethical activity." This sentiment was not prompted by me. "We gather the information for the reports, but gathering is very much a subjective activity, and I have to be certain that the end result is governed by doing the right thing." I mentioned that charities sometimes inflate their fundraising numbers, that others sometimes hide salary and benefit totals.

"Look," she said, "think of development and finance as being two circles in a Venn diagram. When we start to drift, I look for the commonality of goals, and then see where we, the finance and fundraising offices, are apart and try to address that. It would never be within our ethical structure to inflate anything. And if it ever were, I'd want to address it head-on and define why we drifted." Then she said, "We don't play games with goals. We spend a lot of time with one another around here and we make sure we're on the same page."

And I saw how they spend time with one another. Although it's easy to say things like that, it's a lot harder to make it happen. Time, after all, is at a premium, and, that being the case, who would want to spend time with people who look at the world differently and at divisive matters, the way the people in many fundraising offices see those in finance, and the way people in finance see fundraisers? "We're comfortable going to outside experts," Linda said in response to a bevy of technical questions I raised, the answers to which I suspected the organization probably did not have. "We're comfortable saying when we don't know."

At SOME I saw the humility of smart people who were smart enough to know they don't know everything and had the confidence to seek help when they needed it. As a result of close collaboration, development and finance work well together, and neither forgets the most important part of the organization: the programs it provides for the poor. "It's almost that we're embarrassed by our four-star rating with Charity Navigator," Linda Parisi said. "We do our work without regard to gaming the system. It just happens that we do it efficiently and effectively."

But clearly, it doesn't just happen. Every day the people touched by an issue discuss it and determine how to deal with it. The conversations at times must be robust—there is no other way to deal with issues when people have different perspectives—but they are filled with respect. Respect is another important underpinning of ethical behavior and decision making.

A Gala

I had to ask about the group's annual gala. In 2009 it was held at the Mayflower Hotel in Washington, D.C. I wondered if one of the nicest and most famous hotels in the city was an appropriate place to hold a dinner for a charity dedicated to the poor. "You might not believe it," Father John said, "but it's efficient. We always order the cheapest thing—which means it's chicken—and then try to get a really good price. We don't pay the same as corporations. We honor our donors as well as our work, and, on top of that, we raise a lot of money."

I asked to see evidence of that efficiency and within minutes I was presented with the financial breakdown, information SOME is not reluctant to share. The numbers show that the annual gala in each of the prior two years produced just shy of $600,000. The costs were about 23 percent of what was raised. As a ratio for an annual amount, that might seem a little high, but for a discrete fundraising event, it's pretty good. If other charities would be so open about such questions, the public would see that it stacks up well against similar charity dinners. Unfortunately, most charities would balk at providing the information.

The 990

SOME's 990 is also impressive. In 2008 fundraising costs consumed a little over 8 percent of the budget. Almost 89 percent of the budget went to program services. Father John took a salary of approximately $66,000 with another $16,000 given to his retirement. The executive director's salary was $143,000 with another $26,000 given to his retirement.[6] But, to echo Linda Parisi, the director of development, the numbers; are good, its the goal isn't a drive to the numbers but to do the work.

So which of the four pillars are evident in the finance and development offices? All of them. Finance will disclose almost any information of consequence. It works hard to anticipate what people want to know, and so tries to be transparent. When there is a potential conflict of interest, they discuss it openly. And both directors are on top of their departments' activities, exercising a great deal of oversight.

SOME Donor: William Conway

William Conway, a business executive with the investment firm The Carlyle Group, found something to love at SOME. Father John explained that Conway used to ignore street people, but that when he finally looked at some of them, he began to connect. "I used to think that if people were able-bodied, I wouldn't help them out," he says. Today, he feels differently. He gave SOME a $5 million gift so the organization could borrow or raise another $125 million from donors and others, an amount that is intended to put hundreds of homeless into homes. "Until a person has a home, they are always going to be dependent upon the system," Conway said. "I'm kind of solving the problem I can solve."[7]

It's an ambitious project, but one undoubtedly worth undertaking. Part of the magic at SOME is that the staff and board have managed to tell the story in a way that resonates. If a business tycoon who once thought that able-bodied people never needed any help can be influenced, almost anyone can. And that's the effect of combining a good story with technically and ethically competent management.

Father John said that a few years earlier, when the charity was running a deficit and facing a cut in some of its services, an anonymous donor called and said, "We can't let this happen." He followed up with a generous donation. Father John asked the person, who had never visited SOME, if he wanted to stop by sometime. The donor said, "No. If I do that, I may want to give all my money to you." Eventually, the donor did stop by, and although he hasn't parted with all his money he has parted with a lot more since he first saw the face of poverty and the humanity within.

*   *   *

The most important decision a person must make about a charity before supporting it is to determine whether it is close to his or her heart. I hope by now that you understand that the information on a 990, or any evaluation of those numbers, is a poor substitute for evaluating the heart of a charity. Every charity has a purpose, and undoubtedly, there's a cause that every human being in the world can connect to. The National Center for Charitable Statistics at the Urban Institute developed what is called the National Taxonomy of Exempt Entities. The IRS uses the taxonomy to help it categorize charities based on the kind of work each charity performs—education or environment, for example, with many subgroups in each major grouping. The taxonomy categorizes the almost two million charities and other nonprofits in the United States into approximately 400 types of groups. Anyone in the world will find something to love in at least one of the categories.[8]

*   *   *

"You realize, of course," Father John said to me, "that we are literally in the shadow of the Capitol building of the United States. The people in there make decisions that affect everyone in the world. And yet there are 9,000 homeless people," he says without raising his voice. "You would think that if we can tell the rest of the world how to live, we ought to be able to take care of more people right here." Father John Adams is no bleeding heart. He has strict standards. "We hire people who are qualified to do the job," and they do it. The group combines the best of being human: heart, soul, brain, not a slave to numbers and never trying to game the system. He is who he is. SOME is what it is. "I've been asked to expand some to other communities in Maryland and Virginia.

But we can't go beyond DC. We haven't completed our work here yet."

He probably never will. That's the way it is with poverty.

At least until we learn a new and better way to do it, the process described in this chapter is the best way to go about evaluating a charity: Carefully review the written promotional materials and the information on the charity's website, get to know the people who run the place and ask a lot of questions, see if the programs are having any effect by talking to people and reviewing documentation, examine the 990 and other financials, read through its policies, including its ethics policies, and talk to people who support the charity and those who use its services. Ask, too, about disclosure, transparency, conflict of interest, and oversight. And then listen. There are very few wrong answers, except those that show the charity hasn't thought about them much or that they don't matter.

Serving

I served food at SOME. It was an honor. Handing a plate of hot food to a poor person who would very likely go hungry if not for SOME, affected me in a way I'm not normally affected. As I looked into the eyes of each person, I saw a human being. "Look them in the eye and say something uplifting," I was told. "Something like 'Please enjoy your meal' or 'It's good to see you.'" Respect for the poor is a mantra at SOME—an ethos in action—and the people who work there embody that ethos. "It rubs off. A lot of these people are angry," one employee explained to me, "and with good reason. This is the place where they come for respect. They are reminded they are human beings here. And that's an important thing to remember if you're ever going to get off the streets."

Imagine what a person, who may be addicted and emptied and certainly among the poorest in the nation's capital, feels when he trudges in from the street, looking forward to a few minutes of nourishment and protection from the elements. His head is low, probably from either shame or simple weariness. But the man who hands him his plate has been instructed, as I was, to greet him warmly—and with respect.

As it happens, I spent a few days at SOME. One of my appointments to speak with the people and volunteer to serve food there was delayed because President Obama and his family had arranged to be there that day. As more than one person said, "Things were a little hectic." But I was told that the president did what all servers do and said to each person, "Good afternoon. Please enjoy your meal."

Then, in a way ethics textbooks can only dream about communicating but in a way that sums up the effort at combining the four pillars of ethics at charities, dignity was met with dignity.

Chapter Ten

The Voluntary Sector as the Ethical Sector

On Saturday, November 16, 1940, Cornell University's football team was in Hanover, New Hampshire, to play Dartmouth. Cornell was then ranked second in the nation by the Associated Press and was counting on a win that day, as well as one the following week, to earn a national college title. Cornell had won its prior 18 games. The stop at Dartmouth was a formality, really; its record to date that year was 3–4, and the team came into the game as 15 to 1 underdogs. On a messy, frozen field, in a grueling game in which Dartmouth held Cornell scoreless until the fourth quarter, Cornell finally tossed a touchdown pass in the final moments to win 7–3.

It turned out, however, that Cornell needed five downs to score, something that initially went unnoticed by the referees. Game tapes showed the error, and the next day Red Friesell, the head referee, sent a telegram to Dartmouth saying, "I want to be the first to admit my very grave error. The extra down is proved by the motion pictures of both colleges. I assume full responsibility."[1]

Even though Cornell would otherwise have been on its way to a national championship, its president didn't hesitate to acknowledge that it was Dartmouth's game. To the young men who had just arrived back in Ithaca after a journey filled with celebration, he said, "Fellas, we have reviewed the game and it's absolutely sure that we had five downs. I have to tell you that I sent a telegram to the president of Dartmouth that said we deny the win and award it to you." Dartmouth took him up on the offer and accepted the win.

Fifty years later, on Saturday, October 6, 1990, the University of Colorado football team beat the University of Missouri 33–31. There was a lot on the line in that game too. The Associated Press that year ultimately voted Colorado the national champions. But Colorado, like Cornell, needed a fifth down to win against Missouri.

This time, however, no one offered up any corrective apologies, and Colorado certainly didn't "award" the game to Missouri. In fact, the commissioner of the Big Eight, Carl James, said, "It has been determined that, in accordance with the football playing rules, the allowance of the fifth down to Colorado is not a post-game correctable error. The final score in the Colorado-Missouri football game will remain as posted."[2] When asked if he considered forfeiting the game, Colorado coach Bill McCartney, said, "The field was lousy."[3] What that had to do with the controversy is anyone's guess, but it certainly fell far short of calling the president of the university to urge him to award the win to Missouri.

*   *   *

Was the Colorado coach unethical for not giving back the game? Does it matter that the rules of football are precise about saying that the results are determined on the field? The Dartmouth-Cornell game is the only one in college football history whose outcome was decided off the field. Does it matter that Cornell's president Edmund Ezra Day said, "I know Dartmouth and it won't be long before we get a return telegraph saying, 'no, Cornell, you won it on the field' "?[4] It mattered to Frank Finneran, the center for Cornell that season, who said in 2005, "65 years later, we're still waiting for that telegram."[5] The referee's telegram was sent in defiance of the game's official outcome, and, even though everyone in Ithaca was hoping for a response from Dartmouth that never came, Cornell's president sent it without contingency, knowing that a loss would ruin Cornell's chances for a national championship.

Charities in Society

Although it seems otherwise, places like Dartmouth and Cornell, and Colorado and Missouri are charities. So are the Smithsonian, Greenpeace, the Salvation Army, the National Heritage Foundation, Yeshiva, Princeton, the Museum of Modern Art and Stevens Institute of Technology. So are many other organizations working under the umbrella of public support, far too many of which often try to cut corners in their nonprofit compact with that public.

The world is filled with examples of greed and not-so-enlightened self-interest. If it's a problem—and, okay, it may be—why is it a particular problem for charitable organizations? What's so special about the nonprofit world when it comes to ethics?

Because the nonprofit world should be society's ethical sector. The whole idea behind the existence of charities is their potential to do good things; they exist for no other purpose than to help others. That identity is not the result of the charitable deduction or any other privilege Congress may bestow on nonprofits. It's part of the intrinsic role the activities housed inside charities play in society.

That is not to say that government and business are not ethical or that they do not help others. They are and they do—but they do not exist solely to help others in as beneficent a way as charities do. Government's role, according to James Wilson, one of six Founding Fathers to sign both the Declaration of Independence and the Constitution, is to ensure the happiness of individuals. "In a regulated society," he said, "the liberty of every member is increased...for each gains more by the limitation of the freedom of every other member, than he loses by the limitation of his own. The result is that civil government is necessary to the perfection and happiness of man."[6] Although they would disagree where the best point within the spectrum of activity is, political thinkers from Thomas Jefferson and John Adams to Ayn Rand to Barack Obama would all agree that the purpose of government is to provide for the general welfare without infringing on personal liberties. That's not what charities do. Nor is their purpose, as it is for commerce, to generate economic stability and wealth through the exchange of products and services.

Those two spheres of activity have proved inadequate to address the work that charities have been developed to perform.

Alexis de Tocqueville, when he toured the young United States in the 1830s, took note of the "associations" that had sprung up to address the types of social issues in Europe that were paid for by the state, challenges that the government of the United States was too poor to even contemplate in those days.

But it was more than an inability to pay for those services. The concession was then, as it is now, that there are certain functions the government shouldn't even try to perform, and that businesses can't profitably afford to perform. Even the most conservative thinkers, those who think individuals should be left to fully fend for themselves in an unfettered free-market economy in a society led by a hands-off government, welcome the work of charitable organizations. And even the liberal thought leaders among us, those who believe government ought to be more expansive to address more of the needs of the nation's citizens, also think charities play an important role and fill a large void in society. There is no real disagreement about the importance of the nonprofit world, or that it has become its own sector: It does what government cannot and business will not. It follows then, that its purpose is different. If part of ethics is the study of good and bad and right and wrong, then the nonprofit sector is the place to examine those questions in their purest state, without political or economic motivations slanting the discussion. It is for these reasons that the nonprofits comprise society's ethical sector.

That being the case, the nonprofit world isn't in great shape—not even by the standards of those who work at nonprofits. According to the Ethics Research Center in Washington, D.C., most charity executives say they have witnessed unethical behavior.[7]

Obedience to the Unenforceable

A century ago, a jurist by the name of Lord John Fletcher Moulton gave a speech in which he identified "the three great domains of Human Action." The first is the domain of positive law, "where our actions are prescribed by laws binding upon us which must be obeyed," a place he thought was clearly defined. The second domain is that of free choice, in which we enjoy complete freedom. It is "a precious land where the actions of men are not only such as they choose, but have a right to claim freedom even from criticism," a right that permits us to act "without anyone having the right to utter a word of dictation or command." The third is what he called the "domain of obedience to the unenforceable," a land of in-between, where "there is no law which inexorably determines our course of action, and yet we feel that we are not free to choose as we would." This is a place for "freedom of action, but in which the individual should feel that he was not wholly free." Moulton acknowledged that people might divide this domain further, based on what they feel personally about this otherwise undefined tundra of civilizing rules.

Moulton thought that the quality of this middle ground between positive law and absolute choice, in constant danger of being gobbled up by either of the two, is the measure of a great nation. It "measures the extent to which the nation trusts its citizens, and its existence and area testify to the way they behave in response to that trust." He called that place "manners," which may seem a bit light when contrasted with what ethics is all about, but it's not a bad beginning, especially since Moulton applies serious intellectual capacity to his argument.

As an example, he talks of a legislature's right to debate. He pointed out that some legislators in England thought that because their right to debate was unrestricted, they could use it to destroy debate itself, or, at least, to forestall making decisions. This was the result that the absence of restrictions enabled. "The old freedom cannot now be entrusted to the members," Moulton opined, "because when they possessed it they did not respond to it by the exercise of that moral sense which would have led them to treat it as a trust." He lamented the laziness of moral thought that leads people to confuse "can do" and "may do," and said, "Between 'can do' and 'may do' ought to exist the whole realm which recognizes the sway of duty, fairness, sympathy, taste, and all the other things that make life beautiful and society possible." Not only a beauty, which would be a worthy enough goal, but the very possibility of society.[8]

When we look at ethics through this prism, we see it as a study of applying values to a coherent process, and not so much as a rigid determination of right and wrong. Highlighting the search for values, however, does not rob ethics of its element of right and wrong—or of punishment. In a pure sense, ethics is that land where no punishment exists, and enforcement—other than from within—is not possible. Yet we see efforts at enforcement by ethics committees everywhere in the professions and in government. In fact, the principal fundraising association in the nonprofit world has a code of ethics, and determining what to do when someone violates that code is a constant source of serious discussion. One of the code's philosophical underpinnings—and I wish more people would see ethics this way—is that, while punishment may need to be an element or a result in the ethical decision-making process, it is not the goal.[9]

Ethics: Elusive but Persuasive

This is a classroom question: What do ethics and pornography have in common? Students, either because they're too embarrassed or, more likely, really think the two concepts are so opposite each other that they have nothing in common, will often offer up only the silence of confusion. In the 1964 case, *Jacobellis v. Ohio*,[10] Supreme Court Justice Potter Stewart said about pornography, "I know it when I see it." That's how a lot of people think of ethics.

And isn't that a shame? The study of ethics is far too important to remain so vague and called out only on the basis of a feeling.

One of the reasons that the United States holds itself together, despite its divisions, is that everyone claims allegiance to the Constitution. Although not everyone agrees on what all the words in the document mean, we all acknowledge that the Constitution is where our understanding of the law in this country begins.

We have no such altar of ethics. The closest we come in a national sense of our values is the Declaration of Independence. As the Constitution is the country's founding legal document, the Declaration, with its grand aspirations, is our founding ethical document. But we don't scrutinize the Declaration the same way as we do the Constitution. There are no scholars of the Declaration the equivalent of which we find in law schools for Constitutional scholars. Certainly, it has never been amended. Perhaps that's because the Declaration was all about Americans not being under the control of the British, while the Constitution was written with the idea of Americans controlling themselves: One was relevant— its purpose, if not its ideas—for only a point in time; the other was written to be relevant for all time.

If we accept Moulton's premise that ethics is that place of unenforced obedience, this conundrum arises: A document defining ethics that is rigid enough to enforce obedience is no longer within the purview of ethics. As a result, ethics and regulation often collide.

This is why so many people think that ethics is mushy, almost meaningless; the ideal to which we may pretend to aspire but an idea that will never be a tangible part of the real world. If we have to go to court to determine the date of a charitable gift, for example, there are rules. Who's to say, by contrast, what gift-acceptance policies are appropriate for a particular charity? Who's to say we have to follow the rates recommended by the American Council on Gift Annuities? What lawmaker is going to weigh in on how much we pay our nonprofit's president?[11] Sure, people have tried to enforce all sorts of rules relating to these and other matters, but they don't usually succeed, not unless a person's behavior is so egregious, the violation of community spirit so odious, that a line clearly defining right and wrong and thus forced into society's consciousness is crossed. But, as Moulton says, the whole idea of ethics isn't a matter of crossing over clearly established lines; it's a matter of understanding a conceptual territory.

Those of us who care about ethics have to acknowledge all this, that defining and maintaining ethical standards is an uphill battle. But that is not an excuse to dismiss the idea of ethics or to cringe at trying to turn the professions within the nonprofit world into ethical enterprises. We have to stop trying to be like business and understand the truly unique nature of charitable organizations and the truly unique nature of the jobs people who work at nonprofits have.

We certainly have to stop acting as if ethics is intellectually subservient to the law. There is, in fact, no such thing, as I often hear, as the "soft underbelly" of ethics; that the true grit of human interaction is found in the tangible. Nothing could be further from the truth. Even though the ideas guiding ethics are not as clear as the rules found in the law (which are often not very clear at all), they are vibrant with strong meaning and intellectual heft. They go where the law does not. In fact, an ethics document, or any other policy document, written solely by attorneys will almost certainly be flawed and wanting because it will be dominated by legal considerations and short on human and ethical considerations.

*   *   *

Consider another classroom topic of discussion. In the middle of the Civil War, in his short speech at Gettysburg, President Lincoln referred to something that took place "four score and seven years" earlier. The speech was given in 1863; 87 years earlier, the Declaration of Independence was ratified. There's a lesson here: Lincoln was not reaching back to America's founding legal document, the Constitution, as many people might think, in his quest to rid the country of its worst legal crisis seen before or since. He was instead invoking America's founding *ethical* document.

Laws emerge from ethics—not the other way around.

Ethics are Tangible

Ethics seem elusive because we have difficulty getting our heads around the idea; we can't outline it. There is no format. It's not that it's so hard to find people who do the right thing; but we're flummoxed, in part, because we don't have a construct—a blueprint—for knowing what the right thing is, or how to judge what to do. Religious tomes, including the Bible, the Torah, and the Koran, all espouse ethical behavior, but with so many questions that arise from their often-conflicting dictates—Do you kill or don't you kill?—we need a more robust understanding of ethics to actually live in the real world.

The worst idea someone can have about ethics is the one, ironically but understandably, most people cling to in this context: that it is something that simply feels right. People know in their gut what's right, they say, and that informs their decision. While that sounds very nice on the surface, as a principal guide it is actually venomous in a serious ethical undertaking. To paraphrase Stephen Carter, in his excellent and thoughtful book *Integrity*, it is not enough to ask whether our actions are consistent with our deepest beliefs; we must ask instead whether we have done the hard work of discerning whether those beliefs are right.[12] Or, to quote Benjamin Franklin: "For having lived long, I have experienced many instances of being obliged, by better information or fuller consideration, to change opinions, even on important subjects, which I once thought right but found to be otherwise."[13]

What may pass for your ethical understanding of the world and your relation to it may be nothing more than several layers of prejudices reinforced by family and friends, and untested anywhere but in your own head, where they exist, comfortable and unchallenged. That would be fine if you were the only person in the world, but you're not.

So, understanding that there are a lot of people in the world and that many of them are good, let's assert a simple proposition: good people disagree. Some trustees at a charity, who care and are knowledgeable, will think that paying the executive director $500,000, for example, is a good idea. But others will disagree. Without standards, a context, however, for why the disagreement exists, the arguments will go nowhere, and lazy thinking will win the day. That's why places like Stevens Institute of Technology and the Smithsonian, among many others, ended up awarding their chief executives high, inappropriate salaries. "She's worth it, given what others in similar positions are being paid," one person might say. "She may be," another may respond, "but it's too far past our ability to pay and do the other things we need to do." At once, three ideas—money, prestige, and other priorities—are being thrown about without anyone ascribing values to those ideas, or even distinguishing one from the others. But does the person saying that the chief executive is worth the high salary really mean it? Or is he just uncomfortable saying no? There is almost always a story inside the story.

Maybe those who were opposed to the decision by the Boston Museum of Fine Arts to lend the Monets to the Bellagio in Las Vegas really weren't as worried about insurance; maybe they were opposed to lending their name to a gambling community. Maybe they thought that a museum is superior to a casino, that people in Boston, with their rich cultural history, were simply better than the people of Las Vegas, who might be identified with the culture of the mob and the history of sleeze more than with the culture of Longfellow and the history of Revere. Maybe they thought that, but couldn't actually say they thought that. Maybe they made the decision to send the Monets to Las Vegas so that no one would think that they thought such snobby things.[14] Ethics encompasses a process to deal with this difficulty—the difficulty of not being honest.

Ethics is a Process

We must look at what we mean by ethics. In my classes, students often ask, "Is that ethical?" when someone does something he or she doesn't like. At first blush, actions that you don't approve of may seem "wrong," but understanding ethics is more than giving approval. Ethics is a process by which a decision is made, and that process not only uncovers values but also allows you to prioritize them. For what we're really concerned with here are ethics as they relate to our desire to deal with dilemmas. The solution to a dilemma is by definition unclear until an evaluative process takes place. Some dilemmas have more than one right or one wrong answer.

Rushworth Kidder, the founder and head of the Institute for Global Ethics in Maine, says many dilemmas have "right-versus-right" qualities. For example, we are perfectly capable of honoring both justice and mercy, but we must sometimes choose one over the other, as when considering whether to punish someone to the full extent of the law or permit him to suffer less severe consequences in hopes that reduced punishment will better help him mend his ways. Good people will disagree on that question, but they will best resolve their disagreement by invoking and being honest about their values. Both justice and mercy are highly regarded by almost everyone, but, for you, does the one value take priority over the other? Or does it depend on the situation?

There is a process. And it's rather concrete, especially in light of the presumption many people have that ethics are that fuzzy otherworld where nothing adds up and nothing makes sense, except when we agree with the outcome. In fact, when I speak on ethics, some people tend at first to sit at the rear of the room, undoubtedly worried that they are about to be rebuked for behaving badly. In fact, ethics has gotten such a bad rap partly because of people who assume for themselves the role of moralist for everyone else.

The result is a public perception that ethics are relative, so it doesn't matter. People will do what they want anyway. It's true enough, but if we are to have any chance at all of addressing that criticism, and if we are to make sense of our decision making, we must figure out how to generate a guideline.

Clearly, nothing truly complex or fraught with individual interest can be boiled down to a ten-point plan or anything so simple, but we can begin to bring legitimacy to the process, which can turn into a blueprint for organizations that want one, by asking certain questions along the way.

The process might go like this:

> First off, it doesn't hurt to know a little about ethics. There is a world of difference between Kantian principles, which are characterized by a strict adherence to rules, and utilitarian, ends-based principles, which steer us toward considering the greater good as the most ethical course of action. Add to that a third idea, the concept we know as the Golden Rule, an ethic of reciprocity where one treats others fairly and expects to be treated fairly in return. Although most people, when they think about it, will want to apply different ethical principles in different circumstances, they should know what they're dealing with. Thinking about ethics has a long history and is intellectually rigorous. Dealing with real-world issues from an ethics-based perspective may be difficult but life mandates that we undertake the task. Aristotle didn't talk much about what came from his gut. Ethics is not a luxury. It's an essential part of our lives.

> Make sure the question you are dealing with really is an ethical one. Dipping into an endowment's principal may be unethical, but it's also against the law in many states. The law would trump any further consideration of the question. Similarly, did you sign an agreement promising a donor that you would use the money in a certain way? Then you have a legal, contractual obligation to abide by the agreement. If

the understanding was less formal, the charity has an ethical obligation to do what its fundraising representatives said they would do. By the way—aside from the law as we understand it in state and federal statutes—rules and policies at an organization should never trump what is clearly right regardless of what seems immediately convenient.

Gather as many relevant facts as possible—and be sure they're not just the ones you want to know, the convenient ones. If anything should persuade people that ethics is more than fuzzy thinking or a gut reaction, it is this: Facts are crucial. In fact, their absence from so many ethics lectures is one reason the lectures often seem so wooden and unreal. You need to know what's going on. It isn't just a question of how much to pay an executive; it's also a question of how much others in similar positions are paid, the complexities of the job and the skills needed to deal with them, and how filled with integrity the process is that the board used to gather that information. It matters if the person who left a personal bequest to the gift solicitor was otherwise a friend. Information is the engine for all decisions, and it is vital to making sound ethical decisions.

In making any decision, make sure that you're not making an exception for yourself or inappropriately allowing one for someone else. It's not okay to take the handicapped parking spot or to park in front of the fire hydrant even though you will just be a minute. It's not okay for a small number of people on a charity's board to create a compensation package for the executive director without the knowledge of the full board. And it's not ethically permissible for a charity to allow a donor to insist on financially controlling his donation—as in making the investment decisions personally once it's in the endowment—especially when there are other options. Policies are intended for everyone. Always exercise the personal discipline of asking whether you would want others to join you in doing something or whether you want to be a privileged case. You'd be surprised to learn how often people privilege themselves over others.

After making a decision—which is often more problematical than one might think—it is key to keep your mind open to new evidence and new possibilities. One of the problems with declaring a position—politicians are in this corner all the time—is that, for some reason, once we've said it we own it. We can end up defending a position that we are not all that engaged with, feeling the pressure to be right or decisive. This is anathema to the ethical process. Keep in mind the thoughts of Benjamin Franklin, who humbly acknowledged that upon obtaining better or fuller information, he sometimes changed his mind, even on important questions about which he once felt certain that he was right.[15]

How do the issues brought up earlier in this book stack up against this process?

Charities as Business

The assertion that charities should behave more like businesses rankles a lot of charity leaders, yet we see more and more former for-profit directors and other executives being hired at nonprofits. Larry Small, who left Fannie Mae[16] to lead the Smithsonian, is just one example. The logic is that those who have proven themselves in the business world have the skills to lead nonprofits. Of course, inherent in that argument is that business skills are relevant to nonprofit work: If only principles from commerce could be overlaid onto the workings of nonprofits, those nonprofits would shape up.

Putting aside for a moment that some, although certainly not all, of the highest paid people in business are leading endeavors that look a lot more like monopolies—sometimes with a great deal of government support—than organizations that could thrive in the real rough and tumble of a fully free and unencumbered marketplace, it's clear that the business ethos is very different from the nonprofit ethos. For one thing, each legitimately embraces a different concept of "outcome."

Of course, charities need to pay their bills on time and in general run themselves as businesses do. But so do households and individuals, and that doesn't make them equal to commerce.

One recommendation that critics of nonprofits like to put forth is that they should pay their top people more on the theory that if you pay more you'll get more talent.

But nonprofit leaders aren't solely about the bottom line; they are about dealing with social problems that almost never have short-term solutions, which, in the business world, are often expected to emerge within the next one or two quarters. Nonprofit leaders must use a different yardstick from that of their for-profit counterparts because their goals are not the same.

Richard Gerlach, the executive director at SOME, earned a little under $170,000 in 2008.[17] In that same year, Sara Bloomfield, the director of the United States Holocaust Memorial Museum, earned $580,000.[18] Did Sara Bloomfield do three and a half times more for society than Richard Gerlach? That question is so ethereal, you might say. What about comparing their budgets? you might ask. The budget at SOME was about $15 million while the budget at the Holocaust Museum was about $88 million, almost six times larger. By that standard, Bloomfield's salary, using Gerlach's salary as a baseline, is low. On a straight scale, a logic that might legitimately be applied to business, Bloomfield's salary should be just shy of $1 million. Extending that logic even further, Harvard, with a budget of $3.5 billion, should pay its president $40 million.

But the critics of the nonprofit ethos might protest that's not their argument and agree that, clearly, there must limits. An annual salary of $40 million is steep anywhere, and unimaginable at any nonprofit.[19] So the scale and the rationale for the salary argument are good until...it doesn't feel right.

And this is where we enter the ethical arena, when something doesn't *feel right*. Yet, as we have seen, the feel-right concept isn't really helpful in deciding what's ethical, which means that somewhere along the line a process must be applied.

It would be fairly easy to create a formula for determining a director's salary based solely on the charity's budget, and the formula could easily provide for a lessening of the salary growth as the budget grew. That is, an executive salary of $200,000 in an organization with a budget of $25 million would not necessarily translate to a salary of $400,000 when the budget grew to $50 million; it might grow to $300,00—or less—instead. A larger budget would be a factor in determining the executive's salary, but it wouldn't be the only one. The formula could take into account all sorts of things, actually, and the math of it could remain quite simple. The difficult part would be to determine how to apply the math and, of course, figuring out if the charity's success has anything to do with paying its chief executive an extraordinarily high salary. So while the salary decision would become something ethics based when it turned on whether it felt right, it then would require a process that encompassed ethics-based guideposts, such as how the person treated his subordinates, whether his decisions satisfied long-range and still-to-be realized objectives, and his ability to partner with trustees and other leaders to ensure the charity's good standing in the community.

Those guideposts include an examination of results. The argument that large compensation packages attract people with a "proven track record"—jargon from the business world that has found its way into the corridors and board rooms of nonprofits—who will produce results has been elevated to a mantra: Talented people produce results.

Putting aside, once again, that results are elusive in the non-profit world, the for-profit world hasn't done so well with its talent. In fact, the idea of talent—not just at nonprofits but anywhere other than on sports teams—may be vastly overrated when it is tied to organizational leadership. What passes for talent, actually, may be hiding the destructive traits of narcissism.

In a *New Yorker* article from 2002, Malcolm Gladwell argued that talent is overrated. "This talent 'mind-set' is the new orthodoxy of American management," he wrote, as he explored the management theories espoused by the well-known and highly regarded management consulting firm McKinsey & Company, and its influence on an organization that was once one of its biggest clients: Enron. Gladwell said that the leadership at many companies consists of superstars, people who may be smart but who sabotage their organization's efforts with their narcissism. Citing an essay called "The Dark Side of Charisma," Gladwell noted that its authors reported that "narcissists are biased to take more credit for their success than is legitimate." They are "biased to avoid acknowledging responsibility for their failures and their shortcomings for the same reasons that they claim more success than is their due."[20] Similarly, Robert Hogan, a psychiatrist at the Tulsa Institute of Behavioral Sciences, has said of some people who have charisma, "They end up being costly by creating poor morale, excessive turnover, and reducing productivity. Sometimes they can ruin a company altogether."[21]

Does that sound like anyone you know at a nonprofit? I've met plenty of people who would fit this description. Did the Smithsonian fall into the Svengali-like trance of "talent," "results," and "success." Did the Stevens Institute of Technology? Perhaps nonprofit boards, the groups that choose the executive directors and presidents, should ask better, more incisive, and down-to-earth questions before they settle for using the business world's all too often false and irrelevant metrics that, not surprisingly, business itself today finds so wanting.

*   *   *

Perhaps nonprofits should think about the words of Lord Moulton: "I am satisfied that those who have been loyal to duty in the smaller lives that they have led will be loyal in the wider fields in which they are now able to exercise their power."[22] Why not look for the people who have done well on a modest scale, who embody a charitable ethos that intuitively helps them understand that the role of charities in society is to be servants of humanity—that charities are not something to feed from for personal aggrandizement— and forego the search for superstars? But that's just the beginning. We've got to get a handle on tangibly differentiating the effect market forces have on businesses from their effect on charities.

It takes no work and no real brainpower to get out a calculator. It certainly calls upon no intellect that houses a sense of context, and utilizes none of what would commonly be understood as a sense of right and wrong. Drew Gilpin Faust, the president of Harvard—who, by the misguided logarithm noted above, would be making $40 million a year—asked with a note of frustration in the midst of the economic downturn in 2008 and 2009, "Has the market model become the fundamental and defining identity of higher education?"[23]

The same could be asked of the entire nonprofit world.

In a fundraising video, one Dartmouth alumnus said of his alma mater, "You wouldn't run a business this way." He said, "Dartmouth creates a world-class product, discounts the price 56 percent, gives an additional discount for certain buyers...then begs for money."[24] He wasn't being critical. He was pointing out that the school had to look at something other than dollar-defined efficiency to find value. And that can be expensive. The video's narrator reiterated the point. He said that "inefficiency is partly what makes a school like Dartmouth so good. You want efficient? Put a hundred kids in a lecture hall with a professor. Scratch that. With a graduate teaching assistant."[25] The message was that value requires a different calculus from what is used to drive most businesses; value is important at a college—read charity—and, most telling, value is almost always inefficient and expensive, at least in the for-profit way of thinking. Dartmouth used the sentiment to raise money for its annual fund in 2009.

While the spotlight is almost always on the chief executive of a charity, getting past the dollar and close to value is all about board leadership. Jeremy Benjamin, in an article in the Cardozo Law Review's *De-Novo*, discussed the dangers of the marketplace in the nonprofit world. "The duty of obedience counterbalances the fiduciary duties of care and loyalty, which are more subject to market efficiency concerns. Unchecked, market-driven decisions may yield a marketplace of commodities, but not the robust marketplace of ideas essential to a pluralistic, democratic society."[26]

Yet most charities don't go there. It's far easier to look for simple formulas and clichés from the business world than to tackle with originality and insight the problems facing the nonprofit world. But until charitable organizations are serious about facing their own problems, their efforts at addressing the issues they're meant to address in society will be greatly wanting.

The Ethics-Based Mindset

This may all sound so theoretical. Even those who concede that nonprofits shouldn't behave like for-profits may say that nonprofits are hopelessly adrift in knowing where they want to go and how they want to get there, and since the business mindset is the best we've got right now—or so it is thought by some—nonprofits should work within that framework until they figure it out. Indeed, not acting like for-profit businesses is one of the major goals.

So here's an example of an ethics-based mindset—even though the people who had it at the time may have felt they were adhering less to ethics than they were to common sense. New York University, the largest private university in the country, like so many other charities, bumped into Madoff before his fall. In October 2008, Ezra Merkin, who fed money into Madoff's funds, recommended to NYU's chief investment officer that the university invest with Madoff.[27] It was two months before the scandal became public, and there was no obvious reason to think there would be any problems; that is, "obvious," as distinct from a host of other reasons, such as, for example, a market-defying steadiness in the returns Madoff reported.

Yet it is the not-so-obvious question that needs to be asked when it comes to due diligence, and this is what NYU did when it asked Merkin to report to the university on Madoff's investment activities. NYU was doing the right thing—insisting that a number of questions, many of them technical and mundane, be addressed before turning over any money. It didn't need a scandal to put it on edge.

NYU declined to invest with Madoff because Merkin's report didn't answer, or answered badly, many of its questions. It is not difficult to imagine what it wanted to see: trading confirmations to verify that Madoff had actually invested money, for starters. It must have come as quite a shock for university officials to then learn that Merkin, even before he made that request and without mentioning it to anyone at NYU, had already gone ahead and invested some $24 million of the school's money with Madoff. He may have needed to ask for permission, as he should have. Investment managers acting on behalf of their clients are usually permitted some discretion when choosing specific stocks, bonds, or funds, but they are often required, as part of their agreement, to seek permission when the amount to be invested gets to a certain dollar level. Even absent that requirement, an inherent part of the understanding is that the manager will perform his or her due diligence of the fund. When they found out, NYU's lawyers filed a lawsuit in which they said, "Merkin's hedge funds invested NYU's money with Madoff without telling investors or proper due diligence." And further, "The Funds 'feeding' money to Madoff...made a conscious effort to conceal Madoff's involvement from their own investors. This concealment was a requirement dictated by Madoff, which was agreed to by Merkin and other 'feeder' funds."[28]

This isn't just about holding Merkin's feet to the fire, although it is about that; it is also about what fiduciary responsibility means.

Unlike so many people and institutions that invested with Madoff, NYU was able to resist the temptation to throw reason to the wind and invest in a venture that had declared impossible success. If anyone thinks NYU's decision was not ethics-based, he or she should remember that Yeshiva, as well as a lot of other charities that invested with Madoff, clearly did not perform due diligence, at least not at the same level. Why?

It wasn't only the act of due diligence at NYU that was ethics-based; it was the decision to perform due diligence in the first place. At Yeshiva, inside a desire to go along with Merkin's recommendation, the university was making a conscientious decision. It was a bad decision not because the endowment lost money, or even because Madoff turned out to be a crook, but because the principles by which such decisions should be made were not employed. By contrast, in insisting on something other than Madoff's self-reported stock market gains, NYU made a good decision, not because the trustees feared fraud on the part of Merkin or Madoff, but because they employed the principles of due diligence. A value system led to each decision. In a *Financial Times* article about Madoff published in January 2009, trustees of another educational institution where Madoff was on the board were reported as saying they "long had reservations about his reported returns. However, they did not speak up and made no effort to prevent the school from investing with him."[29]

You might wonder whether, if so many individuals and the Securities and Exchange Commission didn't catch on to Madoff, we should have expected charities to figure him out. That's an easy one, at least by the standards of ethical decision making: Charities aren't playing with their own money and so must meet an ultra-high standard of care. As an attorney who works with SEC-related legal issues told me, "Today, in the context of 'due-diligence' and 'standard of care,' the world is a different place from what it was before Madoff." She was referring to how Madoff changed the rules of the game because everyone seemed to believe, without verifying it, that he was actually making trades.

*   *   *

When it comes to endowment investing, everyone agrees that the big issues are that of measuring risk and comparing that risk to possible gains. Risk has to be quantified, but the financial analysis itself does not provide the answer, nor should the financial analyzer be the decider about the acceptable impact if things go wrong. No one disputes the investment acumen of people who run endowments or even those at hedge firms, but a qualitative decision being made based on that information is not the same as the analysis itself. This is an area where charities need to exercise more control over their investment committees.

Let's say, for example that a charity's endowment is $100 million. In a risk analysis, Strategy A has a 40 percent probability of generating an annual return of 15 percent over 5 years; but it also has a 60 percent probability of losing 15 percent of the endowment's value each year during that time. Strategy B has a 90 percent probability of generating a return of 7 percent over the same period of time; it also has a 10 percent probability of losing 7 percent.

If all goes according to plan—and things never go according to plan—Strategy A will result in doubling the charity's endowment to

$201 million at the end of five years, and Strategy B will result in an increase to $140 million. But there's also a fair chance that Strategy A will lose money. If the downside probability plays out, the endowment will be $44 million with Strategy A, while the downside range for Strategy B results in an endowment value of $70 million.

Which strategy should the charity choose (in the real world, there are many more variables)? The charity's managers cannot know until the charity assigns the consequences of not accomplishing its upside objective—and *that* is a qualitative decision. It should be the result of an ethical decision-making process, a process that might very well begin with the question, "What happens if we don't have enough money to serve our clients?" Even a small possibility of losing money may be too much.

The quantitative analysis is only a tool; the process still needs a master architect, a group of people who may or may not be skilled at the analysis but who certainly must be able to apply the numbers and skilled in making qualitative decisions.

Additional Issues

Here is a scattering—eight among many in a growing list—of other issues or questions that charities need to address from an ethical perspective[30]:

> What's the point of a Donor Advised Fund? What's wrong with requiring donors to give money directly to charities, eliminating the useless middleman? In practice they have been a burden on the charities that have agreed to house them with little benefit to show for those charities. On top of that, Congress has had to waste time accommodating them by trying to impose sensible rules. And to what end?

> How can charities make board governance effective? To do that a charity has to decide what it means to be effective. There is no one-size-fits-all blueprint for that. Yet too many charities want to take the easy road and let fiduciary accountability be the only goal, without searching out strategic or generative types of leadership.

> Why should donors receive a full tax deduction, within income limits, for gifts of appreciated property? What moral ground do charities take when they argue for this? While this has not been an issue since Congress repealed the provision in the 1986 Tax

Act that made the appreciated portion of property gifts a part of the Alternative Minimum Tax calculation, it is a legitimate question that charities have never answered, except for saying they want to make it as easy as possible for donors. If charities persuaded Congress to make it as easy for donors as possible, gift amounts would be credits, and not deductions.

Is the issue of donor confidentiality important? Is it right to sell donor lists to make money, as many charities do? Doesn't that impair the integrity not only of donor-charity relations, but of the charity's mission as well? Other than by lamely explaining that the practice generates revenues, charities have never answered this one.

Do we care if we use donor funds appropriately? Why can't charities be clear about how they use donated money? Don't they have an obligation to do that, as well as to define "appropriately," as part of the compact entered into when they receive taxpayer-subsidized gifts? Right now, there is no national discussion about this in the nonprofit arena, and each charity is on its own. Even those charities that do a decent job are unlikely to explain their policies. Think that's not a problem? Consider this thought from Charles Harper, a senior vice president of the Templeton Foundation: "Anybody who trusts a university on a handshake is a fool."[31]

If board-designated funds—as separate from endowments—are in essence rainy day funds, why didn't more charities use them to get through their rainiest day ever—during the economic downturn that began in late 2008? The big savings account we refer to as endowment isn't, usually, all one thing; it has components, and some of that is available to be used any way the board wants to use it. Instead charities, mainly colleges, hoard the money in tight economic times and severely cut salaries and services while increasing fees, such as tuition. "The primary goal of a college endowment," according to an article published in the *Stanford Social Innovation Review*, "should be to protect a school's educational and research programs. Similarly, a hospital's goals should be to treat patients and advance medical research. A museum's goal should be to advance cultural education and preserve cultural heritage. Building an endowment helps to sustain these programs. It should not be the goal of the programs to protect the endowment, cutting them back to sustain or rebuild the endowment."[32] Within state law limits, what would be wrong with reducing the savings account? Although the fund would generate less income in the immediate future, the charity would stabilize its level of services. That, and not a large bank account, is why charities are in business. Building the fund back up to its prior level would be an appropriate task. This is why Congress wonders if charitable endowments should be required to pay a minimum amount to offset their expenses, an amount that is higher than most charities are spending now.

Why do so few charities have an ethics policy? Perhaps it's because the board hasn't gotten around to it and maybe that's because it's not that important.

Finally, what's the problem with more regulation? If there's a clarion call among nonprofits, it's that they don't want more regulation. Some people think there is hardly any regulation at all. Are they right? Charities need to take a stand on this question and answer with intellectual and moral force why regulation is unnecessary while self regulation—the asserted desired state of affairs—has accomplished so little in a world with so many scandals. An example of that: the closed ranks among New York State charities in their fierce fight against a law before the state legislature requiring an ethics course to be taken by fundraisers.

What do all these issues have in common? In addition to employing an intellectually demanding qualitative process, they all require charities to think of themselves as part of a larger community. They ask each to think beyond itself. Properly thought out, they force charities to confront their values on the way to making ethics-based decisions.

One more thing: None of them has an obvious answer.

*   *   *

If nonprofits are society's ethical sector, they should behave that way. As Lord Moulton said: "The great principle of Obedience to the Unenforceable is no mere ideal, but in some form or other it is strong in the hearts of all except the most depraved."[33]

For example, one of the above questions, something we hear about a lot today, centers on a donor's rights. What about turning that around: a charity's rights? As if to underscore the Princeton dilemma, where Bill Robertson sued the university because it did not, in his view, follow the instructions regarding the use of the income from his parents' endowed gift, Jeremy Benjamin, in his law article, says, "Strengthening the duty of obedience, however, raises legitimate concerns. While maintaining public trust is essential, tying the charities' hands of directors to protect donor expectations can handicap the nonprofit sector. Particular concern arises when a donor dies leaving a restricted gift. These dead hand control situations prevent directors from attending to pressing realities the deceased donor may not have imagined, and can require courts to interpret donor intent from gift instruments during costly litigation."[34]

Legitimate concerns, indeed. The issue is vast and complex, and cannot be adequately addressed with the meager arsenal brought to it by those who use only calculators as their evaluative tools and who are looking only for quick results and superstars. Believe it or not—and this really does enter the land of unpopular thinking—the highest paid or the smartest people are not always the best people to dive into such legitimate concerns.

*   *   *

In December 2001, Major Cleo Damon, the head of the Salvation Army office in Naples, Florida, refused a gift of $100,000 from 71-year-old David Rush, who had just won the Florida Lotto. A Salvation Army spokesperson explained, "There are times when Major Damon is counseling families who are about to become homeless because of gambling. He really believes that if he accepted the money, he would be talking out of both sides of his mouth." To which Rush responded: "Everybody has a right to be sanctimonious. I respect the Salvation Army's decision. I do not agree with it, but that is their prerogative." And then, as if to emphasize the ethical dilemma, he said, "There is no bigger gamble than investing in the stock market."[35]

Most people I have spoken to, including my students at NYU—many of whom are already employed at charities—say they, too, disagree; they would have accepted the gift. I'm inclined to agree with them, but I also think it's refreshing when an organization puts its money where its mouth is. That isn't to say the decision was right—or wrong; just that the Salvation Army stood by its own moral compass. That's another thing about ethics—it's not only about right and wrong. While we search for the right thing to do, using the ethical decision-making process as a guide, the goal of ethics is to understand values. Seeking agreement among everyone is a fool's quest. Respecting another's decision, which is to say respecting his or her values, is a more primary goal.

Yes, the Salvation Army is the same group that tried to keep Greenpeace from receiving its share of a bequest on the basis of a technicality. The world is a complex place.

A Few Big Ideas

A good place to begin to make sense of the nonprofit world, with its vague enterprises and unique challenges, is inside Independent Sector's excellent report, "Principles for Good Governance and Ethical Practice," in which 33 recommendations are made within four categories: legal compliance and public disclosure, effective governance, financial oversight, and responsible fundraising.[36] It offers tangible and straightforward ideas so that charities have a way to improve in those four areas.

Independent Sector is a coalition of several hundred nonprofit organizations, and the report, published in 2007, was the product of intense scrutiny by the Senate Finance Committee of the nonprofit world. The document itself came into being after the problems the Red Cross endured after 9/11 and after reporters at the *Washington Post* wrote its exposé of wrongdoing at the Nature Conservancy in Virginia. The Senate Finance Committee held hearings on charitable governance and practice. At the time, in the mid-2000s, charities were getting a lot of unwanted attention.

As a result, the fight between those who wanted more regulation and those who wanted to be left alone at charities was coming to a head. Charities have generally taken the position that they do not need more policing, while regulators take a different view. They see abuses at charities and assume that without regulation abuses will continue unchecked. One regulator in New York thinks the term "self regulation" is an oxymoron. Yet, knowing how imprecise laws generally are, what kind of regulation, if any, should be enacted? And would the inability to enact effective regulation make any further regulation at all a worse solution than the problem? My view is that if charities don't take serious steps on their own to prevent scandals and that betray the public trust, then Congress and the state legislatures, along with the IRS and attorneys general, will have reason to step in.

So, to the degree charities want to be left alone—and certainly if they are to fulfill their promise of growing into the ethical actors they are meant to be on society's stage—they need to urgently embrace their obligations. The nonprofit world is too important for anything less.

While Independent Sector and other organizations, many of which are housed at universities, have attempted to analyze charities, the attempt usually falls short, either because the result is simply to mimic what the business sector is doing: reward the best talent; or because the thinking is vague, academic, and theoretical: charities are good and so their leaders have an obligation to be good.

Hence, the following vision to guide ethical decision-making at nonprofits. Think of each idea within that vision as a supplement to what Independent Sector has compiled—not as additional steps but as deep and ongoing tasks that force a charity to confront its values and embrace their enactment.

Creating and Using an Ethics Policy

No matter how small it is, every charity needs an ethics policy. It's not just a roadmap that, after the road is traveled once or twice, can be shelved. As Independent Sector points out in its good governance document, the policy should be the product of many people's thoughts, and everyone at the charity needs to be oriented and regularly updated on its provisions. The policy itself ought to be updated as well.

Creating an ethics document is not easy. Its development should include examining values and outlining how those values work in everyday life. Not only should the description and consequences of bad behavior be part of the policies, but also policies and procedures that affect how the charity procedurally communicates with the public should be included. To address those matters, in this one example, the charity must determine what it means by "bad," and dissect the process of communicating—often an extremely complex task involving employees in programs, finance and fundraising, and the systems that support them.

Ethics is not a "been there, done that" kind of thing.

Guaranteeing Transparency and Disclosure

Charities should decide what information they will make easily accessible to the public. Documents that indicate the financial health of the organization should be available, but it's possible that many other documents, financial and otherwise, will not be. Determining what will and will not be made available is the result of making difficult decisions. I have no answer to this, but here's an example of a question: Why not make available the salaries of more than just the highest paid people at the charity? The 990 requires only the top salaries to be made public, but should that be the only consideration when it comes to disclosure and transparency? Perhaps the salaries of the administrative assistants should be kept from public view—privacy is a competing value here—but why not go deeper than the IRS requires, especially if by going deeper the public sees what all administrators earn?

And keep in mind that financial statements are only the tip of the iceberg when it comes to providing information about a charity's activities. Board minutes and program evaluations—and there are a slew of other possibilities—should be considered in this context.

Ensuring That Conflicts of Interest and Oversight Are Addressed

Proper oversight means, among other things, taking steps to avoid conflicts of interest. Charities need to make clear to themselves what oversight really means to them. Does it mean making sure the bills are paid, as well as paying attention to other fiduciary matters? Or does it mean taking an active role in determining the charity's future, as the authors in Leadership as Governance outlined? Put that way, the answer may seem obvious, but, because many boards are reluctant to tackle the big questions, the answer is obvious only in broad discussion—doing the real work to exert leadership is detailed, and often difficult and contentious. Deciding whether the Monets would travel from Boston to Las Vegas, as we saw, meant that the board had to do some soul searching about what its responsibilities really were. Financial decisions are almost always decisions requiring leadership and oversight.

Embracing the Nonprofit Ethos

It's far easier to understand what the charitable ethos is not than what it is. It is not a search for profits. It is not accepting arrogance because someone is a superstar. A nonprofit must pay its bills and spend prudently, but it is not a market-based or market-driven business.

The ethical charity will know what this ethos is, and it, like SOME, will act in accordance with those values. If it is good, it will strive to be better. It will embrace one of the best definitions of ethics in the nonprofit world: "Though goodness without knowledge is weak and feeble, yet knowledge without goodness is dangerous, and that both united form the noblest character."[37] The organization knows that not only does it occupy a land where obedience must be paid to the unenforceable, it must also lead in defining and adhering to that obedience. And its leaders know that because nonprofits ask people to do something that's simply not rational—give their money away for little or nothing, in return—a different paradigm must be adhered to. That paradigm is the nonprofit ethos, and ethical charities understand that just because all the questions about this new paradigm haven't been answered is not a reason to fail to understand that they are not for-profit organizations in disguise.

Understanding That Even One Charity Is a Vital Part of the Ethical Sector

Even though it may only be one of almost two million organizations (a little over one million if you count only public charities and foundations) with similar characteristics, a charity must know its special place in society and its responsibilities. While its mission is unique, and its world may seem to consist only of the people it serves, the charity actually is part of a very large world. In many important ways, those people who are served by charity should be able to expect a lot from organizations that profess to help society. Phrases like "highest level of integrity" and "highest ethical values" are only empty rhetoric if the people who say them do so without a commitment to what they mean. Although the nonprofit world is disparate, all charities have a common goal: to serve humanity. Each charity should regularly take the time to educate itself about its work in the context of the of the greater charitable community and with the understanding that it, small as it may be, is important, that it is a part of a larger community, a larger idea, that embraces the good that neither government nor business is equipped to provide.

*   *   *

Organizations are not infallible and they never will be. Thus it is too much to think that we will ever get perfection from charities.

We can't get perfection from places that say they demand it and that have established precise tools to measure progress. So, clearly the idea of generating perfection is inherently unattainable at charities. But what can be done—what must be done—is to assure everyone that charities exist not to be greedy and not to squirrel away money, but to serve society.

The road toward that goal, which seems so obvious and simple but is not, is going to be long and arduous for the nation's ethical sector. And we have to get moving if we have any hope of getting there. As with organizations in the other sectors in society, charities, too, celebrate their technological advances. They rightly celebrate their fundraising sophistication, the efforts that result in over $300 billion donated every year. But in the quest for the best, charities must wonder if in the process of becoming fundraising giants, they are, with the growing challenges generated by that fundraising, also becoming ethical midgets.

We might begin to place ethics on the same level as other, more tangible, goals by starting small or at least with the obvious. There are many examples, but this comes to mind right off: Why don't we willingly acknowledge that cheating or taking advantage of someone else's errors is not acceptable? We can do this by avoiding the kind of tortured thinking that results in "not a correctable post-game error" when it's clear to all who won the football game. If we can get it right on the field of play, we may have a fighting chance to get it right in the much more complex field of life.

Epilogue

In practical matters, the end is not mere speculative knowledge of
what is to be done, but rather the doing of it. It is not enough to know
about Virtue, then, but we must endeavor to possess it and to use it, or
to take any other steps that may *make us good.*

—Aristotle (italics added)

To impose the process of inquiry described in this book on people
who do not actively search for goodness may seem quaint, naive,
or worse. The drug dealers in Colombia, the Mafia, the gangs in
Los Angeles, and even the students in high schools across the country who think it's okay to cheat almost certainly will not embrace
the ethical ideal—not today and maybe not ever. They do not see
how it applies to their real lives. Without a material reason to do
something they won't do it; and, conversely, when given a material
reason they are almost sure to do it. The U.S. government might
talk with the rational people in Somalia, and that may do some
good, but the pirates from that country could not care less about
right and wrong. Yet striving toward an ethical framework is still
crucial to the success of society.

Aristotle wasn't talking about charities. He was talking about
all of humanity. Implicit in his words, from a modern viewpoint,
is a hope that by actually striving to be good (and not just giving
the idea of "good" lip service) we will govern ourselves honorably
and conduct commerce honestly, and individuals will fill in the
ethical gaps left by government and business. Today, charity tries
to fill in the gaps.

But not only the gaps need tending. Some of the essential
elements in the other two sectors also require attention. Charity
will never take the place of either business or government, but, like
the cement that binds the bricks to keep a building strong, charity
must reinforce the buildings of commerce and government, which
are in grave and imminent danger of falling apart. While total collapse may never occur, society would be better served by adopting
best practices rather than shuffling along with the worst.

There is nothing wrong in either of the other two sectors that
an intelligent application of ethics cannot cure. The most logical

place from which a cure might emanate is the charitable sector. Of course, almost everything imaginable is somewhere deep within the phrase "intelligent application of ethics" and the word "cure." Let's understand that actually accomplishing the task, or even making small inroads, is far more difficult than the sentiment makes it sound.

But this is why, despite the difficulties of it all, the sentiment is true. The charitable sector has no political axe to grind and it has no profit motive. The people who serve nonprofits are best positioned to advise business and government on ethics.

But nonprofit leaders aren't there yet. Those at charities are still too concerned with business principles, success of investments, and political machinations, which often subsumes the good they are supposed to be doing for society. The money and machinations have become an end rather than a means. This book's thesis is that charities define the ethical sector of society and therefore must increase their focus on ethics. Once charities adopt an encompassing ethical foundation they can help themselves and become leaders in society.

Not many see it that way, though. If only the senator hadn't had the affair, or if he compromised just a little to help prevent the logjam of ideology. If only the business tycoon hadn't taken liberties with the trust given him by his stockholders, overwhelmed regulators, and a believing public. Think Senators John Edwards and John Ensign. Think Enron. Think mortgage crisis. Think Wall Street bonuses. Correcting wrongdoing isn't only about avoiding something—which is the extent to which most people would go toward solving the problem—it's also about understanding why something shouldn't be done. It's about why some things need to be done.

David Stockman, President Reagan's first director of the Office of Management and Budget, got into trouble by admitting in a now-famous article in *The Atlantic*, that "None of us really understands what's going on with all these numbers."[1] He acknowledged that you can put anything into a computer to make the outcome what you want it to be. The mathematical analysis of many things may seem complex, but often it is not. What goes into the assumptions of such calculations is the core of the matter. And *that* is driven by a sense of right and wrong. Being smart does not make you wise. And the elusive "something more" is a necessary ingredient in the charitable ethos.

Ethics is not a luxury. It's a necessity. And it is subservient to neither the law nor knowledge. The quote in chapter 10 about goodness and knowledge was taken from John Phillips's deed of gift that established Phillips Exerer Academy in 1781.

> But above all, it is expected that the attention of instructors to the *disposition* of the minds and morals of the youth under their charge will *exceed every other care*; well considering that though goodness without knowledge is weak and feeble, yet knowledge without goodness is dangerous, and that both united form the noblest character, and lay the surest foundation of usefulness to mankind.

This was well over 200 years ago, before the Constitutional Convention. The idea of merging knowledge and goodness is not a new idea. So why is it that we have learned so little? The guys at Enron may have been the smartest in the room, but who wants to be in that room? Why do we permit those with technical expertise to drive our sense of right and wrong?

It's because we're not sure. The investing genius knows more than we do. The person at the top got there because she's done something right, and that something is well beyond our capacity to understand. So we acquiesce. And, in a way, that's good. There are things we don't know about and times when we need to follow the lead of others. But we should never do this blindly. We should always ask, "Is this a good idea?" But we don't ask because we're unsure. Too often, we haven't adequately tested our prejudices to honestly own our convictions. So David Stockman's superiors could get away with pronouncements about the budget and the economy that were based on nothing but manipulated computer input that had nothing to do with reality.

How much of our daily input into decisions has anything to do with reality? How many decisions do we make based on slanted input? We see the results every day, from Goldman Sachs and Toyota to the health care debate and wars abroad. The level of dialogue and debate would embarrass the Founders. If they had any idea that this was the type of society they spawned, they may have changed their minds. They made a critical assumption that has not been carried through. While they were hardly naïve—they knew that people and politicians would be selfish and constructed a model of government to deal with that—they could not anticipate that the idea of truth in the face of scrutiny would be subsumed by passion and the desire for profits. The original idea was that the debate would be honest. Differing opinions would be aired and the strongest merits would win the argument. If you doubt this, read the actual congressional record; read the logic within the *Federalist Papers*; read the letters between Thomas Jefferson and John Adams, two political enemies. Nowhere will you see the kind of sickness that led people in this century to gain traction, for example, with the lie that health care proposals called for "death panels." The past is an imperfect place, not the place we usually like to remember or immortalize. But I strongly feel that we have lost the civility of thought and reason and respect that once existed in public discourse and business dealings.

Perhaps it's the subjectivity of most of our ideas that has us in a bind. It may be a curse and a blessing. The blessing is that the English language is so robust we can describe things, people, and ideas with a profound beauty and a rich eye for examination and depth of perception. The curse is the lack of clarity.

The nonprofit sector has a unique opportunity to help improve society. If the problem is that we have not critically examined our convictions, that we have let our lesser angels define our ethics, then charities can be the breeding ground for that examination. Burdened by nothing other than a search for truth and the need to scrutinize and weigh values, charities—with the moral authority they need to begin earning, now as described in this book—can be the natural thought provocateurs of the leaders in business and government.

Why can't nonprofits teach ethics to government and business leaders? Why can't nonprofits lay out the values in arguments and business transactions so that the players and the public will better understand what is really going on? A good example of the kind of discussion would be whether the nation's media health care providers should be nonprofit organizations. Or whether the nation's sources of news—vital to democracy—should be nonprofits, free from commercial pressures. While only government has the authority to regulate, is government the best entity to weigh the values of these questions?

Many people argue that the uppermost intellectual and influential arena of society is the legal system. But I contend that it is the arena of ethics. Why? Because the law, at least in a trial, is incapable of dealing with more than one question at a time. A decision for or against, guilty or not guilty, legal or not, constitutional or not must be determined without the benefit of a broader discussion. Ethics not only permits broader discussion; it requires it. While the law is essential to a civilized society, it sometimes proves inadequate.

This idea may sound radical (to say nothing of its idealism), but it is just the culmination of putting existing pieces together. Borrowing from George Bernard Shaw, Robert Kennedy said in 1968: "Some men see things as they are and say, 'Why?' I dream of things that never were and say, 'Why not?'" Fuse that idea with "goodness without knowledge is dangerous," and you have the best of ideals. Then, combine all of that with an intellectually rigorous approach to ethical decision making and you have the beginnings of a plan.

It is true enough that the conundrum of who is watching the watchers will always be with us. But the authority of the nonprofit sector as the ethical sector is undeniable. With lots of hard work to ensure their sanctity and purpose, those who manage nonprofits can make this authority unimpeachable.

Notes

Introduction

1. Examples of other types of nonprofits include trade unions, political organizations, and restaurant associations, at www.irs.gov
2. The National Taxonomy of Exempt Organizations classifies two million organizations in 645 categories within ten major groups. In addition, the National Center for Charitable Statistics, established in 1982, maintains the Nonprofit Program Classification, which is valuable to researchers because it focuses on what services organizations provide.
3. This information comes from the 990s Harvard and the Getty filed for each organization's 2008 fiscal year. Investment income was calculated as the sum of "dividends and interest from securities" and the "net gain (or loss) from sales of assets other than inventory," at www.guidestar.org
4. The numbers were retrieved from each organization's 2008 990.
5. John Glaser, "The United Way Scandal: What Went Wrong and Why" (New York: John Wiley & Sons, 1994), pp.155–173.
6. Doug White, "Charity on Trial" (Fort Lee, NJ: Barricade Books, 2006), pp.13–21.
7. Estimates of the losses ranged from $50 to $70 billion, but those numbers included Madoff's false profits; the amount of real money that was actually handed over and then lost is closer to $20 billion.
8. Kidder, Rushworth, *Moral Courage*, (Harper, 2005), pp.60–70.
9. Table 25 "Tax-Exempt Organizations and Nonexempt Charitable Trusts, Fiscal Years 2004–2007, at http://www.irs.gov/pub/irs-soi/07db25eo.xls (accessed on 03/05/10); In 2010, the IRS reported a total of 1,789,554 tax exempt organizations as of 2007, 1,128,367 of which were in Section 501 (c)(3).
10. This summary is a composite from information taken from the National Center for Charitable Statistics at the Urban Institute and the IRS. Most people deal with organizations found under section 501 (c)(3) of the Internal Revenue Code.

    In addition to IRC 501 organizations, others defined under sections 220, 401, 408, 521, and 529 are included in the nonprofit totals.

    Not all charities are reported under Internal Revenue Code Section 501(c)(3) because certain organizations, such as churches, integrated auxiliaries, subordinate units, and conventions or associations of churches, need not apply for recognition of tax exemption, unless they specifically request a ruling. American Church Lists reports that there are approximately 378,000 congregations in the United States.

11. The IRS reports in 2009 an audit rate of 1.24%. That rate, however, has increased over the past decade; in 2001 it was 0.61%. At www.irs.gov

12. Two books where Kidder examines this concept are *The Ethics Recession* (The Institute for Global Ethics, 2009) and *How Good People Make Tough Choices* (Fireside, 1995).

One   The Public's View

1. *The London Times*; republished in *The New York Times*, 04/10/1852.

2. See Tocqueville, Alexis de, Democracy in America Penguin Classics (1992). Penguin Classics 2003; first published in 1838; Of special interest to those interested in nonprofits is chapter 5 in Section II, "Of the Uses Which the Americans Make of Public Associations in Civil Life." This is well known.

3. *The New York Times*, 04/17/1897, at http://query.nytimes.com/mem/archive-free/pdf?res=9D02E1DD143DE633A25754C1A9629C94669ED7CF (accessed on 08/12/2009).

   Despite Stanford's well-earned international reputation, students across San Francisco Bay at the University of California, Berkeley, are fond of calling their football rivals a junior college.

4. *The New York Times*, 01/02/1902, at http://query.nytimes.com/mem/archive-free/pdf?res=950CE2DD1530E733A25752C0A9649C946397D6CF (accessed on 08/14/09).

5. "Great Gifts Last Year," *The New York Times*, 04/17/1897 at http://query.nytimes.com/mem/archive-free/pdf?res=9D02E1DD143DE633A25754C1A9629C94669ED7CF (accessed on 08/11/09).

6. The Sherman Anti-Trust Act, passed almost unanimously by both the Senate and the House and signed into law by President Harrison on 07/02/1890, is intended to curb unfair competition in the marketplace.

7. Bloomberg.com, 10/15/09, at http://www.bloomberg.com/apps/news?pid=20601088&sid=aBIvRMQGeMYw (accessed on 12/10/09).

8. R. Jeffrey Smith, "Foundation's Funds Diverted from Mission," *The Washington Post*, 09/27/2004, at http://www.washingtonpost.com/wp-dyn/articles/A55283-2004Sep27.html (accessed on 06/24/2010).

9. Ellen Gamerman, "How Lobbyist's Troubles Felled Columbia School," *The Baltimore Sun*, 05/18/2005 at: http://articles.baltimoresun.com/2005-05-18/news/0505180016_1_jack-abramoff-lobbyist-power-school (accessed: 08/17/2010).

10. National Committee for Responsive Philanthropy, at http://www.ncrp.org/blog/2006/01/abramoff-more-unanswered-questions.html (accessed on 08/30/09).

11. Journey for the Cure Foundation, 2008 Profit and Loss Statement, at http://www.cbsnews.com/htdocs/pdf/JFC_2008_Financial_statements. pdf (accessed on 06/24/2010).

12. *The Washington Post*, 12/ 2/2009, at http://www.washington-post.com/wp-dyn/content/article/2009/12/01/AR2009120104654. html?referrer=emailarticle

13. Rachael Larimore, "The 2008 Slate 60," *Slate*, 01/26/2009, at http://www.slate.com/id/2209476 (accessed on 05/29/2010).

14. http://www.philanthropyjournal.org/about, (accessed on 06/27/2010).

15. "Philanthropy Today,"*The Chronicle of Philanthropy*, 08/31/2009.

16. Charles Piller, Edmund Sanders, and Robyn Dixon, "Dark Cloud Over Good Works of Gates Foundation," *Los Angeles Times*, 01/07/2007, at: http://articles.latimes.com/2007/jan/07/nation/na-gatesx07 (accessed: 08/17/2010). More on investment in chapter 7.

17. *The Boston Herald*, 11/30/2009, at http://www.bostonherald.com/ business/general/view/20091130nonprofits_top_perks_some_get_ low-cost_loans_others_contracts/

18. Adam Smith, "Nonprofit Pay," *Boston Herald*, 11/30/2009, p.22.

19. Amy Bell, "Nonprofit Millionaires," Forbes.com, 12/17/2009, at http://www.forbes.com/2009/12/17/nonprofits-biggest-salaries-personal-finance-millionaires.html?partner=alerts (accessed on 12/18/2009).

20. Marion R. Fremont-Smith and Andras Kosaras, "Wrongdoing by Officers and Directors of Charities: A Survey of Press Reports 1995–2002," The Hauser Center for Nonprofit Organizations The Kennedy School of Government Harvard University, 09/2003.

21. Marion R. Fremont-Smith, "Pillaging of Charitable Assets: Embezzlement and Fraud," Tax Analysts: Special Report, 12/2004, p.334.

22. Ibid, p.342.

23. Associated Press, printed in *Newsday* 08/11/09, at http://www. newsday.com/35m-gift-to-ny-kids-blasted-as-welfare-giveaway-1.1362766?print=true (accessed on 08/20/09).

24. *Law and Order* was the NBC hit of the 2000s that showed its audience the difficulties, often within the context of ethical dilemmas, of taking criminals to court with enough evidence so that the district attorney could have a chance to win the case.

25. *The Chronicle of Philanthropy*, 07/23/2009.

26. Ethics Resource Center, National Nonprofit Ethics Survey, 2007.

27. Ethics Resource Center, summary in president's letter.

28. Paul Light, "How Americans View Charities: A Report on Charitable Confidence, 2008," Brookings Institute, 04/2008.

29. http://www.harrisinteractive.com/harris_poll/index.asp?PID=657

30. Stephanie Strom, "Report Sketches Crime Costing Billions: Theft From Charities," *The New York Times*, 03/29/2008, at http://www. nytimes.com/2008/03/29/us/29fraud.html?scp=2&sq=We%20

really%20need%20to%20take%20a%20good%20hard%20
look%20at%20what's%20going%20on%20in%20these%20orga-
nizations%20light&st=cse (accessed on 12/20/2009).

31. "Are Nonprofits Trustworthy?" The Center on Philanthropy at
    Indiana University and The School of Public and Environmental
    Affairs at Indiana University, 02/2009.
32. 2008 Charity Commission Study Into Public Trust and Confidence
    in Charities, 05/2008.
33. Rockefeller Philanthropic Advisors 2007–2008 Annual Report; p.6.
34. Robert Reich, "Is Harvard a Charity?" *The Los Angeles Times*,
    10/01/2007, at http://articles.latimes.com/2007/oct/01/news/OE-REICH1
    (accessed on 1/20/2009).

Two Regulating and Scrutinizing Charities

1. Although nonprofits don't pay taxes on net revenues or investment
   gains and donors are permitted a tax deduction for gifts to charities, charities generate taxes through their employees, in addition to
   taxes on revenue-generating activities unrelated to their mission.
2. Doug White, *Charity on Trial*, (Fort Lee, NJ: Barricade Books,
   2007), pp.163–178, pp.145–154, and pp.222–223.
3. Harvy Lipman, "Key Senate Aides Propose Sweeping New
   Regulation of Charities and Donors," *The Chronicle of
   Philanthropy*, 06/20/2004, at http://philanthropy.com/free/
   update/2004/06/2004062001.htm (accessed on 12/15/2009).
4. Harvey Lipman, "Increased Regulation of Nonprofit Groups Is
   Unnecessary, New Report Says," *The Chronicle of Philanthropy*,
   11/10/2005, at http://philanthropy.com/premium/articles/v18/
   i03/03003502.htm (accessed on 12/14/2009).
5. "Principles Workbook to Help Organizations Improve Governance,"
   Panel on the Nonprofit Sector—Convened by Independent Sector, at
   http://www.nonprofitpanel.org/ (accessed on 12/20/2009).
6. Adam Meyerson, "Philanthropy Roundtable Concerns About Independent Sector Draft Two," 03/13/2007, at http://www.philanthro-
   pyroundtable.org/content.asp?contentid=540 (accessed on
   12/10/2009).
7. Pablo Eisenberg, "A Lukewarm Effort to Curb Abuses by Nonprofit
   Groups," *The Chronicle of Philanthropy*, 03/31/2005, at http://philanthropy.
   com/premium/articles/v17/i12/12005901.htm (accessed on 12/14/09).
8. Michael Peregrine, "Principal Nonprofit Corporate Law Trends and
   Developments," NAAG/NASCO; Charitable Trust and Solicitations
   Seminar; 10/19/2009; Austin, TX.
9. Court Document, "Memorandum Findings of Fact and Opinion," Kiva
   Dunes Conservation, LLC., E.A. Drummond, Tax Matters, Partner;

Petitioner v. Commissioner of Internal Revenue, Respondent; United States Tax Court; Filed 06/22/2009, at : http://taxlaw.typepad.com/files/kivadunes.tcm.wpd.pdf (accessed: 08/10/2010).

10. Rob Reich, Lacey Dorn and Stefanie Sutton, "Anything Goes: Approval of Nonprofit Status by the IRS," Center on Philanthropy and Civil Society, Stanford University, Draft Report, 10/25/2009, at http://www.stanford.edu/~sdsachs/AnythingGoesPACS1109.pdf (accessed on 06/25/2010).

11. Examiner.com, "An insight into Xavier Becerra's mindset," http://image.examiner.com/page-one-in-national/an-insight-into-xavier-becerra-s-mindset (accessed: 08/14/10).

12. Stephanie Strom, "Charities Rise, Costing U.S. Billions in Tax Breaks"; *New York Times* 12/06/098; at http://www.nytimes.com/2009/12/06/us/06charity.html?scp=1&sq=%22charities%20rise,%20costing%20U.S.%20Billions%22&st=cse (accessed on 12/01/2009).

13. Gateway Sisters of Perpetual Indulgence, http://www.gsoi-stl.org/home_files/home.htm (accessed: 08/14/10).

14. Rob Reich, Lacey Dorn and Stefanie Sutton, "Anything Goes: Approval of Nonprofit Status by the IRS," Center on Philanthropy and Civil Society, Stanford University, Draft Report, 10/25/2009.

15. For the prior three years.

16. IRS, at http://www.irs.gov/charities/charitable/article/0,,id=123297,00.html (accessed on 12/13/2009).

17. Charity Navigator, at http://www.charitynavigator.org/index.cfm?bay=content.view&cpid=628 (accessed on 12/26/2009).

18. Charity Navigator, at http://www.charitynavigator.org/index.cfm?bay=content.view&cpid=43 (accessed on 12/26/2009).

19. Charity Navigator, at http://www.charitynavigator.org/index.cfm?bay=content.view&cpid=484#15 (accessed on 12/26/2009).

20. Francie Ostrower, "Nonprofit Governance in the United States," Urban Institute; 2007, p.1.

21. Ibid, p.8.

22. Remarks of Sarah Hall Ingram Commissioner, Tax Exempt and Government Entities Internal Revenue Service Before the Georgetown University Law Center Continuing Legal Education 06/23/2009 "Nonprofit Governance—The View from the IRS," at http://www.irs.gov/pub/irs-tege/ingram__gtown__governance_062309.pdf (accessed on 12/14/2009).

23. Ibid.

24. Ibid.

25. Ibid.

26. EO-Determinations CPE-Governance; IRS, 05/2009, at http://www.irs.gov/pub/irs-tege/eo_determs_governance.pdf (accessed on 06/19/2010).

27. Doug White, *Charity on Trial*, (Fort Lee, Barricade Books, 2007), pp.111–132.

28. Harvey Lipman, "Key Senate Aides Propose Sweeping New Regulation of Charities and Donors," *The Chronicle of Philanthropy*, 06/20/2004, at http://philanthropy.com/free/update/2004/06/2004062001.htm (accessed on 12/13/2009).

29. Brad Wolverton, "Rethinking Charity Rules," *The Chronicle of Philanthropy*, 07//22/2004, at http://philanthropy.com/premium/articles/v16/i19/19003101.htm, (accessed on 12/15/09).

30. Opening Remarks of Sen. Chuck Grassley of Iowa Chairman, Senate Committee on Finance Hearing on Charities and Charitable Giving: Proposals for Reform Tuesday, 04/5/2005, at http://finance.senate.gov/hearings/statements/040505cg.pdf (accessed on 12/14/2009).

31. Brad Wolverton, "Rethinking Charity Rules," *The Chronicle of Philanthropy*, 07/22/2004, at http://philanthropy.com/premium/articles/v16/i19/19003101.htm (accessed on 12/14/2009).

32. National Taxpayer Advocate, 2006 Annual Report to Congress, at http://www.irs.gov/pub/irs-utl/arc-exec_summary-2006.pdf (accessed on 12/29/2009); the actual number cited was $290 billion, but that number, included in a report delivered in 2006, was based on data from 2001.

33. Brad Wolverton, "Nonprofit Abuses Cost Federal Government Billions of Dollars, IRS Chief Tells Senators," *The Chronicle of Philanthropy*, at http://philanthropy.com/free/update/2005/04/2005040501.htm (accessed on 12/28/2009).

34. This, too, is a broad estimate, derived by assuming a 20 percent effective tax deduction rate—the large donors in the same group with those who don't deduct anything because they don't itemize—applied to $300 billion of donations.

35. In 2004 the IRS devoted $72 million to nonprofit oversight, Marcus S. Owens, "Charity Oversight: An Alternative Approach," The Hauser Center for Nonprofit Organizations, October 2006, at: http://www.hks.harvard.edu/hauser/PDF_XLS/workingpapers/workingpaper_33.4.pdf (accessed: 08/14/2010).

36. This may not be realistic. Even though the potential return might seem to be worth the investment, the total 2008 IRS budget was approximately $11.5 billion. At http://www.irs.gov/pub/newsroom/budget-in-brief-2008.pdf, page 1 (accessed on 06/24/10).

Three   Philanthropy is Big—But Does It Have a Purpose?

1. In 1999 the Gates Foundation changed its name to the Bill and Melinda Gates Foundation.

2. Landon Thomas, Jr, "A $31 Billion Gift Between Friends," *The New York Times*, 06/27/2007, at http://www.nytimes.com/2006/06/27/

business/27friends.html?scp=1&sq=buffett%20gift%20to%20
gates&st=cse (accessed on 06/21/10).

3. The Charlie Rose Show, Public Broadcasting System, 06/26/2006.
4. Albert Hunt, "Numbers Tell a Surprising Story for U.S.," *The New York Times*, 12/21/2009, at http://www.nytimes.com/2009/12/21/us/21iht-letter.html?pagewanted=2&tntemail0=y&emc=tnt (accessed on 12/21/2009).
5. "The Philanthropy 50," *The Chronicle of Philanthropy*, 01/29/2009, at http://philanthropy.com/article/The-Philanthropy-50-Americ/64588/
6. Press Release, The Valley Hospital, 06/16/2008, at http://www.nypsystem.org/press/2008/06/the-valley-hospital-announces.html (accessed on 06/23/2010).
7. "Giving and Volunteering in the United States—2001," *Independent Sector*, at: http://www.independentsector.org/uploads/Resources/GV01keyfind.pdf (accessed: 08/14/2010).
8. Calculations are from the data provided by *Giving USA* (a publication of the Giving USA Foundation) and the Bureau of Labor Statistics.
9. As of this writing, 2006 is the most recent year such statistics are available from the IRS. The document the information can be found is called "Table 1. Form 990 Returns of 501(c)(3) Organizations: Balance Sheet and Income Statement Items, by Asset Size, Tax Year 2006." The 14 percent total is calculated by subtracted government grants from all contributions and dividing by total revenue for all charities.
10. IRS Table 1, "Form 990 Returns of 501 (c)(3) organizations: Balance Sheet and Income Statement Items, By Asset Size, Tax Year 2006."
11. Data from the IRS lag that of other sources. As of this writing, late 2009, the IRS had compiled data through 2006; at that time it reported 237,653 990s from 501(c)(3) organizations. I am estimating the growth through the time of publication to be approximately 300,000. In 2008 the reporting rules changed; the 990 was revised so that, after that time, the income and asset minimums to file 990 (as distinct from the 990-EZ) were raised. Also that year, the new 990N was introduced for charities that take in fewer gross receipts. Effectively, unlike before, other than for religious organizations, all 501 (c)(3) organizations must file their financial information with the IRS.
12. Giving USA Foundation, "U.S. Charitable Giving Estimated to be $307.65 Billion in 2008," 06/10/2009; See also: Partha Deb, et al., "Estimating Charitable Deductions," *Nonprofit and Voluntary Sector Quarterly*, 12/04/2003, pp.548–567.
Estimating Charitable Deductions in Giving USA Revised version: 04/15/2003.
13. *The Chronicle of Philanthropy*, 06/25/2010, at http://philanthropy.com/premium/stats/philanthropy400/index.php?search=search&year=2009&sort=&offset=0 (accessed on 06/24/10).

14. "Key Findings: Center on Philanthropy Panel Study: 2005 Wave," Indiana University, p.1.
15. "World Wealth Report," Capgemini and Merrill Lynch Wealth Management, 2010, p.37, at http://www.us.capgemini.com/DownloadLibrary/files/Capgemini_WWR2010.pdf (accessed: 08/15/2010).
16. "World Wealth Report," Capgemini and Merrill Lynch Wealth Management, 2009, p.35, at http://www.ml.com/media/113831.pdf (accessed: 08/15/2010).
17. "The 2008 Study of High Net Worth Philanthropy: Issues Driving Charitable Activities among Affluent Households," Bank of America and the Center on Philanthropy at Indiana University, 03/2009, p.6, at http://filecache.drivetheweb.com/mr4enh_bankofamerica/502/2008+Bank+of+America+Study+of+High+Net+Worth+Philanthropy.pdf (accessed on 06/26/2010).
18. *Financial Lifeline*; http://www.filife.com/stories/rich-alumni-give-to-needier-colleges (accessed: 08/15/2010).
19. Institute for Jewish & Community Research, 12/11/2007.
20. Ibid.
21. John J. Havens and Paul G. Schervish, "Millionaires and the Millennium: New Estimates of the Forthcoming Wealth Transfer and the Prospects for a Golden Age of Philanthropy"; *Boston College Social Welfare Research Institute* (later renamed: Center on Wealth and Philanthropy), 10/19/1999, at http://www.bc.edu/content/dam/files/research_sites/cwp/pdf/m_m.pdf ;
22. John J. Havens and Paul G. Schervish, "Why the $41 Trillion Wealth Transfer Estimate is Still Valid: A Review of Challenges and Questions," *Boston College Social Welfare Research Institute*, 01/06/2003, at http://www.bc.edu/content/dam/files/research_sites/cwp/pdf/41trillionreview.pdf (accessed on 06/23/2010).
23. Robert Niles, "The standard deviation is kind of the 'mean of the mean,' and often can help you find the story behind the data. To understand this concept, it can help to learn about what statisticians call normal distribution of data. A normal distribution of data means that most of the examples in a set of data are close to the 'average,' while relatively few examples tend to one extreme or the other," at http://www.robertniles.com/stats/stdev.shtml (accessed on 12/29/2009).
24. Holly Hall, "Much-Anticipated Transfer of Wealth Has Yet to materialize, Nonprofit Experts Say," *The Chronicle of Philanthropy*, 04/06/2006, at http://philanthropy.com/premium/articles/v18/i12/12003701.htm (accessed on 01/02/2009). Most of the math is mine, but other results and the raw data came from the *Chronicle* article.
25. Ibid.
26. "The 2008 Study of High Net Worth Philanthropy: Issues Driving Charitable Activities among Affluent Households," Bank of America

and the Center on Philanthropy at Indiana University, 03/2009, p.11.

27. Bank of America Study, p.56.

28. Ibid.

29. Lisa Wogan, "When Wells Run Dry," *Ms. Magazine*, Spring 2005, at http://www.msmagazine.com/spring2005/wellscollege.asp (accessed on 01/01/2010).

30. A good article on the beginning of our tax system, "The First 1040," by Nancy Shepherdson can be found at the *American Heritage Magazine*, 03/1989. The Tax Foundation explored the idea of the reasons for the tax deduction in "Charities and Public Goods: The Case for Reforming the Federal Income Tax Deduction for Charitable Gifts," by Andrew Chamberlain and Mark Sussman, at http://www.taxfoundation.org/publications/show/1191.html; the Stelter study can be obtained at www.stelter.com. Another useful study is one conducted by The Center on Philanthropy at Indiana University, 03/2009; the commentator referenced is Jeff Steele, a planned giving advisor.

31. Barb Arland-Frye, "Thrifty parishioner leaves surprise $1.4 million bequest to his church," Denver Catholic Register, 09/23/2009, at http://www.archden.org/index.cfm/ID/2621/Thrifty-parishioner-leaves-surprise-$1.4-million-bequest-to-his-church/ (accessed on 01/01/2010).

32. *The Chronicle of Philanthropy*, 02/05/2007, at http://philanthropy.com/news/philanthropytoday/1874/charities-battle-over-a-260-million-bequest (accessed on 01/01/2010).

33. *The Richmond Times-Dispatch*, 12/05/2009, at http://www2.timesdispatch.com/rtd/news/local/article/CANN05_20091204–220802/309626/ (accessed on 01/01/2010).

34. Bill Clinton, *Giving: How Each of Us Can Change the World* (New York, Alfred A. Knopf, a division of Random house, Inc, 2007) p.26–27.

35. Gates Foundation website, at http://www.gatesfoundation.org/about/Pages/guiding-principles.aspx (accessed on 12/29/2009).

36. *The Harvard Gazette*, 05/07/2009, at http://news.harvard.edu/gazette/story/2009/05/rockefeller-grants-open-up-world-for-undergrads/ (accessed on 12/29/2009).

37. Arthur Brooks, "The 2008 Legatum Prosperity Index Report," Section 4, Special Topics: Charity and Happiness, Legatum Institute, pp.66–69.

38. Bill Clinton, "*Giving*," (Knopf, 2007), p.210.

39. Author interview, 05/08/2009.

40. That wasn't all. In her will, she left the Salvation Army $1.5 billion.

41. NPR, 11/06/2003, at http://www.npr.org/templates/story/story.php?storyId=1494600 (accessed on 12/31/2009).

42. Elizabeth Jensen, "NPR Points to Shortfall in Cutting 64 Positions," *The New York Times*, 12/08/2008, at http://www.nytimes.com/2008/12/11/business/media/11npr.html (accessed on 12/31/2009).

Four   The Perils of Profit-Making in the Nonprofit World

1. "Table 1. Form 990 Returns of 501(c)(3) Organizations: Balance Sheet and Income Statement Items, By Asset Size, Tax Year 2006," IRS. At the time of this writing, 2006 data were all that the IRS had compiled. The author then extrapolated to estimate the values for 2010.

2. Ibid. Here, the author divided the sum of savings interest, dividends, rental income, and other investment income by total revenues.

3. *The Chronicle of Philanthropy*, 10/29/2009, at http://philanthropy.com/premium/stats/philanthropy400/

4. This estimate is the author's extrapolation of information published in various sources, including the *Chronicle of Philanthropy* and the national Association of College and University Business officers

5. http://www.nyse.tv/dow-jones-industrial-average-history-djia.htm, on the first trading day of 1910, the DJIA was 98.343. On the last trading day of 2009, the average was 10,428.05. This is an average annual growth rate, excluding dividends, of 4.8 percent. Using the endpoints of the Depression era low of 41.22 in 1932 and the all-time high (through January 2010) of 14,164.53 in October 2007, growth was 8.1%. When looking at stock market growth, everything depends on the particular span of time that is used.

6. Even so, there are periods of time, many of them fairly lengthy, when markets have not gone up. Investing may be exciting, but success doesn't come easily.

7. *The Chronicle of Philanthropy*, at http://philanthropy.com/premium/stats/salary/index.php?searchFoundations=Search&Year=2009&order=compensation (accessed on 06/28/2010).

8. Charles Ponzi was in business for the first half of 1920.

9. Yeshiva University Gets Religion, Charity Governance, 04/19/2009, at http://www.charitygovernance.com/charity_governance/2009/04/yeshiva-university-get-religion.html (accessed on 01/15/2010).

10. "Private Foundations: Preliminary Estimates of Madoff Exposure," compiled by Benefit Technology for Nicholas Kristof. *The New York Times*, at http://graphics8.nytimes.com/packages/pdf/opinion/madoff_exposure_7.pdf.

11. "Foundation that Relied on Madoff Closes," Geraldine Fabricant; *The New York Times*, 12/19/2008, at http://www.nytimes.com/2008/12/20/business/20foundation.html.

12. Most people at charities didn't realize the role of the Ezra Merkin as it related to Madoff.

13. This is called "Private inurement," which the IRS describes in the following way: "A section 501(c)(3) organization must not be organized or operated for the benefit of private interests, such as the creator or the creator's family, shareholders of the organization, other designated individuals, or persons controlled directly or indirectly by such private interests. No part of the net earnings of a section 501(c)(3) organization may inure to the benefit of any private shareholder or individual. A private shareholder or individual is a person having a personal and private interest in the activities of the organization." At http://www.irs.gov/charities/charitable/article/0,,id=123297,00.html

14. Andrew Cuomo, "Internal Controls and Financial Accountability for Not-for-Profit Boards," New York State Department of Law: Charities Bureau, at http://www.oag.state.ny.us/publications/internal_controls%20and%20accountability%20for%20NFP%2009.pdf (accessed on 01/30/2010).

15. Jan Gleason, "Growth in Market Value of Endowment Allows Growth in Endowment Spending," Emory University, 02/10/1997, at http://www.emory.edu/EMORY_REPORT/erarchive/1997/February/ERfeb.10/2_10_97endowment.html (accessed on 01/30/2010).

16. http://www.altruistfa.com/prudentinvestorrule.htm

17. Dow Jones Industrial Average, at http://www.djaverages.com/index.cfm?view=industrial&page=reports&show=cumulative-return&symbol=DJI

18. http://query.nytimes.com/gst/fullpage.html?res=9506EFDF1E3EF934A1575AC0A9619C8B63&scp=6&sq=yale%20endowment&st=cse.

19. Tom Lauricella, "Investors Hope the '10s beat the '00s," *Wall Street Journal*, 12/20/2009, at http://online.wsj.com/article/SB10001424052748704786204574607993448916718.html (accessed on 12/21/2009).

20. Ben Gose, "The Boom in Alternative Investments," *The Chronicle of Philanthropy*, 06/02/2006, at http://philanthropy.com/article/The-Boom-in-Alternative/58687/ (accessed on 06/30//2010).

21. Press Release, "Educational Endowments Returned -18.7% in FY 2009," NACUBO-Commonfund Study of Endowments, 01/28/2010.

22. *The New York Times*, December 16, 2008, at http://www.nytimes.com/2008/12/17/business/17yale.html?scp=1&sq=yale%20endowment&st=cse

23. Jonathan Keehner and Jason Kelly, "Harvard-Led Sale of Private-Equity Stakes Hits Values (Update 1), Bloomberg.com, 12/01/2008, at http://www.bloomberg.com/apps/

news?pid=20601109&sid=azBqn85_aRXE&refer=home (accessed on 11/08/2009); and Howard Gold, "Tough Lessons for Harvard and Yale," *MoneyShow.com*, 08/06/2009, at http://www.money-show.com/investing/articles.asp?aid=EDITOR-17401 (accessed on 11/08/2009).

24. Harvard, Private Equity and the Education Bubble. *The New York Times*, 03/03/2009, at http://dealbook.blogs.nytimes.com/2009/03/03/harvard-private-equity-and-the-education-bubble/?scp=1&sq=Harvard,%20privagte%20equity%20and%20the%20education%20bubble&st=cse

25. Gillian Wee, "Endowment Losses From Harvard to Yale Force Cuts (Update1)," *Bloomberg.com*, 07/22/2009, at http://www.bloomberg.com/apps/news?pid=newsarchive&sid=aQn_Cxyu99xY (accessed on 01/30/10).

26. "TSK, TSK, LARRY TISCH," *Fortune*, CNNMONEY.com, 10/26/1987, at http://money.cnn.com/magazines/fortune/fortune_archive/1987/10/26/69714/index.htm (accessed on 01/05/2010).

27. Various author interviews with Eric Swerdlin, president of ChesterCap, in 11/2009 and 01/2010.

28. Raymond James, "An Unconventional Approach," *Registeredrep.com*, 10/01/2005, at http://registeredrep.com/mag/finance_unconventional_approach/ (accessed on 06/30/2010).

Five Do Some Charities Want Too Much?

1. Susan Gilmore, "Charities squabbling over $33 million estate gift from UPS heir," *The Seattle Times*, 03/21/07, at http://seattletimes.nwsource.com/html/localnews/2003628271_greenpeace21m.html (accessed on 02/01/10).

2. Ibid.

3. Stephanie Strom, "Salvation Army Unit Seeks to Gain More of a Huge Gift," *The New York Times*, 02/03/2007, at http://query.nytimes.com/gst/fullpage.html?res=9D07E2DC123FF930A35751C0A9619C8B63&sec=&spon=&pagewanted=all (accessed on 07/07/10).

4. Susan Gilmore, "Charities squabbling over $33 million estate gift from UPS heir," *The Seattle Times*, 03/21/07, at http://seattletimes.nwsource.com/html/localnews/2003628271_greenpeace21m.html (accessed on 02/01/10).

5. Stephanie Strom, "Salvation Army Unit Seeks to Gain More of a Huge Gift," *The New York Times*, 02/03/2007, at http://www.nytimes.com/2007/02/03/us/03will.html?scp=1&sq=di%20stefano%20greenpeace&st=cse (accessed on 02/01/2010).

6. Ibid.

7. Kate Sheppard, "They Only Look Sweet and Benevolent, Ringing Their Little Bells," *Grist*, 03/13/2007, at http://www.grist.org/article/salvation-army-challenges-greenpeace-for-charitable-donation/ (accessed on 04/01/2009).

8. Stephanie Strom, "Salvation Army Unit Seeks to Gain More of a Huge Gift," *The New York Times*, 02/03/2007, at http://query.nytimes.com/gst/fullpage.html?res=9D07E2DC123FF930A35751C0A9619C8B63 (accessed on 07/29/2009).

9. National Heritage Foundation website: http://www.nhf.org/history.html (accessed on 07/09/10).

10. Mary Williams Walsh, "The Charitable Gift Fund Phenomenon: Is It S a Boon for Nonprofits or a Ploy for Investors?" *The Los Angeles Times*, 1999, at http://www.tgci.com/magazine/The%20Charitable%20Gift%20Fund%20Phenomenon.pdf (accessed on 07/09/10).

11. Ibid.

12. Jeff Krehely, "National Heritage Foundation: Pushing Tax Laws to the Limit," Responsive Philanthropy, Summer 2005, at http://www.ncrp.org/files/rp-articles/PDF/RP-Summer-2005-National_Heritage_Foundation_Pushing_Tax_Laws_to_the_Limit.pdf (accessed on 07/09/10).

13. National Heritage Foundation, at http://www.nhf.org/history.html (accessed on 07/15/2009).

14. A noncharity can be a bank or a financial institution, but to set up a DAF it must create a charitable organization just for this purpose, which permit the gifts to it to be deductible.

15. Ibid.

16. Reed Abelson, "Serving Self While Serving Others," *The New York Times*, 05/8/2000, at http://www.nytimes.com/2000/05/08/business/serving-self-while-serving-others.html?scp=1&sq="The%20envelope%20needs%20pushing."%20Houk&st=cse (accessed on 07/15/2009).

17. Ibid.

18. J.J. McNab, "Charity Oversight and Reform: Keeping Bad Things from Happening to Good Charities," statement before the Committee on Finance, United States Senate, 06/22/2004. The two website excerpts immediately prior are also from her statement, as those pages were removed at the time this research was being conducted.

19. Foundation Group, "An Obituary for National Heritage Foundation?" blog, 01/24/2009, at http://www.501c3.org/blog/an-obituary-for-national-heritage-foundation/ (accessed on 07/20/2009).

20. J.J. McNab, "Charity Oversight and Reform: Keeping Bad Things from Happening to Good Charities," statement before the Committee on Finance, United States Senate, June 22, 2004. The two website excerpts immediately prior are also from her statement, as those

pages had been removed from the NHF site at the time this research was being conducted.

21. IRS Notice 99–36, 1999–26 I.R.B. 1; *Charitable Split-Dollar Insurance Transactions*; 06/14/1999.

22. Debra Blum, "Virginia Charity Ordered to Pay $6.5 Million in Damages," *The Chronicle of Philanthropy*; 10/30/2008, at http://philanthropy.com/article/Va-Charity-Ordered-to-Pay/57002/ (accessed on 07/20/2009).

23. Press release, Albert Garcia, Garcia & Martinez; 09/11/2008.

24. The National Heritage Foundation 2008 Form 990, at http://www.guidestar.org/FinDocuments//2008/582/085/2008–582085326-0585a16b-9.pdf (accessed on 09/10/10).

25. William Barrett, "Charity Moved $1 Million Before Bankruptcy Filing," *Forbes.com*, 03/02/09, at http://www.forbes.com/2009/03/02/heritage-charity-bankruptcy-personal-finance-philanthropy_nhf.html (accessed on 07/10/10).

26. Videotaped deposition of Julia Weltmann conducted on Thursday, 01/08/2009, p.60, at http://www.pgdc.com/files/Deposition%20of%20Julia%20Weltmann.pdf (accessed on 07/09/10).

27. Ibid., p.67.

28. "National Heritage Foundation Files for Bankruptcy: Gift Annuitants Among Largest Creditors," Planned Giving Design Center, 02/04/2009, at http://www.pgdc.com/pgdc/national-heritage-foundation-files-bankruptcy-gift-annuitants-among-largest-creditors (accessed on 07/09/10).

29. Julia Weltmann deposition, p.99.

Six   How Long Does the Dead Hand Live?

1. Diana B. Henriquez and David Barstow, "A NATION CHALLENGED: THE RED CROSS; Red Cross Pledges Entire Terror Fund To Sept. 11 Victims," *The New York Times*, 11/15/2001, at http://www.nytimes.com/2001/11/15/nyregion/nation-challenged-red-cross-red-cross-pledges-entire-terror-fund-sept-11-victims.html?pagewanted=1 (accessed on 09/02/2009).

2. The IRS does not permit a donor to restrict a deductible gift in a way that violates the law or generates personal benefits to the donor or his family. For example, a donor may not deduct a gift meant solely to benefit his children at a university, or dictate control over who receives scholarships with the money generated from the gift. If the gift does not violate tax policy, however, it is the attorney general of the state where the charity resides, and not the IRS, that cares about the donors' rights issue.

3. Background Paper, issued by the Robertson Foundation (2009).

4. www.peacecorp.gov

5. Robertson Foundation Certificate of Incorporation (07/26/1961).

6. "Composite Certificate of Incorporation of the Robertson Foundation," as amended through 07/26/1961.

7. In 1961, when the gift was made, there was no "supporting organization" designation at the IRS; Congress tightened the rules on all charities, including foundations, in a sweeping tax act in 1969, which is when the Robertson Foundation became a supporting organization.

8. "Section 509(a)(3) Supporting Organizations," IRS, at www.irs.gov

9. Author interview with William Robertson, 07/15/2010.

10. Ibid.

11. Ibid.

12. "Robertson Lawsuit," at http://www.princeton.edu/robertson/about/issues/

13. These sources are anonymous.

14. Background Paper, issued by the Robertson Foundation (2009). The per-student calculation is based on a total expenditure of $195 million divided by 86 students. That number is $2,267,444; while the per-student point is taken, that number is about $500,000 less than the $2.7 million per student shown in the background paper.

15. John Hechinger & Daniel Golden, "Fight at Princeton Escalates Over Use of a Family's Gift," *The Wall Street Journal*, 02/07/2006.

16. Robertson Foundation Certificate of Incorporation, 07/26/1961.

17. "Robertson Lawsuit," at http://www.princeton.edu/robertson/about/issues/

18. "Robertson Lawsuit—Public Statements," Princeton University, 01/26/2009, at http://www.princeton.edu/robertson/statements/viewstory.xml?storypath=/main/news/archive/S23/29/90M60/index.xml.

19. Ibid, at http://www.princeton.edu/robertson/about/issues/#comp00004656979b00000009f270f5.

20. Ben Gose, "Terms of Endowment: Alleging Misuse of Funds, Donors' Heirs Seek to Reclaim $880-Million in Assets from Princeton University," *The Chronicle of Philanthropy*, 11/15/2007, at http://philanthropy.com/article/Terms-of-Endowment/61601/ (accessed on 08/05/2009).

21. The Banbury Fund 990 (2007).

22. Author interview, 07/15/2009.

23. Ben Gose, "Critics Question Family's Use of Private Funds to Pay Legal Costs," *The Chronicle of Philanthropy*, 11/15/2007, at http://philanthropy.com/article/Critics-Question-Familys-U/61602/ (accessed on 07/30/2009).

24. Robertson News Release, 12/10/2008.
25. Ibid.
26. Princeton News Release, 12/10/2008.
27. "Understanding the Robertson v. Princeton Settlement," at www.princeton.edu/robertson (accessed on 09/30/2009).
28. From a phone conversation with Robert Durkee, 07/08/2009, confirmed by e-mail.
29. Author interview, 07/15/2009.
30. Author interview, 08/10/2009.
31. Vartan Gregorian, "Report of the President, Transparency and Accomplishment: A Legacy of Glass Pockets," Carnegie Corporation of New York (2004), p.7, at http://carnegie.org/fileadmin/Media/Publications/PDF/Transparency%20and%20Accomplishment.pdf (accessed on 06/24/2010).

Seven   Why Good Governance Matters

1. Smithson's biography; Smithsonian Institution, at http://www.si.edu/about/history.htm (accessed on 07/10/10).
2. *Annual Report of the Smithsonian Institution for the Year Ending June 30, 1904.*
3. *2008 Annual Report*, p.32; Smithsonian Museum.
4. The Honorable Charles Bowsher, et al., "A Report to the Board of Regents of the Smithsonian Institution," 06/18/07, p.4 at http://www.washingtonpost.com/wp-srv/style/documents/smithsonian_report_6202007.pdf (accessed on 07/10/10).
5. Ibid, p.3.
6. "Smithsonian Secretary Lawrence Small's Expenses," *The Washington Post*, 03/19/2007, at http://www.washingtonpost.com/wp-srv/politics/graphics/small_expenses.html (accessed on 07/10/10).
7. James V. Grimaldi and Jacqueline Trescott, "Small's House Rarely Used For Business: Ex-Official Got Allowance But Entertained at Museums," *The Washington Post*, 04/19/2007, at http://www.washingtonpost.com/wp-dyn/content/article/2007/04/18/AR2007041802772.html (accessed on 07/05/2010).
8. Ibid.
9. Confidential letter from A. Sprightly Ryan, the Smithsonian's acting inspector general, to the Audit and Review Committee of the Smithsonian's Board of Regents, 01/16/07, p.6.
10. Ibid.
11. The Honorable Charles Bowsher, et al., "A Report To The Board Of Regents Of The Smithsonian Institution," 06/18/07, p.44, at http://www.washingtonpost.com/wp-srv/style/documents/smithsonian_report_6202007.pdf (accessed on 07/10/10).

12. *The Washington Post*, 02/25/2007; p.A-1.

13. Bowsher, ibid., p.4.

14. Elizabeth Olson, "Embattled Smithsonian Official Resigns," *The New York Times*, 03/27/07, at http://www.nytimes.com/2007/03/27/arts/27museum.html (accessed on 07/10/10).

15. Jacqueline Trescott and James V. Grimaldi, "Smithsonian's Small Quits in Wake of Inquiry," *The Washington Post*, 03/27/07, at http://www.washingtonpost.com/wp-dyn/content/article/2007/03/26/AR2007032600643.html (accessed on 07/10/10).

16. Lawrence Small's resignation letter; 03/24/2007.

17. Independent Report, pp.5–6.

18. Robin Pogrebin, "Official at the Smithsonian Resigns After Meeting Transcript Is Destroyed," *The New York Times*, 08/07/2007, at http://www.nytimes.com/2007/08/09/arts/design/09smit.html?scp=1&sq=August%209,%202007%20Smithsonian&st=cse (accessed on 06/20/2009).

19. Charity Governance; 09/29/2009, at http://www.charitygovernance.com/charity_governance/endowment/ (accessed: 08/05/2010).

20. Press release; Office of the New Jersey Attorney General; 09/17/2009, at http://www.nj.gov/oag/newsreleases09/pr20090917a.html (accessed on 07/10/10).

21. Ibid.

22. AG Complaint p.58.

23. Ibid, pp.59–60.

24. Jack Siegel, "New Jersey Attorney General Brings Lawsuit In What Could Turn Out To Be The Nonprofit Case Of The Year—Part II," *CharityGovernance.com*, 09/30/09, at http://www.charitygovernance.com/charity_governance/2009/09/new-jersey-attorney-general-brings-lawsuit-in-what-could-turn-out-to-be-the-nonprofit-case-of-the-year—part-2.html (accessed on 07/10/10).

25. Ibid, pp.44–45.

26. Milgram Complaint, 09/17/09, p.47.

27. UMIFA has now become UPMIFA, the Uniform Prudent Management of Institutional Funds Act; by the end of 2009 most states, including New Jersey, had enacted the new guidelines; see http://www.upmifa.org/DesktopDefault.aspx?tabindex=3&tabid=70 (accessed on 03/01/2010).

Eight   The Four Pillars: The Backbone of Ethics at Nonprofits

1. Treasury Regulations, Subchapter B, Sec. 20.2031–1.

2. Section 3, Philanthropy Protection Act of 1995.

3. The Subcommittee on Telecommunications and Finance Committee on Commerce, United States House of Representatives; October 31, 1995.

4. Louis D. Brandeis, *Other People's Money and How the Bankers Use It*, (New York: Martino, 2009), at: http://www.law.louisville.edu/library/collections/brandeis/node/196 (accessed: 08/17/2010).

5. University of Louisville, Louis Brandeis School of Law, at http://www.law.louisville.edu/library/collections/brandeis/node/191 (accessed on 01/13/2010).

6. Brandeis, ibid.

7. Berkshire Hathaway, Inc., "An Owner's Manual," A Message from Warren E. Buffett, Chairman and CEO, 01/1999.

8. Center for Consumer Freedom, at http://consumerfreedom.com/about.cfm (accessed on 07/10/10).

9. In May 2003, the *Washington Post* wrote a series of articles under the heading, "Big Green: Inside the Nature Conservancy," about the problems at the environmental nonprofit.

10. Doug White, "Charity on Trial," Barricade Books, 2007, pp. 145–154.

11. The Nature Conservancy, "Accountability and Transparency of The Nature Conservancy," at http://www.nature.org/aboutus/leadership/art15505.html (accessed on 11/14/09).

12. GuideStar posts the 990s of almost all charities in the United States, at: www.guidestar.org

13. George Santayana, "Life of Reason, Reason in Common Sense" *Scribner's*, 1905, p.284.

14. Noach Lerman & Rafi Blumenthal, "YU Endowment Shaken By Madoff Storm, Loses $110 Million," *The Commentator*, 08/12/09, at http://www.yucommentator.com/2.2830/yu-endowment-shaken-by-madoff-storm-loses-110-million-1.297188 (accessed on 07/11/10).

15. "Right From the Start: Responsibilities of Directors of Not-For-Profit Corporations," New York State Office of the Attorney General Charities Bureau, p.5, at http://www.ag.ny.gov/bureaus/charities2/pdfs/Right%20From%20the%20Start%20Final.pdf; the Charities Bureau website is: www.charitiesnys.com

16. Thomas Silk, cited in "Good Governance practices for 501 (c)(3) Organizations: Should the IRS Become Further Involved?" *The International Journal of Not-for-Profit Law*, Volume 10, Issue 1, 12/2007.

17. Janet Frankston Lorin, "Millstein Letter Helped Keep Yeshiva Money on Path to Madoff," *Bloomberg.com*, 01/01/09, at http://www.bloomberg.com/apps/news?pid=newsarchive&refer=home&sid=agi2s78EFGR4 (accessed on 07/11/10).

18. Jack Siegel, "Yeshiva University Gets Religion," *CharityGovernance.com*, 04/14/09, at http://www.charitygovernance.com/charity_governance/2009/04/yeshiva-university-get-religion.html (accessed on 07/11/10).

19. "Good Governance Practices," IRS, at http://www.irs.gov/pub/irs-tege/governance_practices.pdf (accessed on 08/20/2009).
20. Shannon Colavecchio, "New FSU President Signs Contract for $395k, Plus Bonuses," *The Miami Herald*, 01/12/2010, at http://www.miamiherald.com/news/southflorida/story/1420549.html (accessed on 01/25/10).
21. Holly Hall, "College President Receives Controversial Fund-Raising Bonus," *The Chronicle of Philanthropy*, 01/21/10, at http://philanthropy.com/news/prospecting/index.php?id=10708 (accessed on 01/26/10).
22. Stephanie Strom, "Donors Sweetened Director's Pay at MoMA," *The New York Times*, 02/17/2008, at http://www.nytimes.com/2007/02/16/arts/design/16moma.html?scp=1&sq=Modern%20art%20Trust%20director%20lowry&st=cse (accessed on 01/26/2010).
23. Mary Jo Layton and Lindy Washburn, "Hackensack University Medical Center's Board Adopts Policies Designed to Clean up Conflicts of Interest," Newjersey.com, 11/20/2009, at http://www.northjersey.com/news/Hospital_tightens_its_ethics_rules.html (accessed on 01/26/2010).
24. Michael Rispoli, "Witness Says Hackensack Hospital's Hiring of Coniglio Was a Sham," *The New Jersey Star-Ledger*, 03/30/09, at http://www.nj.com/news/index.ssf/2009/03/witness_coniglio_hire_unnecess.html (accessed on 01/25/10).
25. 2007 990, Hackensack University Medical Center.
26. www.boardsource.org.
27. Richard Chait, et al., *Leadership as Governance*, John Wiley & Sons, 2005, p.107.
28. Ibid, p.106.
29. Ibid, pp.109–110.
30. Geoff Edgers, "MFA's Monets: Dicey Deal? Museum Defends Loan to Las Vegas Gallery," *Boston Globe*, 01/25/04, at http://www.boston.com/news/local/articles/2004/01/25/mfas_monets_dicey_deal/ (accessed on 01/25/10).

Nine   Inside a Good Charity

1. http://www.blacktie-stlouis.com/about_blacktie/ (accessed on 12/20/2009).
2. Colleen Westberg, "Our Featured Nonprofit—Gateway to a Cure," Blacktie-Missouri, undated, at http://www.blacktie-stlouis.com/non-profit/archive2.cfm?id=50 (accessed on 12/20/2009)
3. Bev Chapmen, KNBC, 11/09/2007, at http://www.youtube.com/watch?v=ftDrRyK6_nk (accessed on 12/20/2009).
4. "Slow Miracles," *So Others Might Eat*, (Abolet Publishing, 2009), p.13.

5. SOME website, at http://some.org/about_history.html (accessed on 07/11/10).
6. 2008 990, So Others Might Eat.
7. Thomas Heath, "Carlyle Tycoon Lowers his Gaze to Discover a Vision," *The Washington Post*, 01/21/2008; the information is a compilation of my conversation with Father John on 02/19/10 and the *Post* story.
8. National Center for Charitable Statistics, at http://nccs.urban.org/classification/NTEE.cfm (accessed on 07/11/10).

Ten   The Voluntary Sector as the Ethical Sector

1. Cory Bennett, "Part II: The Fifth Down Game," *The Cornell Daily Sun*, 11/08/2007, at http://cornellsun.com/node/26006 (accessed on 02/08/10).
2. Associated Press, "College Football: Colorado Victory Stands," *The New York Times*, 10/09/1990, at http://www.nytimes.com/1990/10/09/sports/college-football-colorado-victory-stands.html (accessed on 02/10/10).
3. Joe Pasnanski, "Viewpoint," *Sports Illustrated*, 10/08/2008, at http://sportsillustrated.cnn.com/2008/writers/joe_posnanski/10/08/daniel/?eref=sircrc (accessed on 02/10/10).
4. CBS, "1940 Cornell v. Dartmouth. Famous 5th down Game That Prevented a National Title," 10/25/2006, at http://www.youtube.com/watch?v=QKvefN4PmT4 (accessed on 02/10/10).
5. Ibid.
6. California Republic, at http://www.californiarepublic.org/CROhld/archives/Columns/Galles/20071106GallesWilson.html (accessed on 12/15/09).
7. Holly Hall and Peter Panepento, "Half of Charity Employees Report Seeing Ethical Lapses," *The Chronicle of Philanthropy*, 04/17/2008, at http://philanthropy.com/article/Half-of-Charity-Employees/60786/ (accessed on 12/20/2009).
8. The Right Honorable Lord Moulton, "Law and Manners," *The Atlantic Monthly*, 07/1924, Vol. 134—No. 1.
9. A good article on this point is "Doing the Right Thing," printed in the January/February issue of *Advancing Philanthropy*, which is published by the Association of Fundraising Professionals. The article can also be viewed at http://www.afpnet.org/Ethics/EnforcementDetail.cfm?ItemNumber=967 (accessed on 10/01/2009).
10. Nico Jacobellis, the manager of an Ohio movie theater, was convicted for obscenity after he showed the movie "The Lovers." The Supreme Court overturned the conviction.

11. In 2010 New Jersey governor, Chris Christie, said he wanted to cap the salaries of the top-earning executives to $141,000, for any non-profit social service agency with a budget over $20 million, at http://www.nj.com/news/index.ssf/2010/04/nj_gov_chris_christie_aims_to.html (accessed on 06/19/10).

12. Stephen Carter, *Integrity*, (HarperPerennial, 1996).

13. Benjamin Franklin, attributed to him during the Constitutional Convention, 09/17/1787.

14. These few sentences are meant only to make a point. There is no evidence the trustees of the Museum of Modern Art thought anything so spurious; in fact there is much evidence that they made their decision with the best of intentions and with the highest honor.

15. A rigorous explanation of the steps involved in ethical decision making can be found in Rushworth Kidder's *How Good People make Tough Choices* (Fireside, 1995).

16. Fannie Mae is an unusual for-profit company, a government supported entity with private shareholders.

17. So Others Might Eat, IRS Form 990, 2008.

18. United States Holocaust memorial Museum, IRS Form 990, 2008.

19. Only Lawrence Ellison, the head of Oracle, earned more than $40 million in 2009. According to FoxBusiness, he made almost $85 million. But 2009 was a down year, http://www.foxbusiness.com/story/markets/business-leaders/list-earning-chief-executives/ (accessed on 06/18/10).

20. Malcolm Gladwell, "The Talent Myth," *The New Yorker*, 07/22/2002, pp.28–33.

21. Daniel Goleman, "The Dark Side of Charisma," *The New York Times*, 04/01/90, at http://www.nytimes.com/1990/04/01/business/managing-the-dark-side-of-charisma.html?pagewanted=1 (accessed on 07/13/09).

22. *Atlantic* article.

23. Drew Gilpin Faust, "The University's Crisis of Purpose," *The New York Times*, 09/01/2009, at http://www.nytimes.com/2009/09/06/books/review/Faust-t.html (accessed on 09/24/2009).

24. Ernie Parizeau, at http://www.dartmouth.edu/~alfund/why_give/business_model.html?utm_source=Fire+Engine+RED&utm_medium=email&utm_campaign=June_Email1_Video_NonDonors (accessed on 11/12/2009).

25. Ibid.

26. Jeremy Benjamin, "Reinvigorating the Nonprofit Directors' Duty of Obedience," *De-Novo*, Cardozo Law Review, Yeshiva University, 03/2009, vol. 30–4, pp.1681–1683, at http://www.cardozolaw-review.com/content/30–4/BENJAMIN.30–4.pdf (accessed on 02/15/2010).

27. "Interactive Timeline: The Fall of Bernard Madoff," *The Financial Times*, 01/26/09, at http://www.ft.com/cms/s/0/cc1ceb9e-ebd5–

11dd-8838–0000779fd2ac,dwp_uuid=b7a8d610-caaf-11dd-87d7–000077b07658.html?nclick_check=1 (accessed on 02/10/10).

28. *New York University v. Ariel Fund Ltd* 08- 08603803.

29. Brooke Masters, "Madoff: Off the fairway," *The Financial Times*, 01/26/2009, at http://www.ft.com/cms/s/628a2dba-ebdd-11dd-8838–0000779fd2ac,dwp_uuid=b7a8d610-caaf-11dd-87d7–000077b07658,print=yes.html (accessed on 02/02/10).

30. In putting forth these questions, despite how they are worded, I am not implying a correct or preferable answer; in my consultations with staff and boards, I often propose an alternative, or often even offending view to get people thinking.

31. John Hechinger, "Big-Money Donors Move to Curb Colleges' Discretion to Spend Gifts," *Wall Street Journal*, 09/18/2007, at http://online.wsj.com/article/SB119007667292230616.html (accessed on 11/15/2009).

32. Burton A. Weisbrod and Evelyn D. Asch, "Endowment for a Rainy Day," *Stanford Social Innovation Review*, Winter 2010, at http://www.ssireview.org/articles/entry/endowment_for_a_rainy_day/ (accessed on 12/30/2009).

33. John Fletcher Moulton, "Law and Manners," *The Atlantic Monthly*, 07/1924.

34. Jeremy Benjamin, Ibid.

35. The Associated Press, "Salvation Army not taking Lotto Winner's $100,000 donation," *The Gainesville Sun*, 01/02/2003, p.2B, at http://news.google.com/newspapers?nid=1320&dat=20030102&id=hCYSAAAAIBAJ&sjid=fusDAAAAIBAJ&pg=4423,234838 (accessed on 02/15/2010).

36. Panel on the Nonprofit Sector, "Principles for Good Governance and Ethical Practice: A Guide for Charities and Foundations," Independence Sector, 10/2007, at http://www.nonprofitpanel.org/Report/principles/Principles_Guide.pdf (accessed on 03/05/10).

37. John and Elizabeth Phillips, Original Deed of Gift to Phillips Exeter Academy, 05/17/1781

Epilogue

1. William Greider, "The Education of David Stockman," *The Atlantic*, December 1981, at http://www.theatlantic.com/doc/198112/david-stockman (accessed on 10/15/2009).

Index

Page numbers in *italics* refer to illustrations.